PRIVATE VIEW

PRIVATE VIEW

by

Walter de la Mare

with an introduction by
Lord David Cecil

FABER & FABER LIMITED
24 Russell Square
London

First published in mcmliii
by Faber and Faber Limited
24 Russell Square, London, W.C.1
Printed in Great Britain by
Western Printing Services Limited, Bristol

INTRODUCTION

by

LORD DAVID CECIL

Here is a collection of Mr. de la Mare's essays on literature. As might be expected, they are unlike those of
anyone else. His criticism is as unashamedly personal
as that of Charles Lamb. In his view all criticism must be, for
reading a book is inevitably a largely personal affair. 'It is
alike the despair and the solace of human existence,' he says,
'that we can divine little more from the world of men or books
or of solitude than we bring to them . . . the mind is a mirror
that can reflect no more of reality than its clearness and circumference can command. It is experience that searches us,
rather than we who search experience. Beauty itself depends
for its being, less on that which reveals it than on him who
perceives it.' In these essays therefore Mr. de la Mare does
not aspire to sit in final and Olympian judgement on his subjects,
but only to make us look at them for a moment through his eyes.

This means we see a lot we should not see otherwise. For
Mr. de la Mare's eyes are wonderfully unlike those of most
people. We watch him meditating with a characteristic dreamy
intensity on Tchekov or Vaughan or whoever it may be. As he
meditates, he discourses; not dogmatically and loudly but
hinting and questioning in an undertone, as it were, as he tries
to clarify to himself the impression he is receiving. Through these
hints and questionings this impression is conveyed to us: and
as we read one essay after another, we get a more general
impression of his highly individual response to literature.

Two things make it individual. First of all it is more inextricably of a piece with his attitude to life in general than is so with
most critics. Most critics see life and art as separate, and con-

v

sciously relate them to each other. The 'aesthetic' critic speaks
as if art were more important than life: if a book is imaginative
and well written, he cares not if it squares with the facts of actual
experience. The 'rational' critic, on the other hand, takes for
granted that life is more important: ultimately he judges an
author by how far he does or does not give us a true view of
what he calls the 'real' world. But Mr. de la Mare does not see
life and art as separate. To him the world of imagination is just
as 'real' as the world he sees round him in the street. Hamlet
is as much a living man in his eyes as are his friends, the Forest
of Arden as actual a place as is the New Forest. To disbelieve
in the Forest of Arden on the ground that it is not like any forest
in a geography book would be to him meaningless. If it has been
seen by Shakespeare's imaginative eye it exists, in any important sense of the word, at least as intensely as any so-called 'real'
forest.

Yet the very fact that Mr. de la Mare believes so completely
in the world of art means that he does not exempt it from the
standards of judgement that he applies to the world he sees
round him. The aesthete's amoral attitude is impossible to him.
If Hamlet is as real as a friend, why then, he must be judged in
the same way as one would judge a friend. However skilfully
an artist may present his imaginary world we are justified in
condemning it if it offends against our moral sensibilities. Mr.
de la Mare is enthusiastic about Thackeray's sharp insight into
human nature and his casual, dexterous art, but he thinks there
is a mean streak in his conception of humanity; and that this is
a blot in his books. And he has no hesitation in saying so.

The second outstanding characteristic of Mr. de la Mare's
criticism arises from the fact that he himself is a creative writer
whose imagination is always irrepressibly at work; with the
result that what he sees is inevitably tinged with the colour of
his own temperament. He interprets other authors in his own
terms. This appears most memorably in his verses on Shakespeare's characters, or in the delicate fantasy of *Henry Brocken*
where the hero travels through a dream country inhabited by
figures from literature; Jane Eyre, La Belle Dame sans Merci,
and so on. In his critical essays, Mr. de la Mare has not the
scope for his interpretive genius to display itself so freely and
boldly. But even in these the same spirit is at work. Instinctively

he looks in the works of other authors for imaginative qualities
akin to his own. He notes anything in them that is subtle or
mysterious or tender. This has unexpected results. Defoe, for
instance, was for the most part a prosaic, earthbound spirit in
love with hard fact. But there was also in him an unexpected
romantic strain that made him delight especially in such facts
as are unusual. It is this strain that Mr. de la Mare perceives
and emphasizes. His portrait of Defoe is therefore not the usual
portrait. We are shown his figure from Mr. de la Mare's highly
individual angle of approach and bathed in the shifting, mingling
lights and shadows of Mr. de la Mare's transfiguring vision.

Imaginative criticism of this kind runs the risk of being more
imaginative than critical. The portrait is fascinating, but a bad
likeness. Mr. de la Mare wonderfully avoids this danger. For
he always keeps his eye on the object he is drawing. Though
the aspects of it, which he chooses to stress, may be unusual,
yet they are there; and they are profoundly characteristic.
Brilliantly he discriminates the quality, or combination of
qualities, which gives an author his individual flavour; as when
he says of Barnes, 'the fine observation Barnes displayed so
effortlessly and unassumingly is the observation of a man who
glances up in reverie, and saturates the small thing seen with
the quiet dream and emotion out of which he saw it.' Or of the
people in Hardy's poems, 'these characters are mysterious and
touched with a kind of strangeness or romance, as indeed all
humanity is mysterious when, viewed searchingly, it is off its
guard.' Or of Bridges, 'he is the poet of happiness—not of
mirth, gaiety, joviality, Bacchic abandon, but that of a mood, or
rather, a state of being, in which mind and heart are at one, a
balance between joy and solemnity such as delights and solaces
us in the music of Handel, as beauty and its reflection are at
one when a child, stooping over some green, quiet, sky-reflecting
pool, stays rapt in the contemplation of the half-dreaming picture
it meets there in the water.'

And Mr. de la Mare's praise is as exact as it is warm. His
words isolate and define; they do not blur their subject in a
general misty rhapsody of enthusiasm which leaves limitations
unprecise. Listen to him on Henry James's novels. 'Only in a
hyper-civilized and introspective society such themes would
be possible. They are the last least ramifications of the tree of

life. We see what Mr. James sees, but with the passive eye of
reverie rather than with the active eye of the imagination. He
deepens and subtilizes rather than broadens and volumnifies.'
And after this passage Mr. de la Mare goes on to enforce his
point by contrasting Henry James's confined intense vision of
life with the free unpredictable open-air sweep of Tchekov's.

He leaves us disposed to appreciate both authors better than
we did before. Indeed, his criticism is seldom destructive. Mr.
de la Mare is not interested in writers who have no positive
gift to bring him. This is no defect. People do not write intelligently of authors with whom they have no sympathy: they do
not get close enough to them, even to perceive their faults
accurately. By implication Mr. de la Mare reminds us of an
important truth; namely, that the first essential purpose in
literature is to delight us. His example teaches us another lesson
too. By concentrating always on the individual author and not
wasting his time in vague, high-sounding generalizations on
the nature of art, he directs our eye to the fact that every genuine
work of literature is of its nature unique, and must be judged as
such. Most critics forget this. They erect iron laws of what is
good and bad which involves them in condemning one artist
for no better reason than that he is unlike another. How few
critics, for example, seem able to admire both Donne and
Bridges; for they judge Bridges's poetry by a standard acquired
by reading Donne's, or vice versa. In this book Mr. de la Mare
shows us it is possible to enjoy both authors wholeheartedly.
Incidentally, he also shows us how to enjoy Mr. de la Mare.
For his critical essays, as much as his poems, are themselves
works of art; an exquisitely wrought expression of the same
odd, profound beautiful vision of reality.

PREFACE

Even Hogarth's genius will never now, I'm afraid, woo me into a soul-felt admiration of his Industrious Apprentice. And yet, even a glimpse of his ragamuffins, idling on their road to ruin—callously playing pitch-and-toss on the lid of a venerable sarcophagus in that sombre city churchyard of his—immediately sets me closely scrutinizing each one of those sharp and haggard countenances in turn. Why so injudicious a predilection? Can it be due to a remote echo of ancestral bagpipes and the strains of *Auld Lang Syne*? Would Apollo, even at Aphrodite's behest, have ever consented to bestow his Golden Apple on the Goddess of Industry? Many of us live by industry, and some of us for not much else; but has any hero ever died for her!

However that may be, in respect to the contents of this volume, Industrious Apprentice its compiler certainly must have been. And Industrious Apprentice he has remained ever since. Even apart from their origin, the pages that follow may claim the same dubious merit. They are the outcome of a laborious sifting. They represent a mere fraction of the reviews and the like which were contributed years ago (and with how affectionate remembrances now) to the *Times Literary Supplement*, to the *Saturday Westminster Gazette*, and to the *Edinburgh Review*.

And, first, I wish to express my thanks for the generous help given me by the Editor of the first mentioned of these, and especially for his letting me have a detailed list of contributions of so remote a date. Without this help I should have been unable to retrieve many of them—some on War-print so fragile that it flaked away at its folds under one's finger-tips. Not so, a prodigious bound copy of many months' issues of the *Saturday Westminster Gazette*. This—and how much else—I owe to Naomi

ix

Royde-Smith (Mrs. Ernest Milton) whose literary counsel and encouragement in those far-away days were of priceless value, and indeed still remain so.

Much the greater part of this amassed material had been left unvisited until recently. Then—more Industry!—I began to browse over it again. A long time was thus consumed, and not always with joy! Experiences of a similar nature, unconnected with journalism, must have been familiar to Rip Van Winkle. Perhaps even Robinson Crusoe—when at length, poor soul, he had distinguished himself by becoming a really ancient mariner —cajoled himself into revisiting his Island; and then discovered to his dismay that so much of it was only quantities of sand.

An unforeseen event in this reading was that so many writers who were at that time early in their careers and had afterwards fallen into temporary neglect, were now, one after the other, so radiantly rearising into the literary firmament—writers, too, after my own heart. Not by any means that in the interval their books have remained unread or unreadable. Concerning plainly 'good' books of certain kinds popular taste changes slowly. Many of them indeed are now safely among the Classics—and in their first editions represent a small fortune! Popular *affection* goes deeper yet, and its inmost interest is more profoundly concerned than is that of any surface mode or cult, or perhaps of the inordinately highbrow. And how often, as with feminine fashions, the literary mode will veer back to an earlier generation's, with an almost childish gusto and the serenest self-satisfaction. Mode or no mode, recent reunions with my early Wilkie Collins', with the *New Arabian Nights* and the Rajah's Diamond, with Jules Verne's *A Journey to the Centre of the Earth*, with *The Diary of a Nobody*, proved them for one old devotee as irresistible as ever.

It seems odd that this prolonged toiling through so many thousands of words (*not*, alas, 'the best words in the best order') proved, on the whole, to be more surprising than insupportable. This, I fancy, was due to self-interest, to vanity, to an inveterate curiosity, to apprehension, and to that order of industry which is closely akin to idling. Apprehension was certainly an enticement to go on. Through all those years what might one *not* have been guilty of—the blunders, the absurdities, the conceits, the heinous inaccuracies, the blindness, the wanton enthusiasm! Well, there was a crop of these ample enough. But what of wheat among the tares?

It was the case of an old man well into his seventies—and words still his merchandise—finding himself in the presence again of an exceedingly close but abandoned relative of less than half his age. I came to be aware of this phantom more and more clearly as I went on. And yet how difficult it remained to decide on the positive differences revealed in this ghostly, memory-haunted syllabling between such long-severed selves. Often of course there was a pleasant tinge of patronage, and a complaisant, complacent sense of 'making allowances', accompanied by that cheapest of all smiles, one of superiority.

Far more frequently the boot was on the other leg. This vanished creature, as it seemed to me, was not only more assured, less wandery, more securely based, and more confident in the expression not only of his convictions but of his 'views', than is his literary Grandpapa, so to speak. Also he could write a good deal better, and apparently with far greater ease, and I never knew what he was going to say next. A queer little proof of the confidence (though heaven would bear ringing witness to the far-away toil and travail) will be found in so much the latest of the brief papers that follow—of only last year. After reducing myself to a state of abject despair in the composition of this little excursion into a theme as delicious as some childhood memory of a field of buttercups and daisies— the coming of age of Peter Rabbit—I all but decided that it was too outrageously bad to submit it to the Editor who had asked for it. However, in it went; tombstone though it may be. That, among so many hundreds of reviews, the last of them should have proved all but fatal!

At length in these perusals I began to faint by the way. And then, a friend in need and a friend indeed came to my rescue, Mr. Alan Pringle—himself very appropriately the *son* of an old friend. With rare kindness, patience and pertinacity he sifted the quarter of a million words which I had submitted to him into what follows. To him too I owe its arrangement. He has added the source and date of every entry, the title of the book reviewed, and the name of its publisher when it first appeared. It may since then have been in other hands.

Not that there were no repinings over the massacre thus involved! So many admirable and memorable books endeared by memory, and a delight to revisit even in a review, and so many writers who thus failed to be of the present company. Writers so familiar as Cunninghame Graham, Arnold Bennett, Wells, 'Q', Montague James, let alone such verdant perennials as John Clare, Canon Dixon, Meredith, Montaigne, Aksakoff, Jane Austen, Hans Andersen, Kipling, Swinburne—to mention at random so few of so many.

Mere space in those halcyon days for the reviewing of poetry and *belles lettres* seemed of no more account than—well, than the current Income Tax. Two full columns, for example, of the *T.L.S.* were lavished on me (and not a line too many) for the reviewing of Mr. Ralph Hodgson's 'Song of Honour'. Even for such a poem as this, the fate of a star confined within a tomb would be of far more frequent occurrence in our own constricted age.

Personal memories of these old years abound of course, but I will indulge myself with only a few. My first book-review in the *T.L.S.* (*The Potters of Tadcaster*) appeared on October 1, 1908. I had by then (as Disraeli declared was the fate of critics in general, let alone reviewers) failed as a *writer*. No fewer than three books had then appeared, two of verse, and one, an extravagant romance, *Henry Brocken*. And by 1908 their financial 'takings' for the author had amounted to a deficit occasioned by his purchasing the copyright of two of them for £20. I had also contributed two or three reviews to *The Bookman*. And now, having emerged from the City and the service of the English branch of the Standard Oil Company, I was a free-lance. The problem—an acute one—was how to keep the point of it sharp—if only on behalf of a celestial little family of four. Earlier in that year I had been invited by Edith Sichel to her house in Onslow Gardens for yet another of our 'pow-wows'—delectable talks about books and so forth—*and* to meet Mr. Bruce Richmond, the editor of the *T.L.S.* Edith Sichel had a rare subtlety in her friendships, and a wonderful mind for a younger writer to feed upon.[1]

More vividly even than ever I recall that auspicious afternoon and the prolonged dark smiling contemplative 'look' I exchanged with my fellow guest across the tea tray. Coming

[1] On another such occasion I was presented to André Gide who was in need of someone to teach him English.

events cast not only their transitory shadows before them but may prove on retrospect to have been crucial sign-posts at Destiny's cross-roads, and, too, some sort of 'Everlasting' flower in bud. Whether they are contrived by Providence, or are the outcome of an inscrutable design, or the issue of 'pure chance' (perhaps the most strangely fallacious concept—unless of course it is a witless factor—in the Life of Man) there is not the space in this brief Introduction to attempt to decide!

Anyhow, it was the little golden key presented to me that afternoon which turned the lock in an invisible door. Never had a novice an editor so all-forgiving and so generous. Later, and I seldom fail to remind him of it, my first leader—a 'three-decker' —came along. Its subject was Edgar Allan Poe, already an old and dangerous flame of mine. Delighted and appalled and against time I at last sent back my proof of this. It arrived next morning—not too late—but heavily revised with an excessively soft lead-pencil—after a damp night! In parts it must have been smudged beyond retrieval. None the less about three weeks afterwards there followed—with no more than three syllables of reproof—another sovereign chance, the *Poetry of Barnes*.

Naomi Royde-Smith must, I think, have been absent from the office when there reached me on another occasion a volume from the *Westminster Gazette*, entitled *The Use of the Sabre by Cavalry in War-time*. Treasure Trove, indeed! and of an exemplary order. For perhaps the first time a book had come my way the subject, and therefore the contents of which, were *completely* strange to me, whereas so many of its predecessors had provided me with, say, no more than seven-eighths of the knowledge and information which I had gained by reading them for review. I wallowed in it. Alas, before even having dipped pen in ink for what I am convinced would have been the most brilliant achievement in letters there came a card from the *W.G.* to break the news that the volume had been intended for its military correspondent.

It is to Spender that, apart from much else, I am indebted for a priceless piece of advice. This was in reply to an enquiry concerning what little recipe he would suggest in the way of composition to any novice who had declared himself in need of it. Grizzled silver hair, unexpectedly light-brown eyes, he pondered a moment. Then, 'So, I think, to write,' he said, 'as to need no punctuation.' I was reminded of an 'impot' given me at school after I had passed over yet another 'dictation' paper: 'This will never do, de la Mare. Write me out fifty commas.'

On a later occasion, with Miss Royde-Smith he was scanning her make-up for her next week's issue which contained, to my joy, a rhyme entitled 'Nobody Knows':

> *Often I've heard the Wind sigh*
> *By the ivied orchard wall,*
> *Over the leaves in the dark night,*
> *Breathe a sighing call,*
> *And faint away in the silence,*
> *While I, in my bed,*
> *Wondered, 'twixt dreaming and waking,*
> *What it said.*
>
> *Nobody knows what the Wind is,*
> *Under the height of the sky,*
> *Where the hosts of the stars keep far-away house*
> *And its wave sweeps by—*
> *Just a great wave of the air,*
> *Tossing the leaves in its sea,*
> *And foaming under the eaves of the roof*
> *That covers me.*
>
> *And so we live under deep water,*
> *All of us, beasts and men,*
> *And our bodies are buried down under the sand,*
> *When we go again;*
> *And leave, like the fishes, our shells,*
> *And float on the wind, and away,*
> *To where, o'er the marvellous tides of the air,*
> *Burns Day.*

Whereupon he turned to her, a faint puzzlement in his face: Dear me, I hadn't realized that there was a Burns anniversary this week! . . .

Of the weeds and wild flowers in the unkempt and adorable garden of literature once-current reviews of books are perhaps among the least likely to survive *Time's* busy salt, arsenic and hoe. Some of them are welcome 'strays'; some are worthy of the truest remembrance. Still, most of them are among the Ephemerides; they 'haste away so soon'. As did these.

CONTENTS

CONTENTS

Novelists and Story-tellers

CREATIVE CRITICISM*

The most cautious reader of Mr. Henry James's *Notes on Novelists*—cautious, that is, in the consciousness of his own limited equipment and possibly indiscriminate view of the matter in hand—may at least for his comfort and salvation realize in part the integrity, the consistency, the penetration, depth, and fineness of this comprehensive body of criticism. The practice, the science of criticism, so far as English literature is concerned, seem to Mr. James to be shamelessly in abeyance just now. The 'conscientious' reviewer may hack off a fragment and retire to his corner thanking his stars if Heaven has granted him a plum. The great public, a hydra with as many hungers as heads, may devour books as it devours staling sandwiches, on the long journey of human existence—this one substantial with a story, this one gristly with a plot, this one dubiously savoury with erotic caviare, and this other remarkably 'true to life'. But it is all pretty much in the void. And to define what is meant by truth in the art of the novelist, and what is meant by literature as distinguished from its raw material, is, in general, as much a needless luxury of the intellect as it is to be quite clear on what one means precisely by 'life'.

These *Notes on Novelists*—and were there ever notes so luminous, so ramified, so persuasive, so systematic?—are, broadly, concerned with just that truth, and that literary significance. And as regards what, we imagine, Mr. James means in this volume, by life, we can burrow after it, hunt for it, and blissfully break straight out on it, no less surely than we can find it prepared for our more intimate spiritual recognition in his novels. Mr. James's beloved technicalities may for the most part be intended for the consumption and delectation of the chosen 'tribe' itself—the writers of fiction. His view of it is to that

* *Notes on Novelists.* By Henry James (Dent).

3

extent esoteric. But because fiction holds up, or should hold up, an all-searching, all-collective, and reflective mirror to humanity, such criticism woos our purified and disciplined vision back to the great original, with a renewed ardour, a finer curiosity, a cleaner knowledge of what to look for and where to look. 'The effect . . . of criticism is to make our absorption and our enjoyment of things that feed the mind as aware of itself as possible, since that awareness quickens the mental demand, while this in turn wanders further and further for pasture.' We are to find reasons for our interest. Thus only can that interest grow more various. Appreciation must keep pace with the extent and multiplicity of the appetite. Then literature, no less than life, will wait on both.

How Mr. James's mind won the freedom of *his* vast and teeming province of human existence *A Small Boy and Others* and *Notes of a Son and Brother* supremely, abundantly testify. What rich and various crops he has garnered therefrom are for all to share in his novels. Now comes this criticism, to thresh other men's corn, to separate with pertinacious flail grain from chaff. Never can there have been a writer who so assiduously covered the field, who so liberally, so copiously, and yet with such anxious circumspection and pains showered upon us his enormous haul. Ravage and rummage it as best we may, it will be broad shoulders that can carry off a tithe of its bulk and a truly discerning eye that can select its rarities.

These notes, then, cannot but convict one of a desperate inadequacy. They cover twenty years of profound reflection, of reflection in some cases twice and thrice re-scrutinized. They consider the complete achievement of Balzac, George Sand, Flaubert, and of Zola. D'Annunzio, Dumas the Younger, Matilde Serao, Stevenson surrender their secrets to an analysis as patient as it is unfalteringly drastic, and in the process suffer distillation. A complete circuit is made, the inmost shrines illumined, of that Gothic pile of verse—from the stones of whose too opulent fabric judicious selection might have erected a veritable classic of prose fiction—*The Ring and the Book*. Charles Eliot Norton is befriended as only the tenderest and loyalest consideration can befriend. And the 'Novelists of the Younger Generation' now discreetly marshalled beneath the more encouraging banner of 'The New Novel', may review once more the aromatic relics of their 'squeezed oranges', the punctiliously assorted crumbs from each large and fruity slice of their plum-cakes. One essential pendant is, we may trust, only temporarily wanting—'Henry James as Critic'.

It is not a slight, though it be an instinctive tribute to Mr. James to realize that it would entail a stretching of the term beyond its natural and convenient capacity to refer to him as a writer of genius. And this in spite of the fact that his work so consummately justifies Carlyle's fallacious truism that genius implies only a transcendent capacity of taking trouble. Genius is often in fact a resplendent facet in what is otherwise a more or less commonplace gem seemingly unaccompanied by any pains whatsoever. This present supreme talent that can from books create their authors, that can from the fruit of the tree of life extract such fastidious essences and has so far explored the secret gloom and shine of the human heart and the queer, entangled, restless intricacies of the human mind as to leave by comparison the scientific psychologist a mere child intent on a comparatively new puzzle, that has so refined the art of fiction as to reveal most of its practitioners as mere happy, splashing, vigorous and rather noisy and indiscriminate paddlers saturated in the mere flood of actuality—of this talent at least one thing can be said, it gleams, not in such unique flashes and glimmerings, but steadily and lucidly and temperately. To survey it, abounding in its own sense, is the reward for the reader of these Notes. It is its benevolent equality with the best and most spacious that distinguishes and isolates such criticism. As the novel itself should be,

'it is a blest world in which we know nothing except by style . . . but in which also everything is saved by it, and in which the image is thus always superior to the thing itself . . . . Style itself, moreover, with all respect to Flaubert, never totally beguiles, since even when we are so queerly constituted as to be ninety-nine parts literary we are still a hundredth part something else.'

Could so many ponderable truths be packed into fewer words? It is this complete 99 per cent that stands revealed here; a generous faculty of appreciation, a catholic yet scrupulous taste, a grace of proportion, of construction, that is never a mere gift and yet is one of the rarest and least-recognized of gifts, a tempered plasticity and flexibility of mind as of method, abundance without superfluity, and of detail reduced to the last possible tenuity, that is yet as essential to the large effect as is the tilt of a cherub's nose to the edifice it smiles upon.

This is only a crude attempt to catalogue elusive components. For, above all, there is that general pervasive, human presence, of which we are continually, as it were, in the midst—as if a grave dignitary of an ancient ritual, distinguished no less by his office than in his person, should bless this whole wonderful new creation of the living breathing world of literature, a prelate who, in spite of the ceremonious vestments sacred to his calling, can still accept or dismiss with a familiar gesture of the hand and with a smile of eye and mouth as far removed as courtesy and indulgence can be from the merely hieratic.

Times Literary Supplement, Oct. 15, 1914

THE LESSON OF THE MASTERS*

There is a tradition in the publishing trade—a timid, trembling edifice of apprehension founded upon hard cash—that the great public cannot be cajoled into reading collections of short stories. It is too much of an effort—this reiterated attempt to master preliminaries. As soon as the names of the chief characters in a novel are grasped the reader may take his ease and leisure in its broad acres. The short story, if it is anything better than an anecdote or a sketch, entails no less single and concentrated an act of attention—and then it is all over and one must begin again with the next. A whole lifetime, indeed, may be the raw material of a short story, no less than of a novel. But no life is a concatenation of short stories. Only by an impulsive or deliberate imaginative arrangement, a crystallization, by the creative and elucidating influence of an idea, can life or any fragment of life be isolated and given the necessary form and finality. So essential must the presentation be that there is little room for more than a self-sacrificial glimpse of the writer. He is there; but so are the faint airs in an enclosed garden that one is aware of only because of the fragrance and music they bear. The range of the short story is none the less as wide as human nature, and its variety as various. The lyric affords an even narrower accommodation; but Herrick is Herrick and Donne is Donne. Could there be a sharper and more arresting contrast in the mastery of a particular art than there is between the short stories of Tchekov and those of Mr. Henry James?

The series of little volumes that happens to make its first appearance at the same moment as *The Steppe* is an excellent notion. If, so it had been decreed, it had been intended as a con-

* *The Aspern Papers; The Turn of the Screw; Daisy Miller; The Lesson of the Master*. By Henry James (Martin Secker). *The Steppe and Other Stories*. By Anton Tchekov (Heinemann).

7

tinuous feast of many courses, Mr. James's public would scorn not to have faced the discipline of absorbing his short stories one after the other. But there *is* a completeness in the self-contained. Each one of these little books is an invitation not only to the re-enjoyment of the thing in itself, but to an analytical enjoyment, too, of the method, the gesture, the ritual, the unwavering, un-wearying precision, economy, and intention of Mr. James's art and craft. *The Lesson of the Master*, indeed, affords precept as well as example. The great St. George, with the pathos of a shameless candour, presses on his young admirer the self-, the all-denying sacrifice he has abandoned. He is now nothing better than a weary, wasted, used-up animal, inextricably involved in the lush pastures of success. But this adoring neo-phyte has written a book, *Ginistrella*. It has, the master assures him, the quality which 'fortune distils in a single drop at a time'. 'Have you it in your heart', he entreats him, 'to go in for some sort of decent perfection', not for the sake of the plaudits of the mob, not for the sake of domestic ease and a dear little family, but of 'the incorruptible silence of Fame', of the two or three who know, and, above all, of the one—one's self, one's conscience, one's idea, the singleness of one's aim? 'But the artist, the artist,' pleads the young man, discountenanced at the thought of becoming a mere disfranchised monk, of surrender-ing the beautiful Miss Fancourt, 'isn't he a man all the same?'

St. George had a grand grimace. 'I mostly think not.' Overt does go in for a decent perfection; in two years has attained it, and finds himself again hankering after the fleshpots of Egypt. We leave him with the ironic speculation whether, in spite of the fact that Mr. and Mrs. St. George found the new work really magnificent, this young man, dedicated by nature to intellectual rather than personal passion, did not discover his true audience to have diminished by two-thirds to just 'the one'.

In all Mr. James's short stories the theme no less than the practice is the attainment of some kind of perfection. Their conflicts—tragic or ironic, simple or bizarre—are of the spirit. They describe, illustrate, disentangle such problems, such situ-ations as only a subtle and profound mind, engaged in an all-scrutinizing and dissecting practice of life, can be fully aware of. Delicate—but none the less vital—altitudes and attitudes of con-duct are their inspiration. Daisy Miller, freshly plucked from the unsophisticated wilds of Schenectady, audacious and innocent, crude and courageous, 'dares' the tribal law, defies a far from Catholic Rome. She was dying to be exclusive herself. 'Well, guess we are exclusive, mother and I. We don't speak to any-one—or they don't speak to us.' And poor Winterbourne, learned in ladies, picks his fastidious way through the decencies and gallantries, and the fleeting impulses and revelations of a warm but faltering heart. Even at the vividest he sees her—the inmost self of this beautiful, uncouth, and noble child of liberty—only in vague and baffling glimpses. 'The girl looked at him through the fine dusk'; that was their first brief spiritual *Ave*. 'He felt her lighted eyes fairly penetrate the thick gloom of the vaulted passage'; that was their final farewell. She lacked a cer-tain indefinable fineness, whispers the celestial witness, the all-seeing providence, of these human entanglements. 'But whether or no being hopelessly vulgar is being "bad" is a question for the metaphysicians.'

That being hopelessly bad is not being vulgar is one of the minor enlightenments of *The Turn of the Screw*—though the turn itself is of the screw of 'ordinary human virtue'. Mrs. Grose comes as near as any of Mr. James's characters to an inadequate realization; his governess, with her queer little flutters, her im-passioned self-dedication, faintly recalls no less delightful a pro-totype than Jane Eyre. The preparative prologue is, if anything, a trifle forced and disproportionate; and its first sentence, 'I remember the whole beginning as a succession of flights and drops, a little see-saw of the right throbs and the wrong,' has a flourish of the master hand some little distance beyond Jane Eyre. But what story in the whole region of fiction can match its deliberate, intentional, insidious horror, the sense and presence of gloating, atrocious, destructive evil which it conveys, the steady, cumulative intensity of the 'awful hushed cold inter-course' between living and dead, of the blind groping of love amid the debauched innocence of childhood? The very names convey a devilish innuendo. The actual confrontations of Quint and of Miss Jessel (as fine and as rare and as clear in imaginative poise as that between the wretched thief of privacy, loyalty, and tenderness and poor Miss Tita in *The Aspern Papers*), between anguished child and that hideous demon, with 'white face of damnation', are evidence of a subliminal world that centuries of psychical research can only supplement. If there are stories of impulses, actions, crises in life that cannot be written, and stories that should not be written, then *The Turn of the Screw* is a triumph against impossibility and a venture unmistakably on the verge.

Yet we trusted our guide and he redeems his pledge. Involved, obscure, secret human relationships are the fabric of these short stories. Their characters draw the reader by the finest of threads into the mind—the world—of their creator, by presenting life in the terms and against the background of a penetrating and complex consciousness. Only in a hyper-civilized and introspective society such themes would be possible. They are the last least ramifications of the tree of life. We see what Mr. James sees, but with the passive eye of reverie rather than with the active eye of the imagination. He deepens and subtilizes rather than broadens and volumnifies. He advances by a sequence of infinitely precise insinuations, intimations, contrasts, references, slowly ripening his idea in a kind of animated suspense. He rarely, as it were, comes into the open. He does not strike the rock, setting free a gush of waters. He distils the distilled. We are as little likely to meet Nature here as to meet Milton's Jehovah. Even beauty is an influence rather than a presence. To return from such stories to the outer life is to come out of a clear, secluded, soundless chamber into the raw glare and din of the street. Consummately at his ease in park and pleasance, the artist in Mr. James would as lief face limbo or the American prairies as Tchekov's 'Steppe'.

And yet *The Steppe*, though it merely describes the long journey to school of a little boy, first, in a screeching, rattling *britchka*, with his uncle, a hard, dry man of business, and his old friend Father Christopher, a wise, tender-hearted, devout old priest, and next on the top of one of a trail of wagons piled high with bales of wool under convoy of half a dozen *moujiks*; and though at first sight it is as a story formless and without definite aim or idea, yet it not only gives life and actuality—indeed, the whole history—of its many alien characters and at the same time brings the heart and mind and senses of childhood back again, but it positively flings open the gates of earthly existence. We are no longer cabined in by our little civilized hopes and fears and riddles and anxieties—here is space, nature, mystery, the rich wide amazing earth stretched out beneath the serene and baffling smile of God. A queer God—who 'alone knows why'. Space unfolds ever widening horizons; and time, it is but an impassioned pause in eternity. We hardly realize the art of the telling, the selection, the shifting of narration, the insinuated instruction. It is all so bountifully naïve, sweet-natured, and easy. Like a soundless and distant lightning, a half-hidden personality plays over our minds, the personality of a wise, warm, and delighted nature, gifted with a miraculous purity of the senses. A few words and Moses Mosevitch, the innkeeper, stands before us, garish, pallid, unctuous, succulent, obsequious; or the fabulously wealthy and powerful land-owner Varlamov, just as the one's legs or the other's little cob might bring them in person. So, too, the child's sleepy vision of the Countess Dranitska—a line or two of description, and presto, she is a Goya. Melancholy and joy, beauty and ugliness, goodness and evil, they are but the shifting lights and shadows of humanity. It is all one to Tchekov, so be it that every one, 'even the angry frogs', *live* every minute of life. 'For we only live once.'

'A man does not require three *arshins* of land, nor a farmhouse, but the whole earth, all nature, in the fullness of which he can express all that is within him, and especially the freeness of his spirit.' This abounding love and animation and delight make the very rocks of the Steppe the symbol of some mysterious wisdom, its windmill an angry and imprisoned spirit, its solitary green slim poplar tree a dryad lovely, naked, solitary, adream. The cruelly tragic becomes endurable, and pain too, and grief, tyranny, folly, viciousness. Of such is life. It is as difficult to conceive what Tchekov would have made of *The Turn of the Screw* or of *The Aspern Papers* as it is to see what Mr. James would have made of *The Hollow* or *The Gooseberry Bush* or the infinitesimal *Grief*—though it is attractive to surmise. Masters both, each in his own sphere, we can read and be grateful. For the one the life of the world within, for the other the life of the great world without. But as soon as the distinction is made, memory is thronged with vivid refutations of it.

Times Literary Supplement, May 13, 1915

TCHEKOV'S LETTERS*

'My God,' cries Tchekov in a letter to his sister from Tomsk in 1890, 'how rich Russia is in good people!' He was bound on a self-imposed journey of three thousand miles by road—leagues of it under floods—from Moscow to the convict settlement of Sakhalin. Wearied to the bone with endless night travel, want of sleep, and bad food, scandalized to find that Tomsk could supply a dinner only of eggs and milk, at which his soul revolted, he could yet express this fullhearted benediction. Of the Tatars, 'they are good people'; of the Poles, 'they are good, hospitable, and very refined people'; of the Jews, 'they enjoy universal respect. I saw a tall thin Jew who scowled with disgust and spat when the "President" told indecent stories; a chaste soul; his wife makes splendid fishsoup.' If, he decides, it were not for the cold and the officials, Siberia would be the richest and happiest of lands. But Sakhalin? 'While I was staying in Sakhalin I only had a bitter feeling in my inside as though from rancid butter; and now, as I remember it, Sakhalin seems to me a perfect hell.' It is the richness and abundance, the sense of these dark, immense, sea-like spaces and interlinked horizons, the extremes of culture and primitiveness, of rapture and misery as of landscape and weather, and the swarming variety of character, caste, and kind that cannot but astonish the English reader of these letters.

We sigh: but is it in envy or astonishment or in self-gratulation? It brings home to us a rather restricted insularity, even in our literature, that narrowly verges on the parochial. We may mope a little like caged birds surveying high summer in the woodlands. We may take refuge in Shakespeare (Tchekov's first thought in Venice was of Desdemona), in Dickens, and Byron.

* *Letters of Anton Tchekov to His Family and Friends.* Translated from the Russian by Constance Garnett (Chatto and Windus).

But what wonder that our younger novelists, as Henry James declared (though he spared little room for the Russians!), so intemperately squeeze out the juices of their insignificant tangerines? Even our Kipling, our Conrad, our Cunninghame Graham are small comfort. They strew exotics at our feet; we can few of us at first hand appreciate more than a tittle of their witness, or share more than a corner of their field of experience. London, it is true, is a large place; England, in parts, a peerlessly lovely; the Empire reflects the journey of the sun. But for two solid months, in his leather coat, his sodden felt boots, with his precious coffee and his unopened bottle of brandy, Tchekov could gallop from station on to station, and however uncouth were his fellow-creatures, they were his own countrymen. He was in Russia; still at home.

Nevertheless, his one reference to England is not uncomforting. It came from Hong Kong, in a letter to his friend Suvorin, the editor of the *Novoye Vremya*:

'I went about in a jinrickshaw . . . and was moved to indignation at hearing my Russian fellow-travellers abuse the English for exploiting the natives. I thought: Yes, the English exploit the Chinese, the sepoys, the Hindus, but they do give them roads, aqueducts, museums, Christianity, and what do you give them?'

We may pause a little blankly at the Christianity, and scan not without irony the museums. But what in fact is Russia's gift to the world at large? According to one intimate observer it promised some years ago to be the mystical faith and love of Mary as opposed to the benefactions of Martha. Today it is Bolshevism.

Yet men of Tchekov's generation are still alive in Russia. Today, if he had survived, he would have been only sixty, and these letters surrender the clearest possible picture of a mind and temperament the energy and resilience of which, though his in a peculiar degree, we cannot but accept as representative of cultured Russians in general. It was a temperament, with all its fine sanity, keen perceptiveness and imaginative comprehension, subject to violent extremes of enthusiasm and lassitude, delight and dejection. 'God's world is a good place' is a generalization that must be set off against 'Life is a nasty business for every one' and 'our society is exhausted, hatred has turned it as rank

13

and rotten as grass in a bog, and it has a longing for something fresh, free, light—a desperate longing.'

Tchekov may assert that 'it is essential in this world to be indifferent', but mere protracted indifference, or a continuous balance and moderation of mind, apart from the 'coldness', the impersonality, of the true artist, was never habitual. A candid outpouring of emotions and ideas which, if we share, we are apt to keep secret or to suggest with a self-defensive reticence, is the chief characteristic of his letters. As they proceed they become less impulsive and objective, more reflective and subdued. His cries are from the heart; there is no stuff in his bosom too perilous to share.

'There is no discipline in me: I don't understand what is happening in my soul: I have a passionate desire to talk to you. My soul is in a ferment: I do not know who speaks through my lips —God or someone else; I have no religion: of late I have been devilishly suspicious and uneasy: there is a sort of stagnation in my soul . . . and personal life. I have no passion: you complain that my heroes are gloomy—alas, that's not my fault. This happens apart from my will. . . . I am a man who enjoys life. In any case, as I work, I am always in excellent spirits: all these sentences are fragments torn from their context, but from a context full of soul fragments.'

So, too, in his last letters from Badenweiler, the little spa to which he fled to die:

'There is so much German peace and order here. . . . Today at dinner they gave us boiled mutton—what a dish! . . . I am gasping and dreaming of getting away. But where to go?'

Peace and order, boiled mutton, a destination: what a problem! And yet, 'Above all be cheerful; don't look on life so much as a problem—it is, most likely, far simpler.'

For most of us that is so; though it may not be all honey and complacency to explain why. It is a question of race as well as of environment and personality. In spite of the early and full maturity of Tchekov's mind and intellect we seem to retrieve in his letters the consciousness and sensibility of childhood with all its vividness and absorption. So also the stage, on which he moves, dreams, and acts—furiously and incessantly—resembles the setting now of a folk-tale, now of a dramatic ballet. Its men and women are so 'real', so contrasted and salient in effect, that we

14

believe in them, live in them, as much (or as little) as we believe
and live in characters in fiction; though perhaps Russia alone has
produced the variety of fiction in which they flourish with so
little restraint and sophistication. They come and go, appear and
vanish, like the patterns in a kaleidoscope, or figures on the
'screen'.

In one of his letters, for instance, Tchekov describes the
household of his friend Madame Lintvarzov. 'It is a family
worth studying.' There is the old mother, 'very kind and rather
flabby', who reads Schopenhauer, goes to church to hear the
song of praise, and treasures every fleeting contact with the
world of art and literature. Her eldest daughter is a doctor; to
the peasants a 'Saint'. She has a tumour on the brain, is an
epileptic and totally blind, yet she stoically laughs and jokes,
and listens to Tchekov's stories as he reads to her on the veran-
dah, while fully aware that she is about to die. The second
daughter is also a doctor, a gentle creature, exquisitely sensitive
yet scrupulous to morbidity, a zealous manager of house, estate,
and stables, who yet, apparently, 'has not been happy for a single
instant, and never will be'. The third is a vigorous, sunburnt
girl, a passionate Little Russian patriot, with a loud voice and a
laugh that can be heard a mile away. She goes to Shevtchenko's
grave as a Turk goes to Mecca, wears stays and a bustle, and
looks after the housekeeping. And so on; and we know not
which astonishes us the more—the bizarre models or Tchekov's
effortless portraiture.

With the presences, and voices, and exuberance of human
beings as various and unusual as these the letters abound. The
scenes they occupy are no less sharp and clear and 'atmo-
sphered', and are apparently merely the forefront of an immense
background of time as well as of space. Not only race and history, but the fabulous, the extreme romantic, are in their blood.
They are the work of the creator's imagination rather than of his
thought and intention. They belong to a species every member
of which appears in some degree to be a sport. Even their commonplace is tinged with fantasy. They are like beings of a former
life re-encountered in dream or seen under the influence of
drugs.

Such was his raw material as a writer, though he never wrote
directly from nature, but let 'memory sift the subject'. He him-

self, as he is depicted in his brother's Biographical Sketch and is
made manifest in his letters, might well have been one of his
own characters. He was the grandson of a serf who had bought
his own and his family's freedom ('at 700 roubles a soul, with
one daughter thrown in for nothing') from a nobleman, the
father of Tolstoy's friend Tchertkov; and Tolstoy, of all men,
was the man Tchekov loved best. Tchekov's father opened a
'Colonial Stores', and, loving music and art better than business,
failed and fled. At sixteen Anton—a lively, high-spirited, non-
sense-loving, mimicking boy—went to Moscow, earned his own
living there, and paid for his education. He studied medicine and
became a doctor. When he was nineteen he published his first
story. Thenceforward his life was a furious race against consumption, and, though success dropped like the gentle rain
from heaven, an endless fight for the means to live and to display his energies:

'My soul longs for breadth and altitude [he writes in 1892],
but I am forced to lead a narrow life spent over trashy roubles
and kopecks. . . . My heart aches from the consciousness that I
am working for money, and money is the centre of all I do. This
aching feeling, together with a sense of justice, makes my writing a contemptible pursuit in my eyes: I don't respect what I
write, I am apathetic and bored with myself, and glad that I
have medicine which, anyway, I practise not for the sake of
money. I ought to have a bath in sulphuric acid and flay off my
skin, and then grow a new hide.'

Medicine, as he said, was his lawful wife, and literature his
mistress, but he could be at ease with neither. Peasant patients
flocked from miles around to the house which he had bought,
and heavily mortgaged. He gave them his skill and charity. The
thought of the horrors of its life drove him to Sakhalin. 'To do
something, however little, for medical science'—he made a
census of its 10,000 convicts and settlers, and talked to every
one of them. He fought the famine of 1892, and the cholera. In
1894 he became a member of the Zemstvo. He organized the
census at Melihovo, built a high-road and three schools, a fire-
station and a belfry for the church surmounted by a cross of
looking-glass which flashed out in sun or moonlight over the
country a full eight miles. Meanwhile he wrote like a madman,
one act of a play a day, a tale in twenty-four hours, till, apart

from reviews and *feuilletons*, his 'score' amounted to a round three hundred 'signatures'. Yet the country house, in which he maintained a 'whole organization', was continually thronged with visitors; they slept in every room and in the passages. He was the life and soul of the company he loved; 'when I am alone, for some reason I am frightened.'

Out of this flooding life and experience, guided by the two ideals of art and science, he made his stories, and the complete philosophy of his practice as an artist might be woven together of extracts from his letters. His one desire was personal freedom. The artist's—the 'objective writer's'—concern, he maintained, is not problems, not preaching, not specialization, but to be an impartial witness. He should state, not solve. Justice should be more precious to him than the air he breathes. However difficult it may be, 'owing to the conditions of technique', to combine art and science, at such marriage the artist should aim. In his early twenties, he tells Grigorovitch, he had come to the conclusion that 'an artist's instinct may sometimes be worth the brains of a scientist, that both have the same purpose, the same nature, and that perhaps in time, as their methods become perfect, they are destined to become one vast prodigious force which now it is difficult even to imagine'. Six years afterwards, and eleven years before his death in 1904, he laments to Suvorin:

'Let me remind you that the writers who we say are for all time or are simply good, and who intoxicate us, have one common and very important characteristic: they are going towards something and are summoning you towards it too, and you feel, not with your mind but with your whole being, that they have some object, just like the ghost of Hamlet's father, who did not come and disturb the imagination for nothing. . . . And we? we! We print life as it is ("one smells the hot rolls"), but beyond that—nothing at all. . . . Flog us, and we can do no more! We have neither immediate nor remote aims, and in our soul there is a great empty space. I don't know how it will be with us in ten or twenty years—the circumstances may be different. . . .'

For this volume we owe yet another debt to Mrs. Garnett—to her courage, assiduity, and skill. She has made a selection from the total of eighteen hundred and ninety letters published by Tchekov's family. (The letters to his wife, whom he married in 1902, have not yet appeared.) The translation is in an admirable English that smells neither of the lamp nor of the Russian. But one small question is whether the dots that are so freely scattered through her pages are Tchekov's, or her original's, or her own. They are at times provocative.

Times Literary Supplement, Feb. 12, 1920

AT THE WORLD'S END*

'Every work of art', said Flaubert, 'contains a particular element proper to the artist's personality, which, quite apart from the execution, seduces or irritates us.' This is certainly true of the art of Mr. Conrad. The particular element is not one that appears and reappears like the shimmer of a precious metal in a fragment of quartz or the vacancy of dream in a quiet eye. It is something which dyes his whole story, every human being in it, scene and word, and seals them as exclusively their author's as do the characters of his own signature. So pervasive and intense is the influence of this personal element that for Mr. Conrad's reader it is not merely a question of liking or disliking his work, certainly not of being just amused or bored by it. Either, when we open the pages of *Victory*, the spell of the old familiar seduction instantly re-envelops us, and we greet it as with the long-drawn sigh a child puffs out at sight of an unutterably rich and bespangled Twelfth Night cake. Either we return to it from time to time as with the half-shudder of expectation with which a young man sallies out to meet the loved and secret (even, maybe, illicit) fair in the profound hush of a world of summer and an ascending moon. Either this; or we are irritated, shocked, repelled.

If fascinated, we acquiesce; if repelled, we criticize. Can the secure life we know and complacently flourish in be *this*? Should the underlying philosophy, mood, obsession of a piece of fiction be almost as intolerable as the stare of a pagan god? Come the faint and tepid airs of our spiritual zone from these exotic, heavy islands menacing with the untranslatable thunder of their surfs? Can such horror dog our secret minds, and we unaware? Are there really and truly men around us of a more deadly and conscious evil than that of the devil we have laughed out of

* *Victory*. By Joseph Conrad (Methuen).

19

court? And really! are the trivialities of right and wrong, the little cowardices, uncharities, and inhumanities, so vital? How, indeed, shall we ever be able to call our small souls our own if this is the shuddering test to which the Infinite has submitted them?

And here there seems to be a paradox. If it is the solemn and ironic gravity of the scrutiny which Mr. Conrad bends on life in these remote islands, Samburan and Sourabaya, if it is his conversion of the tawdry commonplaceness of existence into a tragedy never more appalling than when he mocks it as grotesque, never more profoundly significant than when so instinctive a creature as Lena risks even ravishment at the hands of the foul and pitiless Ricardo for the sake of her bright and selfless love, if it is this desperate import which Mr. Conrad pours into mortal affairs that may irritate and shock, how can these qualities possibly seduce? 'Life is so hideous', wrote Flaubert, again in one of his letters, 'that the only way of enduring it is to avoid it. And it may be avoided by living in art, in ceaseless search for truth rendered by beauty.'

Of much of Mr. Conrad's truth to 'reality' most of us cannot judge but by his own aid. 'I am not likely', he remarks—how needlessly only his public could assure him!—'to offer pinchbeck wares to my public consciously.' Faced indeed with the expert's little dish of diamonds, even the veriest novice soon realizes that unless all his gems are paste, none can be. It is only by means of Mr. Conrad's imaginative experience that we can be transported to his island of Samburan. It is only his imagination that could body forth for us precisely such a monstrosity as that 'insolent spectre on leave from Hades', that 'merry skeleton', the truly gentlemanly 'Mr. Jones'. And even Mr. Jones, we have to remember—in the eyes of the philosophical dreamer, Axel Heyst (alias 'Mr. Enchanted Heyst', alias 'Hard Facts Heyst', alias 'Mr. Blasted Heyst', himself another 'perfect gentleman', as 'we of the islands' summed him up)—*seemed* to be nothing more awful than an envoy from the outer world, and nothing more substantial than an apparition and chimera. So, too, with Schomberg.

This typical Teuton, the incarnation not of recent animosities, but of 'old, deep-seated, and, as it were, impartial conviction', has appeared twice before in Mr. Conrad's world. Here his 'grotesque psychology is completed at last'. Axel Heyst is a Swede. In a moment of unconsidered compassion he cheats this corpulent hotel-keeper, Schomberg, of a friendless, drifting young English girl, Lena. And Lena had seemed to Schomberg like a ripe fruit, not only ready to drop into his mouth, but which would prove a delicious antidote to the extremely dry distaste for his battered, fear-besotted wife. His frenzied lust gives him cunning, not courage. When the emaciated Mr. Jones, his pock-marked lieutenant, Ricardo, and their servant, the baboon-like Pedro, storm his respectable veranda, this precious German, torn betwixt wounded vanity and terror of such a trio, hints of other spheres. There is hidden, ill-gotten treasure in solitary Samburan, he leers, where the noxious and eccentric Heyst lives in sin with the girl he has stolen. So the trio take a boat and put to sea. 'Let me undo the button of your shimmy.'

This Schomberg *lives*: and so too Pedro, and so too lives Wang—Heyst's cautious and scrupulous major-domo; not because they exactly resemble any Teuton or alligator-hunter or Chink we may have had the fortune to meet. And thus too—with its criss-cross construction, as erratic in its progress as the knight in chess, but as competent wastelessly to cover the board —thus too lives *Victory*, solely by virtue of its having itself been lived in, incident by incident, word by word, by one 'in ceaseless search for truth rendered by beauty'. It is for this reason that such a story may wholly 'seduce' even far less serious, search-ing, devoted, compassionate souls, because, perhaps, they, more used to the melting mood, have found life not so much hideous as difficult and perplexing, because they also may have been occasionally troubled by a detached view of the universe. 'Sup-pose the world were a factory and all mankind workmen in it. Well, he discovered that the wages were not good enough. That they were paid in counterfeit money.' It is in these words that Axel (vainly) attempts to explain to Lena the pessimistic views on life of the elder Heyst—the dead and gone philosopher whose heavy, gilt-framed portrait on the flimsy wall of mats broods on in the pregnant heat of Samburan. 'Man alone can give one the disgust of pity' is one of this philosopher's icy aphorisms. And again, 'Of the stratagems of life the most cruel is the consolation of love.' And again—

'Men of a tormented conscience, or of a criminal imagination, are aware of much that minds of a peaceful resigned cast do not even suspect. It is not poets alone who dare descend into the abyss of infernal regions, or even who dream of such a descent. The most inexpressive of human beings must have said to himself at one time or another: "Anything but this!" ...'

'We all have our instants of clairvoyance'—Mr. Conrad proffers the magic crystal. We peer into it. And we see this familiar life of ours, heightened and deepened, charged with phantasmal terror, carnal disgust, with a thwarted, venomous, and phantasmal evil; and transfigured with humble dutifulness, self-sacrifice, courage, scorn of pain and of death. And confronted with this miracle—whether of verisimilitude or of transformation—those of us who are not irritated are seduced. Our little ceaseless search has also for a moment found rest and solace—'in truth rendered by beauty'.

Times Literary Supplement, Sept. 30, 1915

THE DYNASTS*

Without arrogance or uncertainty, it is surely possible to congratulate posterity upon its inheritance of Mr. Hardy's *The Dynasts*. Here is a book, if ever there was one, concerning which we feel we can predict with assurance that it will survive far beyond our own transitory generation. First published in three volumes, which appeared as each was completed, it is now issued in one; and its range, the breadth and boldness of its conception, its unity in complexity, its inexhaustible creativeness are the more manifest. For more than twenty years, Mr. Hardy tells us, this vast theme lay as it were in process of gestation in his mind. 'On a belated day, about seven years back', it was outlined. And now here is this 'panoramic show', this 'Spectacle in the likeness of a Drama', a Gargantuan achievement that can claim to be a national as well as an individual triumph, secure, living, and complete.

It is no wonder that Mr. Hardy had to beat about to find terms in which to describe his work. 'Epic-Drama', even, is a hardly satisfactory 'cross'. *The Dynasts* is at present, indeed, the only representative of a new species in literature. And not only is it a species singularly original and unforeseen, but so integral and organic is this new birth that for the moment there seems no probability of improving upon the model, no promise of evolution. This at least may be said: many years of what, so far as art is concerned, can only be a short life will have to be devoted to the accomplishment of any work that attempts to follow Mr. Hardy's astonishing example. Many years, too, of the life of how rare a genius, how masterly a mind, of how entranced and curious a student of history, character, consciousness, and life.

* *The Dynasts*. An Epic-Drama of the War with Napoleon, in three parts, nineteen acts, and one hundred and thirty scenes. The time covered by the action being about ten years. By Thomas Hardy (Macmillan).

Of these four absorbing studies, that of consciousness, perhaps, has been the means of supplying what is the most unusual quality in *The Dynasts*. The psychological novel that with the meticulousness of a chemist's balance weighs individual motive, and with the subtlest touches of an etcher frets in the lights and shades of individual character, is now no new thing in fiction. Every dramatist, too, in his presentation of action is compelled to concern himself with that inward conflict of the will, that inward impulse of the instincts and of heredity from which action proceeds. In fiction character is presented either from the point of view of the author, with a running explication or commentary, as with Meredith; or from the point of view of one of the characters themselves, as with Mr. Henry James. In drama the characters must present themselves in speech and action, without intrusion of the dramatist, straight to the spectator's intelligence. *The Dynasts* stands midway between these two forms of art, and is the outcome of a fusion of both methods.

Not only does it far transcend the ordinary novel in scope and conception, but, while keeping true to the actual human experience and actions it sets out to present, it bathes both these, and the innumerable characters and wills, influences and motives that brought them about, in an atmosphere of pure imagination, an imagination with the powers of a creative, all-seeing spectator to whom the whole complex drama is but a succession of mental phenomena. The reader's consciousness is Mr. Hardy's stage. He translates, as it were, the macrocosm without—that world of a Great Historical Calamity, or Clash of Peoples—into terms of the quiet brooding world within. Beneath the thraldom of a magician's wand we are at the same time the master and the sport of his puppet-show, of which Europe, spread out in fancy from London to Moscow, is the narrow, changeful scene. Just as in actual life the imagination wanders like Ariel, now soaring until the sea is but a darkish wash of colour round continents like the fretted fragments of a child's puzzle, now hovering in extraordinary closeness over Stephano and Trinculo, hob-nobbing with Caliban; so we wend our way through *The Dynasts*, incessantly conscious of man's mortal, corporeal insignificance, yet conscious, too, of the illusion of space and time and of things material, incessantly conscious of our own immortal gravity and calm, and of the inward voices.

For what are Mr. Hardy's 'Phantom Intelligences' but inward voices—the spies, the witnesses, the spectral companions of the life within? Do we not every day hear the lamentable Pities chaunting from afar as we scan our morning paper's tragic crop? Who has not tapped at times, willy-nilly, that subconscious butt of racial and hereditary experience from which emanates the thin trickle which we call the wisdom of 'the Ancient Spirit of the Years'? Who has not listened with horror-stricken surmise to the voice of Rumour, and vainly endeavoured to cast off the brooding presence of the Spirits of the Sinister, who haunt every approach of the mind with their blighting cynicism? Is not even the Immanent Will that momentary sense which sometimes visits us of a kind of potential omniscience and omnipotence in ourselves? With such complete mastery Mr. Hardy marshals these scenes of battle and famine, of Brighton gala-night and Commons' sitting, of Wessex Downs and Moscow snows and the bogs of Walcheren, with such subtlety of management he shows his characters, great and little, as 'acting while discovering their intention to act', that, whatever our wonder and delight or horror and revulsion may be in surveying his vast spectacle, we are very rarely stirred out of the trance in which he binds us. Under his spell, indeed, we hardly realize the stupendous difficulties of the achievement. We are in thrall to a dream—and to a dream that comes at times very near to crossing the border-line of nightmare.

But in all this we are only attempting to express what Mr. Hardy himself makes clear in his preface—using, too, much the same terms. 'Readers will readily discern', he writes, 'that *The Dynasts* is intended simply for mental performance and not for the stage':

'[But] in respect of such plays of poesy and dream a practicable compromise may conceivably result, taking the shape of a monotonic delivery of speeches, with dreamy conventional gestures, something in the manner traditionally maintained by the old Christmas mummers, the curiously hypnotising impressiveness of whose automatic style—that of persons who spoke by no will of their own—may be remembered by all who ever experienced it.'

'Curiously hypnotising impressiveness'—that phrase exactly sums up the extraordinary quality in *The Dynasts* which we have been trying to describe. But there is no need to wait for that genius of stage-craft towards whom Mr. Hardy in this passage seems to be wistfully peering. Open the covers of this book, and instantly the intense and intimate commerce begins. Stealthily and hitchlessly the scenes clear, brighten, fade, and close; out of the 'unapparent' voices speak. 'Life is a show, and now we know it,' but when the last page is turned how extraordinarily significant have become those persons 'who speak by no will of their own', how strangely fateful their conventional gestures, and how curiously quiet a sense of responsibility has edged into our minds. Where, if not within, we are tempted to ask ourselves, is the sole reality of life; and what is this world but a chequered ball in whose hieroglyphics we may read on close scrutiny something of the destiny which has made us children its momentary possessor in the garden of eternity?

But this lapse into the vague and metaphysical occurs only after one's reading of *The Dynasts* is done. Otherwise—if any such trend, that is, grew too obvious or insistent during the reading—the author would not be the supreme artist he is. Simply as a piece of literature this Epic Drama is inexhaustibly fascinating. Any attempt to criticize in detail must be left to the writers of such books as will almost inevitably come to be written around it and its various aspects. One or two things, however, insist on notice in even the most casual survey—Mr. Hardy's power of imaginative visualization and his peculiar gift of words. We say visualization, but it is something more than this. Only a sixth sense could so transport us where it will. Never before have 'stage directions' been the masterpieces of narrative they have become in his hands. The whole world of *The Dynasts* is haunted. Throughout it we are in much the same condition of suspense of mind as that which follows on the 'knocking' in *Macbeth*. Shakespeare's porter must, indeed, be one of Mr. Hardy's favourite characters. But never is this hauntedness more apparent than when occasionally a countryside, a room, empties itself of Man:

'The wind continues to prevail as the spot is left desolate, the darkness increases, rain descends more heavily, and the scene is blotted out . . .

'The two multitudes lie down to sleep, and all is quiet but for the sputtering of the green wood fires, which, now that the human tongues are still, seem to hold a conversation of their own.'

As for Mr. Hardy's words, they are wraiths of reality, a kind of phantom presentment of things themselves in all their most peculiar significance; but things, let it be said, always and ever in relation to Humanity—in all its guises and complexities the true protagonist of this drama:

Mock on, Shade, if thou wilt! But others find
Poesy ever lurk where pit-pats poor mankind!

Saturday Westminster Gazette, 1910

AFTER THE WESSEX EDITION*

Not many of the critics who had the insight and the confidence to foretell a great future for the author of *A Pair of Blue Eyes* are likely to enjoy the satisfaction of reviewing *A Changed Man*. When Mr. Hardy's first novel appeared, Dickens had been dead only three years, Thackeray ten, Tennyson was still chiselling out his *Idylls*, Browning steadily growing more obscure. Wilkie Collins was not yet fifty, Mr. Bennett and Mr. Galsworthy were six. None the less, Mr. Hardy, unlike the young writer of today (who may publish his memoirs almost before he has had time enough for any substantial future), was then well over thirty. Forty years have passed, complete literary constellations have risen, and some have set, and here is this collection of twelve new short stories, showing a power still unabated, a zest and interest in life and humanity known only to the beloved of the gods who die young though they live to be a hundred.

A Changed Man consists of fragments that have now been redeemed from various magazines, but escaped inclusion in the Wessex edition of Mr. Hardy's works. They range in date of composition over more than a third of a century. Close analysis might suggest many interesting comparisons, but one tendency is more or less clearly manifest, a tendency away from romance and comedy towards the tragic and satirical. *A Mere Interlude* was written twenty-eight years ago, *Enter a Dragoon* only fourteen. Had their dates been reversed, it is more than probable that the conclusions of these stories would have followed suit. Selina and her little Johnny of the latter story would then have been spared their grim encounter with that too, too respectable widow with *her* little Johnny at their amorous Sergeant's grave, and Baptista of the former would hardly have taken so philo-

* *A Changed Man*. By Thomas Hardy (Macmillan).

sophically to her second husband's four plain, gawky girls. It is a sorrowful but unquestionable fact that if comedy by comparison with tragedy appears a far more artificial treatment of life, then the happy ending may so often seem a piece of mere self-indulgence. That being so, the editor who steadfastly resisted the hanging of Tess may have spared his readers a pang, but it must remain uncertain whether the Recording Angel will credit him with the kindness.

Men and women, for one's own little personal purposes, may be roughly divided into two kinds—those who we think would make 'good' characters in fiction and those who would not. A different kind of goodness is at stake. Uriah Heep may be no less absorbing than Bazarov, Tom Jones than Becky Sharp, Sir Willoughby de Patterne than Heathcliffe, Long John Silver than the Vicar of Wakefield. But although, at first sight, this is a selection of extremes, the type of each of these characters is fairly common. Bazarov is cosmopolitan, however essentially a Slav he may be; Heathcliffes come to tragic ends far south of Yorkshire; Beckies, Pecksniffs and Peggotys in varying solution may be perceptible in most social circles; De Patternes (almost) in every milieu. According to the degree of our hospitality, so will be the warmth of our welcome. An intense dislike, a fervour of distaste may be our main response to any such presence, but that need not imply eviction—possibly quite the contrary. The phantom makes no material change, whether or not a phial of *elixir vitae* or a pinch of Mandragora is in his waistcoat pocket. He owes us whatever life is his for the time being: that's all.

There are some scores of men and women in *A Changed Man*. And Mr. Hardy makes us realize them as few of us *realize* even the closest of our friends. One or two of them, the Duke in *What the Shepherd Saw*, Monmouth in *The Duke's Reappearance*, and, to a lesser degree, Monsieur G—— in *A Committee-Man of the Terror*, stand, like Saul, head and shoulders above their fellows; but not because they are, as men, of nobler stature, but because as Dukes and so forth they wear high heels. It must be confessed that their office, the gewgaws of their fate and station, have a little obscured their humanity. The baron in *The Romantic Adventures of a Milkmaid*, again, just suggests the strut and the well-worn beards of such barons as tread a

more picturesque and condensed stage than that of life. What
Byron is to the poetic norm, so these scintillating figures are to
the human; conspicuous for the most part in the comparatively
inessential.

But they are as rare as they are rich. They decorate and
enhance Mr. Hardy's stories as a patch, a pencilling, and a
tinge of rouge may set off a woman's beauty. More queerly,
when the whole book is read, theirs, it is discovered, is an
inexplicable, superfine touch of mocking fantasy. They stand
out against the soldiers and lime-burners, the merchants and
farmers, and shepherds and ploughmen, the schoolmistresses
and dairymen's daughters in much the same fashion as a
cockatoo burns gaily in an old maid's parlour. For Mr. Hardy's
men and women are nearly always quiet, ordinary folk, 'light-
natured, hit-or-miss' souls, most of them, in what, at first, seem
ordinary circumstances. Beauty—dark or fair, flashing or quiet,
buxom or slim—and beauty that must fade (*timor mortis
conturbat me*) is the chief distinction of his women. Individualized
they may be, every one of them—as individual as their names,
Laura and Alicia, Caroline, Christine, Baptista. But it is
Femininity, however diversely personified, that is the woof of
all Mr. Hardy's novels, as Masculinity, soldier's or dreamer's,
Don Juan's or recluse's, is the warp. He takes them up in turn
as deftly and surely as a connoisseur a piece of old Bow or
Chelsea. 'Be living now, and happy,' he seems to say to them,
'increase and multiply if you can; for that is why you are here.
Is it not so?' he adds, turning sharply on his reader. And then
the circumstances that seemed so ordinary prove to be only
empty space wherein the spider is softly, pauselessly, to spin his
web. These lovers are flies, once light and bright of wing; and
Fate all in good time will suck them dry. And that Fate, too, is
a crooked, surely a crooked and monstrous creation of this
prodigious and prolific mind.

Like all preternaturally real people, Mr. Hardy's characters
are also a little like ghosts. For they have one and all come out
of the house of imagination into which all our fellow-beings
must go if we are really to understand them. And he not only
places them in space, the space of memoried scenes, but in perspective of time. We survey them not only through air and sunlight, and, scrutinizingly, through the dusk of evening, but

through the years. His stories, even the shortest, with few exceptions, are therefore not episodes and incidents, not snapshots, but, like so many of his lyrics, histories—'minor novels' is his own deliberate phrase. He chooses not single and final crises, but the survival of them for his theme. *The Waiting Supper* is a happy, candle-lit meal of which Nicholas and Christine are forbidden a single taste. Now her own vacillating heart, now a mere mishap in strategy, now Nic's angry pride, now her husband's malice; and then, for years and years, that husband's chill and passive fish-gnawed anatomy in the weir, his gold watch dangling against the cage of his ribs, keep these lovers apart, their four too sanguine candles steadily guttering towards the dark.

And at last—'"Is it worth while after so many years?" she said to him. . . . "Let us be joyful together as we are, dearest Nic, in the days of our vanity". . . . He fell in with these views of hers to some extent. But occasionally he ventured to urge her to reconsider the case, though he spoke not with the fervour of his earlier years.' The sheer wear and tear of life—even the most ardent are in some degree doomed to capitulate to that.

So, too, in *A Mere Interlude*. It is not the fate of poor Charley, the headlong and confident bridegroom, who, watched by Baptista from her window, went down to bathe their first glad morning, disappeared, appeared again, looked back, and at last, like 'a small waxen object' in the distance, emerged from the nook that had screened him, crossed the white fringe of foam, and walked (out of earthly existence) into the undulating mass of deep-sea blue; nor is it so much that she was destined a few nights afterwards to lie between dried-up old Heddegan (whom she had so lightly and featly dodged) and a thin partition that alone divided her from the body of her drowned Charley—it is not this, but Baptista's after-life that Mr. Hardy had most clearly in view—though he tells us very little about it, and that little of cold comfort.

The truly tragic in mortal life, indeed in these and other of his stories, (and life in Mr. Hardy's fiction is richly but rigidly mortal), is usually not death but the prolonged survival of it, not passion but trembling hands and a cold hearth, not fire and tempest but the hungry moth and its progeny, and the diligent rust. Love is Time's fool, and an old fool, in most of these

stories. There is irony even in the title of *A Changed Man*, for
while the zealous Captain Maumbry (turned parson) sleeps the
sleep of the dead at Durnover Cross, an even slower and
conscious change is creeping upon his remorseful widow. Her
lover, Vannicock, brings the little bag back that she had taken
as her whole luggage upon her mad and muddled flight. 'Laura
received it and absently shook it out. There fell upon the carpet
her brush, comb, slippers, nightdress, and other simple neces-
saries for a journey. They had an intolerably ghastly look now,
and she tried to cover them.' There is languor, an accent of the
perfunctory, in Vannicock's renewed proposal. What had come
between them? No living person; only an insistent shadow.
And as time went by 'their feelings seemed to decline from their
former incandescence to a mere tepid civility. . . . Mrs. Maumbry lived and died a widow.' Moreover, the word husband has
received little lustre from the Vannicocks of life, and Laura's
dilemma was therefore two-horned.

Mr. Hardy's readers soon grow familiar with 'that intolerably ghastly look'. He teaches them his own satirical satisfaction
with a hapless suitor 'too old to put an end to himself for such
a reason as love', and with poor mortals who 'resign themselves
to circumstances'. 'Howsomever,' says one of the Sidlinch men
who have come to bury the body of the self-destroyed soldier at
the cross-roads on Christmas Eve, 'howsomever, the Lord's
will be done, since it must, whether or no.' And we can comfort
ourselves by reflecting that Mr. Hardy knew the end of his
stories at their beginning, that scars physical or amorous tingle
only upon rainy days and are otherwise almost pleasantly
reminiscential, and that *our* sad fates will come when they must,
but that we need indulge in no excoriating anticipations. Moreover, art completes a pattern; current experience is a medley of
loose ends.

And because art designs and fulfils, we can read without tears
the most plangent narrative that this master of the desolating
will gladly consent to knit for us. He loads his dice maybe, but
he plays a vivid game. It is a deep and spacious beauty that survives in memory, even when Luke, in *The Grave by the Handpost*, can bear remorseful solitude no longer, and dies at the
cross-roads beneath which his father's bones lie pinned by the
suicide's stake to Mother Earth.

Few English novelists can compare with Mr. Hardy in the depth and significance he gives to life by unifying it with that of the great world without. Harassed, trapped, circumvented, worn-down though his puppets may be, he bestows on them not only nerves and hearts and bright eyes and dancing feet and good appetites, but he sees to it that their little toy-dramas shall be magnificently staged. Twilight is in collusion with their sorrow, a red sun peeps in on a blushing Margery in her hollow elm, *all* night echoes to the 'carol'-singers and their tuned instruments, ranged roundabout the gallows-like handpost; even the moss speaks, in its humble fashion, under the stress of the blast, as the buffeted pilgrim goes to keep his 'Tryst at an Ancient Earthwork'.

For if there is little witness to any loving Providence in Mr. Hardy's stories, there is a richly humanized Nature. Wild flowers in the hedgerow are not more children of earth than his Wessex folk, with their beautiful voices, their easy grace, their impulsive, headstrong youth, their sententious marrowy old age. They are born, they grow up, hope and strive and desire, some of them marry, a few repent, many in a monstrous conspiracy of mishap perish. So, too, may we; consoled (or pestered) to the end by the dream of immortality, but at last 'content to have so far been, as to have a title to future being'. If, however, to survive in the grateful remembrance of man-kind be the most that mortals can expect of days they shall never see, then happy indeed and in their still-enduring heyday are Laura and Alicia, Caroline, Christine, Baptista—and happy even their tortured men-kind!

Saturday Westminster Gazette, Nov. 1, 1913

SAMUEL BUTLER'S NOTE BOOKS*

'All philosophies, if you ride them home, are nonsense,' said Butler, and he intended no disparagement of nonsense. His *Note Books* prove that he rode home every philosophy that came in his way for sheer delight in the exercise, and that he never failed to be refreshed when he reached his journey's end. The one thing he hated was stagnation. Though 'in a way death may be said to be better than life, it is in a very small way': as for dying—that process has absolutely nothing to commend it. Wherefore try all things, be anything, do anything, so long as you escape a life that is nothing better than a 'long lingering death-bed'. He tilted against everything taken for granted—whether in morals, or science, or art, or in conduct. Reputations enraged him because they are usually mausoleums—and very few of his august contemporaries escaped his hail of 'bricks'. 'Agreeable' ideas were his aversion because they are usually moribund, and only a vigorous shaking and a few back-somersaults can reanimate them. He kept his eyes wide open, but dearly enjoyed a peep out of the corner. He loved the wrong side of a fact or a theory—where the quality and workmanship are most evident. His mind was sanctuary to forlorn causes. He not only adopted them but fathered them, and in his company they ceased to be forlorn. His was an inveterately questioning mind—the mind that is not so much seeking for answers as for fresh questions. Butler pursued truth, though 'its pursuit is chimerical'. And though there is no permanent, absolutely unchangeable truth, there are countless vivifying and astonishing points of view. Truth, he thought, should be 'played pretty low down'. 'Pit-truth is more true to the stalls than stall-truth to the pit,' while a little bit of absolute truth

* *The Note Books of Samuel Butler.* Selections arranged and edited by Henry Festing Jones (Fifield).

34

might 'dissipate the universe'. So Butler sat in the pit (occasionally in the gallery) and enjoyed both his company and the privilege of expressing his real opinion about the great play, the rest of the audience, and the actors—tragic or farcical—who were doing their best.

He himself never wanted, or at least never attempted, to 'bring down the house'. His *Note Books* were not actually intended for publication, though he hoped that a few friends might perhaps turn them over at leisure; possibly that the few might prove many and not exclude the worthiest of his foes. They gradually became a well-stocked aquarium of thoughts and whims and fantasies which now and then supplied the readers of his books with an appetizing if peculiar dish. Ideas little and great, grave and jocose, were confided to them. He wrote first to please himself, and then perhaps to shock a ghostly Mrs. Grundy, or Professor Dryasdust, or Rev. Mr. Wilkinson, peering over his shoulder. His egotism is more obvious than real, though it is real enough. 'He is a poor creature who does not believe himself better than the whole world else.' But a sense of humour suffices 'to keep a man from all sins except those worth committing'; and Butler's humour plays everywhere—nowhere more lightly and luminously than over his deepest gravity.

Thoughts after all are as much secretions of feeling as of mind. And though Butler's thoughts for the most part resemble cold steel, he often uses his victim 'an if he loved him'. A sudden warmth and kindliness at times kindles his words, and imagination, born as it were of his passion for 'common simple straightforwardness', here and there lifts his prose into a region not far removed from that of poetry. That a poet indeed he was—and one disdaining verse—is proved by the last few pages of this volume.

But the *Note Books* defy summary or analysis, crammed as they are with speculation and wisdom, irony, satire, pranks, quips, and stories. Any page will set the wits to work, amuse, arrest, provoke. Now and then their *obiter dicta* will test even a strong stomach. The shut mind had better approach them warily—they might blow its hinges off. To Mr. Festing Jones their manageableness and much of their charm and value are due. His index is not less invaluable than the arrangement of his superabundant material—this mute quizzical setting side by side of apparently contradictory extravagancies, each illuminating each. Some of the notes, indeed, had Butler's editor for origin: 'Jones said he had not much conscience, and what little he had was guilty.' If only a like small but very guilty conscience might inspire every editor! As Bacon said: 'You may take *Sarza* to open the Liver; *Steele* to open the Spleene; *Flowers* of *Sulphur* for the Lungs; *Castoreum* for the Braine; but no Receipt openeth the Heart, but a true Frend; To whom you may impart Griefes, Joyes, Feares, Hopes, Suspicions, Counsels, and whatsoever lieth upon the Heart, to oppresse it, in a kind of Civill Shrift or Confession.' Sarza, steel, sulphur, castoreum, all are here; here, too, the priceless friend that has done so much to ensure Butler's 'only true' immortality, and that of a duration far exceeding his own hope—'a good average three score years and ten'.

Edinburgh Review, Jan. 1913

'POUR LES MILITAIRES'*

If a novelist's style willy-nilly bears the impress of his temperament, not less clearly his complete fiction is a kind of representation, in the large, of his life, outlook, character, and surroundings. The novels of Disraeli, for instance, of Richardson, of Dickens, the plays and lyrics of Shelley, the very nonsense of Lear—all are so many full- (or part-) length looking-glasses in which one can survey over each shoulder in turn, in colour, angle, movement, a sort of composite reflection of their respective authors. And Miss Lee's memoir of Ouida shows that even an almost fabulously popular novelist may be actually, and in reverse of this process, a vivid and faithful replica of his evanescent masterpieces.

An attempt positively to live Ouida's novels would, maybe, pass the wit of man. None the less, Ouida herself succeeded in this. She was born on New Year's Day, 1839. Her father was a witty, unprepossessing Frenchman, who managed to teach his native language in the schools of Bury St. Edmunds; and to remain 'mysterious'. He would disappear for months at a time. Not even Madame Ramé was aware of her husband's precise pursuits. It was all guesswork; and guesswork suggested 'secret societies'. Romance, then—even though it was a little dubious in kind—watched over Ouida's cradle. She was precocious. At twelve she was already a politician, a scorner of Louis Napoleon, an ardent free-thinker. At fourteen she wrote a history of England, and fell in love, not once, but as often as the tinder of her heart was enkindled by the faintest spark of masculine kindness. This lean, lanky girl in a crinoline was already an ardent lover of Nature, with a passion for dogs and horses. Her human sympathies were more or less restricted to one sex.

* *Ouida: A Memoir.* By Elizabeth Lee (Fisher Unwin).

In April 1859 (her twenty-first year), she contributed to Harrison Ainsworth's *Miscellany* her first story, entitled 'Dashwood's Dog, or the Derby and What Came of It'. The 'secret agent' had long since vanished into secrecy, and the burden of keeping up the kind of home which mother and daughter had been accustomed to now lay entirely upon her young shoulders. But 'Fame in a stoale of purple set with eies' was well on its way. In '65 she met her true friend and publisher Baron Tauchnitz, and offered him *Strathmore*, which had been, she assured him, 'most triumphant' in America. In '66 she sent him *Chandos*, 'the most brilliant of my books'. And two years afterwards the *Revue des Deux Mondes* is introducing to its readers 'Un écrivain dont l'exubérante imagination, la verve facile, l'esprit courant, la désinvolture aristocratique ont appelé l'attention du public anglais'.

This insular public was soon to be scandalized 'par les audaces dont ils n'ont pas l'habitude', by subjects of a luridness at which even 'les Dickens et les Thackerays' blanched. But Ouida was contemptuous—'Je n'écris pas pour les femmes, j'écris pour les militaires.' Her very name fell like a reiterated knell upon Victorian drawing-rooms. Some fifty novels were her final score— and that implies twenty-four years of hard work at least— fully enough to keep 'les Thackerays' permanently pallid. Our own question is not so much who now concocts lavish and garish romance 'pour les militaires', but who is not shocking?

Tongues even in '65 had begun to wag over this 'dangerous' young person. It was whispered that she was none other than the scandalous Miss Evans, the author of *Adam Bede*, whose death, Ouida said long afterwards, without mentioning names, had left only one novelist still living capable of writing good English. Her mother inquired in vain the name of the husband who had divorced Louise. Louise herself lived on in an ever-increasing blaze of splendour and notoriety. She gave dinner parties to officers and gentlemen, who were invited to talk *au naturel*; and thus, like the Claimant, their vivacious, exacting hostess picked up of an evening what she could put to signal use next day. *Puck* proves the soundness of her views on entertaining—not without a tinge of cynicism. Later in life, when these dashing parties at the Langham Hotel were brilliancies of the past, Henry James, who, like Ruskin before him, paid willing tribute to Ouida's ardent love of Italy, was to give a somewhat acidulated account of her personality: 'She was *curious*, in a common, little way . . . a little terrible, and finally pathetic, *grotesque.*' His comment is also *curious*—and in a similar way.

But in her heyday Ouida's grotesqueness took a less obviously pathetic form. Celebrities flocked to meet her and were often tartly entreated. Critics sincerely flattered her. Whyte Melville found *Puck* a 'first-rate, first-class, first-flight novel'; Lord Lytton commended her delicate grace of style; great artists paid 'homage' to *Ariadne*, and '*really* understood it'. She sunned herself in adulation. She gowned her mother in black for foil to her own bright satins. Half Florence—but not more than half—was at her feet. William Allingham described her in his diary as 'dressed in green silk, with a clever, sinister face, her hair down, small hands and feet, and a voice like a carving knife'. Twenty years later as pungent an observer was impressed by her 'tallowy skin, her straight black hair, red nose, her *décolleté* gown of blue glistening silk, covered with lace resembling a curtain, the skirt very short to display her beautiful feet, cased in blue satin shoes'. And even that faithful witness was not of her own sex. Such is the malice of notoriety. But Ouida insisted on attention, though she detested mere newspaper publicity. And *Friendship*, which split half Florence into quarters, shows to what extreme even in those modest days the craze for public confession could lead her.

Her extravagance was a byword. She had a noble contempt for money, and was always at her wits' end to obtain it. She fed her infatuated dogs on truffles and squandered the rest of her income on litigation. She even went to law against a lawyer. Her vanity was as naïve as it was magnificent. 'My fame, my power', exclaims this 'idol of the great world'—and this, even to her publisher! None the less she had the sagacity to perceive that she was probably merely a passing fashion—as transitory an object of worship as the golden calf. 'I think you will find *The Massarenes* worth 1,000 Trilbys.' 'Keep my book at the *head* of your advertisement. You have nothing to equal it.' 'Dear Mrs. Thornton,—As you were so kind as not to ask for an autograph, I send you mine. Ouida.' But her courage matched her egotism. She feared no man and nothing when her convictions or her most genuine and ardent sympathies were at stake. The dumb

animals never had a more eloquent friend. No dread of conse-
quences, no sacrifice of time or of money could daunt her. She
had strong views and expressed them in strong terms to strong
men, and she was bitterly vindictive. Rhodes, Chamberlain,
'that madman' Gladstone, even Queen Victoria, were victims of
her violent pen. She abhorred commercialism, militarism, and
socialism. She loved beauty and fought boldly against oppression
and injustice.

But evil days came. She outlived her vogue and many of her
friendships. An abominable outrage at the hands of a vile land-
lady undermined her health, and vain attempts to obtain redress
impoverished her when she could no longer make money at will
and at ease. A cold moonlight night, spent with her four dogs in
a cab in the piazza of the railway station at Viareggio, caused
blindness in one eye. She was humiliated by well-intentioned
but vulgar offers of charity. Yet her last tragic days found her
spirit unbroken, her vanity still the most precious of consolations.

Ouida always hated memoirs. 'To possess any interest they
must be treacherous—in general to the dead.' In hers is only
the treachery of truth. A garish reputation quickly fades. The
thankless mob that enjoys being titillated, shocked, derided,
defied, turns at last the coldest of cold shoulders on a favourite
by whom it is merely bored.

Times Literary Supplement, March 26, 1914

THE COMPLETE WORKS OF THACKERAY*

One by one the Shades of the great Victorian era are facing that exacting ordeal—the celebration of a centenary. The chorus of adulation and gratitude—or of detraction—is occasionally apt to drown the level voice of criticism; which being so, silence perhaps, after all, is best, the silence of those who need no reminder to quicken loyalty or to rekindle affection. The generation that in its teens eagerly devoured and exulted in Thackeray, that waited breathlessly month by month for his 'parts', is now—well, where, alas—or not alas—are the snows of yesteryear? Tastes and interests imperceptibly change, though, rarely, the elder generation usually thinks, for the better. But that the old delight in Thackeray is not faded, that the interest and fascination of his work are far from being a mere question of auld lang syne, is proved, if proof be needed, by the publication [1911] of two complete editions of his works, in twenty and twenty-six volumes respectively.

The Centenary Biographical Edition includes a series of portraits, one to each volume, depicting Thackeray at every age and in every pose (one or two of them not without a trace of benign superciliousness). Of these one of the most interesting exhibits him at the age of three—a little boy in skirts, standing on a pedestal surmounted by a pile of books and embracing his mother, while his father, a picture of grace and preternaturally tall, reclines beside them in a chair. The most amusing is Fred Walker's delighted sketch of the back view of a four-square and formidable personage holding a hat—Thackeray at forty-nine. *The Centenary Edition de Luxe* is de luxe indeed. It contains bibliographical introductions by Mr. Lewis Melville, and no

* *The Centenary Biographical Edition of the Works of William Makepeace Thackeray.* With Biographical Introductions by his daughter, Lady Ritchie. 26 vols. (Smith, Elder). *The Harry Furniss Centenary Edition de Luxe of the Works of Thackeray.* 20 vols. (Macmillan).

41

fewer than 2,000 illustrations, a fourth of which are new for the occasion, by Mr. Harry Furniss.

The virtue, and the most dangerous feature, of all 'Complete Works' is their completeness. To know all—is to be compelled to excuse much. And from even the most cordial in face of any such 'all' a sigh of longing *may* escape for a definitive edition, of any favourite author, whose completeness shall signify inclusion only of the best. Given Mr. Right for its arduous execution, the arrogance of sponsoring any such achievement might at least be condoned in busy days like these, when, so far as books are concerned, about nine months of every twelve bid foul to drown us in a reiterated spring tide.

Genius it would seem seldom comes unaccompanied into the world. In 1809 Tennyson was born, in 1811 Thackeray. In 1912 the hundredth anniversary of the birthdays of Robert Browning and Dickens was appropriately celebrated. With only a degree of appropriateness, let it be added, in Browning's case. At a celebration under the auspices—was it?—of the British Academy, Henry James, wide black-ribanded pince-nez on nose, tranquilly, drily and 'meticulously' softly blew—not his poet's trumpet—but blew up his poet's claims as a novelist, and Arthur Wing Pinero, less softly, made hay of any pretensions accepted by his Society to be a consummate writer of plays. The two novelists, like the two poets, so nearly contemporary, are invariably but capriciously associated. In aim and outlook, temperament and gifts, both pairs were leagues asunder. The discernible influence of each on each is very slender. A popular welcome as wide as theirs, refulgent perhaps a little too early for Tennyson, too belatedly for Browning, cheats even the wildest dreams of the people's chosen versifiers of today. It is hardly less saddening than surprising to learn that the mid-Victorians at least *bought* some quarter of a million copies of Coventry Patmore's *Angel in the House* (a feat rivalled much earlier by Martin Tupper's *Proverbial Philosophy*). The fastidious easily stomach the success of what they deride; but what of this Angel? Six-winged she is not; but her mount was no parochial Pegasus.

Both our novelists also wholeheartedly luxuriated in the love of the many; but Thackeray's was perhaps the more enviable fate for an artist—he won the idolatry of the few. He left novels —great and small—not only for a wide public, but for a select

and exclusive clan. He wrote for the most part books about
gentlemen for gentlemen, a limited source of inspiration; and he
penned them with a rather too close attention fixed on the para-
sitism, the affectation, and pretentiousness which gentility
brings in its train. 'My vanity would be to go through life as a
gentleman, as a Major Pendennis,' he said once, and was ever
ready to maintain, somewhat to the chagrin of Bohemia, that a
man of letters may not only be that, but a man of fashion too.
On the other hand, he more than once deplored the fate that he
lived at a time when reverence for rank, birth and fine manners
was in rapid process of disintegration and dilution; when, that
is, mere money had begun not only to talk too loud but also to
invest in the seats of the mighty; when the snob had become
almost as powerful as he was ubiquitous. Snobs, indeed, from
the Snob Royal to the snob literary, haunted Thackeray's
imagination as midges haunt the shades of evening. And he
poured out on them so fierce and deadly a fusillade of contempt
and abhorrence as to annihilate, if not the species, a few, surely,
of its *subs*. But then, how few of us refrain from all snobbery,
direct or inverted? Is there not a disquieting trace of it in this
passion for showing it up?

Thackeray faced and scrutinized his limited but conspicuous
section of the world of mankind with a mind now fascinated, now
repelled. And in either mood his was a survey from his privy
gazebo so searching that in extent and detail it forms for his
period a kind of universal gazetteer. We read him, and there
passes before our eyes an astonishingly lifelike panorama of the
social London of his day, thronged with figures in a direct and
natural relation each with each, and grouped in a design that is
neither arbitrary nor fantastic. And yet what is the intrinsic and
final meaning of it all to a mind intent on the less shallow riddles
of life? Against what background of mystery, of the beyond,
do these puppets enjoy, or rebel against, their being? Why do
Tolstoy and Tchekov stir and deepen heart and understanding,
and why does Thackeray so frequently awaken little better
than a transitory but absorbed curiosity, often sharpened by
aversion?

The very term and thing, Victorianism—and it has received
its full measure of ridicule and belittlement, has now a peculiarly
local provenance. And if Thackeray had overheard the charge of

provincialism that has been levelled against him, he might well have invited his Age to come to his defence. The lords and ladies he loved to etch and the circumferential fringe that basked and fawned in their rays or feebly strove to conceal itself from their influences were busied about many things, but not much troubled, as Jeames expressed it, by 'the mite and madgisty of existence'. 'Our history—is of the world and things pertaining to it.' And 'you belong to your belongings, my dear,' remarked Lady Kew to Ethel Newcome. But although the age that sees itself reflected in Thackeray's mirror was by comparison with much of the past (another day than ours will concern itself with the present) a transient and superficial phenomenon, it is difficult to believe that it went its way content with quite such impoverished and flaccid ideals. 'I ask you to believe', he wrote in his preface to *Pendennis*, 'that the person writing strives to tell the truth.' But it is not so much the truth that is vitally material, as what kind of truth, and the truth concerning what particular object. And we cannot help surmising that the apparent deadliness of the world without seemed to him to be some kind of apology for a rather marked reticence regarding the world within.

It is indeed an unusual experience in reading Thackeray to feel that we are face to face with a man who is pouring out his whole heart to us. On many of the great questions he is at least reserved. 'What a situation for a man! for a philanthropist', he said of Steele, 'not to dare to look in the face of the religion he adored.' But even after that comes an illustrative reference to 'jeering creditors', grocers, butchers, and small-coal men. We read of Heber 'committing his case to the quarter whither such pious men are wont to carry their doubts', and catch a faint flavour of Gibbon. It is because Thackeray more than once deliberately announces himself to be a moralist (an office only indirectly the novelist's) and openly avows that preaching is the humorist's real forte, that we begin to wonder why the cumulative effect of his books is so unsatisfying. His powers were in a measure checked and impeded by a certain ingrained self-distrust and diffidence, increased possibly by too assiduous a practice of analysis and introspection. The habit seems to have grown on him of writing down (not necessarily far down) to a lesser self—to the self, that is, which gets on in the world, is seen of men, is respected and respectable. He preached back, as it were, at his youth, and forward at an age that might find him hardened and unapproachable. He made a god of good sense, and endeavoured to counteract the poverty of its ritual by burning incense at the shrine of sentiment, or muttering rather savage asides in the porch. And good sense is not, and never will be, the inspiration, although at its highest it must be the fundamental condition, of great art.

The world for Thackeray, indeed, had early played the jilt; and after that experience a man's first and worst temptation is to salve his vanity at the expense of his fickle mistress. Thackeray was by nature exquisitely sensitive, and to the sensitive solitude is an indispensable refuge; but he was also, when his mood and company allowed him to be, an extremely sociable and clubbable man, and never really wearied of the booths and crowds, the craft and artlessness, the tinsel and gingerbread of the great Fair. He could guffaw and huzza with the many, and he could take his place apart with the few, aloof, ironic, tolerant, contemptuous, maledictory, but still an engrossed spectator. At school the little boy with a head so big as to excite an entirely needless anxiety concerning its contents in an observant aunt was inclined to be idle. Every day Dr. Russell used to begin at him, 'Thackeray, Thackeray, you are an idle, profligate, shuffling boy.' How many such boys have idled into eminence! He was abused, he said, into sulkiness, and bullied into despair. But even in these early days he discovered a kind of retaliatory enjoyment in checking, so to speak, 'Violets, bright blue violets', against 'Cabbages, bright green cabbages'. His Cambridge was only Charterhouse on another scale. And when Thackeray went out into the world, comparatively easy in pocket, rich in gifted and faithful friends, generous, approachable, enthusiastic, the world, as is its wont, treated him in much the same fashion as the horse-dealer treated Moses Primrose. He rode boldly into the lists, and had a fall.

The experience left him sore and still more at odds than ever with the conflicting elements of his temperament. And through the life that followed—early to be darkened by a sorrow past even time to heal—we seem to watch his struggle to come to terms, to make peace between them. He faced what could be only a transitory defeat bravely and doggedly, and although the first hope and resiliency of youth were gone past recall, he had not lost the invaluable power of losing self and self-consciousness together in sheer riotous fun and gaiety. '"God save the King!"' cries Captain Hedzoff in *The Rose and the Ring*, 'executing a demivolte, two semilunes, and three caracoles.' And the feat was never beyond 'Old Thack's' dignity or fits of depression either. It is this perennial fountain of high spirits, this fecundity, this endless, lucid, unchecked rivulet of words that never cease to astonish us. But given that temperament and that early disillusionment, it is not much to be wondered at that when, after *Punch* and journalism, *Yellowplush*, *The Snobs*, and the satirical *Catherine*, Thackeray turned with hoarded thought and feeling in *Vanity Fair* to portray life as it actually is—it is not surprising that his work should then present rather the outlook of a blasé and world-ridden sexagenarian than that of a young man still midway in his thirties. But the pitiless cynicism of the book is certainly not more remarkable than its grasp, its boldness, its acute insight into character and motive, and the placid assurance with which the now practised author arranges his vast, packed canvas. None the less there must be something, some secret life-giving grace and beauty denied to any record of life that leaves such an aridity and sourness behind it. Only the partial truth is here. Compared with it the Vanities of Ecclesiastes are consolation indeed.

In the greatest writers analysis attempts in vain to discover the process that has transformed experience into literature. Poetry is the sudden blossoming, after long and hidden growth, of roots deep in the earth and of boughs in heaven. Genius advances from intuition to intuition with an absorption untroubled and unperplexed by inessentials, and compels life to its own ends. Talent sits before its models and takes infinite pains over what genius may not even have consciously ignored. In Thackeray's work we see, now tending to one side, now to the other, a complex blend of these different and to some extent antagonistic methods. He assiduously copies; he is impelled to create. Now it is a comprehensively detailed transcription; now it is, with that resounding slap on the knee, 'Genius, by God!' —even if the particular passage, the defeat of Becky Sharp, which evoked his tribute is to some tastes by no means his happiest. Just our ordinary inquisitive everyday selves follow critically and unmovedly, with wits cold but keen, nine of his long chapters. Comes the tenth, and for a moment, we sit enthralled by some sudden exquisite simplicity. A brilliant searchlight has probed into the back of our hearts. Simply as a question of art, capacity, and accomplishment, what reader of the *Irish Sketch Book* could foresee that *Barry Lyndon* would be its vivid outcome? The bees of the imagination have turned common honest honey into a treacle on which to nourish a Queen. It is not only the first real book that Thackeray finished, it is the first of the few books of the best Thackeray—a Thackeray undividedly in love with his task. Barry is alive, a free spirit, snapping his fingers at a possibly aghast creator. He is of the blood of Becky. Only towards the end of this novel does Thackeray really break the spell, and clasping a voluminous footnote to his bosom, climb into the pulpit. Barry is the first revelation of so many to follow of what his characters could do with Thackeray when he gave them *carte blanche*; when, that is, he did not, like a restless anxious mother, keep tidying up and preening, exhausting his children with too much attention, constantly asking himself that disastrous question for a man afire with an idea, 'Now, what will they think of this?'

His work was a great labour to him. 'Oh, the struggles and bothers—oh, the throbs and pains about this trumpery!' He knew only too well the desperate hours that must sometimes be spent in brooding over a watched pot. Yet in the end, he once confessed, his novels for the most part wrote themselves. 'The characters once created lead me, and I follow where they direct.' But that kind of following is the arduous pursuit of Ariel. And Thackeray, as that punctiliously industrious maker of books Anthony Trollope reiterated again and again, was not only inclined to be too lax and dilatory with himself, he was not always loyal and diligent enough to be worthy of his characters. In *Pendennis*, in *The Newcomes*, even in *Esmond*, caprice or tiredness or inattention blurs their outlines. They are consummately alive for pages and pages together, then comes a moment when the hand falters, the grip relaxes. The man who could immortalize Harry Foker and Costigan could, we feel, have made a better thing of Mirobalant; the creator of Becky and Blanche must have nodded a little over Laura Bell. The narrative flows and ebbs, wavers, halts, diverges. In most of the novels there is a conspicuous absence of what Matthew Arnold delighted to call *architectonicé*. There is, too, a rather indolent uniformity of personality and fate in his heroes. The young man fights and duels and gambles, recovers from a severe attack of calf-love, and returns after maturer adventures to the still faithful heart, magnanimous and passive enough, through all trials and tribulations, to have tarried his time. Thackeray's virtuous people, moreover, have a restricted range of virtues, in the exercise of which intellect (as with Meredith) or passion (as with Hardy) have not, as a rule, much to say. And his vicious are at least uncomplicated enough to have been definitely and precisely inveighed against in the Ten Commandments. Nor, however vigorously he rattles the box, does he readily convince us that his dice are unloaded. He saw to it that in his own novels at any rate no 'swaggering young scapegrace' should get as much 'plum-cake' as fell to the lot of Tom Jones. He affirmed a little lugubriously that 'since Fielding no writer of fiction among us has been permitted to depict to his utmost power a Man. We must drape him and give him a certain conventional simper.' On the other hand, Eve, he thought, was not much the worse for doffing a 'smirking paradisical nudity'. The pivot of the matter is the word 'permitted'. Really independent minds are apt to take French leave. It is possible, too, that Boccaccio, Sterne, and perhaps Fielding himself would have echoed the complaint.

Thackeray certainly stayed his hand, withheld his 'utmost power', well on this side of excess. And yet the reader cannot but become conscious, not only that Thackeray's mind was too sedulously occupied with the meaner aspects of life, with what was for him its wrong side, but also that at times innuendo is going all but as far as innuendo can, and that it is not invariably balanced by any enkindling revelation of the more unearthly and heroic impulses and ideals. Though Charlotte Brontë could find no greater fault than a disquieting flippancy in her hero— 'Thackeray is unique. I *can* say no more, I *will* say no less,' Harriet Martineau was not so easily pacified—'I confess to being unable to read *Vanity Fair* from the moral disgust it occasions.' Moral disgust is a somewhat rare attitude towards fiction in these days of life for life's sake. Still, man naked as he came into the world would be infinitely preferable to the vixens, the sharpers, the cads, the unco' guid, the 'whitened and raddled old women', the mean and the mercenary and the matchmakers over whom Thackeray laboured with conscience unperturbed, with a probe so skilful, and with an averted nose.

An ever-present consciousness of his audience is some explanation of this peculiar limitation and of this peculiar predilection. Reading his lectures on the English Humorists we almost hear the rustle of moiré silk, the warm but gloved applause, the unanimous patter of congratulation. Was this the man we should have liked to live with? he asked his hearers concerning Swift, so sure of his answer that the panic outbreak that follows against the 'dreadful Dean', and the too audible sob over the lamentable fate of Stella, seem a little supererogatory. The author that is to deepen our lives with the intensest moments, with the full-charged moods of his men and women, must refrain his own personal emotions and keep them low. Thackeray could not deny himself the joy of addressing the jury, and in so doing often made havoc of his case.

In his art he is curiously unequal. At his best—how well-nigh faultless that best can be! 'Esmond', said Pater, is 'a perfect fiction'. It is of one piece, on one level, mellow, reticent, complete. And death claimed the author of Denis Duval with power renewed, romance revivified, magic easily his own again. 'There came a broadside from us—the first I had ever heard in battle'—these are its last words. And though by no means Thackeray's first broadside, Denis Duval promised unmistakably to be his most resounding one. Let him but escape from the trammels and fret of the life immediately around him, from the itching of old wounds and the chatter of tongues, and a perfect serenity comes into his work—an ease, a mastery, an atmosphere, beyond the attainment of the greatest of his contemporaries. His talent was as wide in scope as his genius was supreme by fits and starts. As essayist, The Roundabout Papers, shrewd, whimsical, at peace, place him with Addison and Steele, if a good way beneath Lamb and Montaigne—his bedside companion. Poet he could not be, fearing an inmost seriousness almost more than cant. But even his lightest ballads are often flawless in form; crisp, and natty. Even Jeames can break into a lyric in which burlesque fails to conceal a real impulse towards beauty:

E   49

When moonlike ore the hazure seas
In soft effulgence swells,
When silver jews and balmy breaze
Bend down the Lily's bells;
When calm and deep, the rosy sleap
Has lapt your soul in dreams,
R Hangeline! R lady mine!
Dost thou remember Jeames?

It is beloved Tom Hood, mis-spelt; and Walter Scott had a finger in the melody. Nor was this finish a facile achievement. For though the immortal 'little Billee' was the offspring of a few minutes at a concert in Rome, Thackeray once confessed to having given four mornings' hard labour to the writing of six lines of verse. He rarely describes nature—this devotee of Pall-mall; but what delicate tender glimpses of evening and night, vignettes of peace and solitude, beautify as if at haphazard his novels. And at times to what real quietness of hope and regret, love and rapture, his people come. Who can forget the voice welcoming Harry, filling the old words with an emotion never to leave them again: 'He in tears that soweth reapeth a joyful harvest'? And even the renowned but perhaps just questionable *Adsum* could be paralleled by moments certainly not less moving and memorable.

The years have gone by, and the 'Life' Thackeray characteristically shrank from contemplating has not yet been written. Much of that life, and the man himself willy-nilly, are lucidly in his books for any reader of insight. And in the prefaces to the *Biographical Edition* are what for many people is an infinitely better thing than any biography, formal, extraneous, and disproportionate—Lady Ritchie's store of memories, gilded with the sunshine of childhood, bringing with such sure and simple touches as her father himself might have envied his very presence before our eyes.

Times Literary Supplement, June 29, 1911

DANIEL DEFOE*

The enduring influence of most great writers, and of all poets, springs out of a lifelong conflict between the world of their imagination and the great world of sense. It is rather their unlikeness than their resemblance to their fellows that distinguishes them; the rareness of their qualities, not the superabundance of those common to all. 'They give the heavenly manna of idea on which the noble mind can feed,' as Mr. Masefield says in an Introduction to this volume of singular insight and distinction. Popularity regarding such men, either during their lives or after they are dead, is therefore mainly an illusion. For popularity is only the smile that comes into the face of a generation seated before its favourite author with palm outstretched, asking not a bluntly truthful delineation of its fortune or 'character', but for a little dexterous yet fulsome flattery. There is, however, another greatness almost as rare as theirs, and sometimes shared by them, which consists in the mere universality of a writer's attraction—the attraction of the ideas and characteristics of the vast majority of men become lucid and articulate. Such writers, because, though fashions may change, the crowd that follows them changes but little, inherit a continual following both from the many and the few. Their writing is of the earth, their ideal substantive and rational, their subject-matter the texture of daily and common life. But of all such writers none surely ever crept so low, and kept so close to the normal intelligence and experience of mankind as Defoe.

Few have had the gifts and the opportunity. 'If he valued any of his writings,' Mr. Masefield thinks, 'he valued those volumes of party journalism by which he had helped on the cause of liberty.' But we need not too loyally follow an author's preferences. And party journalism, or pamphleteering, is not the best

* *Defoe*. Edited by John Masefield (Masters of Literature. Bell).

school of immortality. Little that Defoe wrote for the Press, or for his patrons, is likely to attract even the most diligent reader of today. The fact, however, that he launched from Newgate and unfailingly produced with his own pen his little four-paged *Review* three times a week for nearly nine years, contributed everywhere, and compiled about 250 complete works besides, proves, quite apart from the thirteen fortunes he made and lost in trade, politics, and literature, how courageous, volatile, quick-headed, and 'unabashable' this dark, spare, middle-aged, hawk-nosed champion and idolater of the people must have been. That his gift for romance survived such appalling industry is the most remarkable fact of all. It wore down and impoverished much that a quiet and grave life leaves untarnished, but it completely failed to quench his youth and spirit, his sublime naïveté, his zeal for life and for the attention of the busy, fractious world of men.

Defoe charms and endears us, yet we scarcely know how or why. His humour is little else than a kind of shrewd, or coarse, or ingenuous good sense. We become conscious again and again in his stories of a real kindness and pity for the outcast, the unfortunate, the suddenly abased, the simple, and the misled. But it is seen only in glimpses, and for the most part is stifled by a robust worldliness, the keenness, haste, and blindness of the practical man, by just such a cold and weary indifference as horrified the creator (and destroyer) of Little Nell, when Crusoe dismisses Friday with a terse 'They let fly about 300 arrows, and to my inexpressible grief killed poor Friday,' and deletes his island as if with a sigh of relief. 'I have now done with my island and all manner of discourse about it. And whoever reads the rest of my memorandums would do well to turn his thoughts entirely from it.' Even Moll's lamentable remorse and terror of the hangman cannot expunge a deed of heedlessness such as this!

So far as his portrayal of humanity is concerned, it is impossible to believe that Defoe knew, either intuitively or by study, so little of his own adult nature, of his own vivid and active intelligence, as the insensitive superficiality of his men and women would seem to imply. However clear and intense their early life may be, it dies out at last, like a slowly expiring candle, simply, it seems, because he continues to write on about

them with reiterated effort long after his interest has faded away
and tedium has set in. 'Defoe's creed', says Mr. Masefield, 'was
earnest and solemn, the temper of his mind was earnest and
solemn.'

And yet, in spite of this, nothing seems to be less the outcome of any deep earnestness than the moral interludes and
reflections that interrupt his stories—rarely, however, when
their intrusion would be destructive of their dramatic interest.
The repentance into which he drives all such wicked characters
as escape the gallows or Virginia comes only from the soreness
after punishment, never from a broken spirit and a contrite
heart. Has he left prosperous a more despicable Worldly Wise-
man than the sententious Quaker in *Captain Singleton*? And still
we feel it is all due to their author's perfunctoriness, that he
knew mankind more profoundly than he had the patience or
inclination, or than it seemed worth while, to show. Betty,
indeed, before she becomes Mrs. Flanders, might easily have
inspired Thackeray; there is a French vivacity in the earlier
chapters of her history; and one of her many husbands reminds
us unmistakably of the art of Mr. George Moore. 'Let the
naturalists explain these things, and the reason and manner of
them: all I can say to them is to describe the fact,' exclaims
Crusoe, almost petulantly, after that touching cry from the
heart, 'O that it had been but one—but one soul saved!' And
his petulance echoes across almost with the force of a direct
challenge to Mr. Henry James.

But Defoe left a good many other things to the 'naturalists',
poetry among them. Of all that he wrote, his verse least brings
poetry to mind. Yet, as in all good work that deals directly with
life, he has left in his prose innumerable passages that are, as it
were, the clarified actuality out of which poetry is made, that
marvellous description, for instance, of the comets in the *Journal
of the Plague*:

'In the first place, a blazing star or comet appeared for several
months before the plague, as there did the year after another, a
little before the fire; the old women remarked . . . that those two
comets passed directly over the city, and that so very near the
houses that it was plain they imported something peculiar to the
city alone. That the comet before the pestilence was of a faint,
dull, languid colour, and its motion very heavy, solemn, and

slow; but that the comet before the fire was bright and sparkling or, as others said, flaming, and its motion swift and furious. . . . Nay, so particular some people were, that as they looked upon that comet preceding the fire they fancied that they not only saw it pass swiftly and fiercely, and could perceive the motion with their eye, but even they heard it; that it made a rushing, mighty noise, fierce and terrible, though at a distance, and but just perceivable.'

It is significant that he lays the burden of this fantasticalness upon the backs of the old women, 'and the phlegmatic hypochondriac part of the other sex, who I could almost call old women too'. Here and there he actually lingers on the strange borderland of poetry. In a passing reference, perhaps, to daybreak and the sea; in his 'transports' of fear, despair, and of gratitude; certainly, too, in a wistful thought of Crusoe's that possibly long after he has sailed away the parrots will still be calling him over the lonely island, 'Robin Crusoe, Robin Crusoe!' and there will be none to heed or answer.

In the event, however, 'that broken-down mariner', as Mr. Masefield ungraciously calls him, leaves a disenchanted island behind him, the abode of hated trespassers on our fancy—Spaniards and futile pirates, and that complete bore and masterbuilder of wicker-work, Will Atkins—when, that is, he at last sails home. For Defoe's mind concentrates itself on the foreground, the tangible, the immediate present. It is too restless and too busy for profound insight or fixity of purpose. No more than any of his contemporaries does he seem to have looked with conscious longing or remembrance or hope upon nature. His colourless scenes are like woodcuts, sharp and clear. 'His fondness for the industry of man limited his sympathies,' but he compels us to share his rapture in silks and velvets, in a midwife's graduated bills, and in such works of art as in *Captain Singleton* 'put our artificer to his trumps'. And though *Roxana* in her autobiography grows almost eloquent over her charms of face and shape and unpainted skin, it is little else than a simpering confidentiality across the counter.

It is, in fact, the absence of these aesthetic and introspective qualities in Defoe that is the secret of his peculiar power. It enabled him to concentrate his mind, to the exclusion of everything else, on the world without. The objective reduced to its common denominator was his instinctive aim. He had waited upon life at its crudest and barest, and had thus acquired so wide a knowledge and so packed a memory of actuality that when he chanced to turn to story-telling for a living it poured out with all the novelty of an unfailing invention. Art seems needless when mere instinct can produce such a little masterpiece of verisimilitude as *The Apparition of Mrs. Veal*. It epitomizes Defoe's method—of sedulously accumulating detail till the result has all the tang and substantiality of fact. The reading of his stories at their best therefore has the clearness and force of an actual experience, an experience, too, far more vivid and precise than that which most of us can gain for ourselves. And since Defoe's reality is never that of the modern 'realist', who walks the world spying out the inconspicuous refuse of experience, but always carries with it the personality and the humanity of its medium, nothing breaks through his narrative but what came there of its own immediate appeal and carried its full significance. Such romancing has all the fascination of one of those matter-of-fact dreams in which we are spectators of our own actions without the possibility of interruption from within or without. It is a complete absorption of the senses in which the faint rumour that accompanies conscious life is stilled—the condensed spectacle of the peepshow.

To attain this effect a story must of necessity be a direct, personal narrative. There must be no meddling by any third party. It is partly for this reason, we think, that all Defoe's stories break every now and then into his peculiar undramatic dialogue; not merely, as he himself asserts in one place, for the sake of brevity, but in order to avoid any interference with what mainly occurs in talk—a voice speaking, a voice replying. Not for him the psychological aura, the half-tones, the subconscious syllabling of the 'naturalist'. So elementary a reality could, of course, be peopled only with elementary intelligences. Defoe's characters, greatest and least (and little more than a moral hairsbreadth divides them), never shock us with our own inferiority. They are just such obvious and everyday creatures as we must all appear to be to the great outside world that knows not even so much as our names. Their good and evil are as primitive as the good and evil with which a common jury is concerned. If indeed it was conscious craft that made Singleton and Crusoe men so modest and ordinary in their extraordinary circumstances, it was a craft that sprang from pure genius. Defoe descends with such limpid ease to the level of the boy who reads of these amazing and harmless heroes that he comes near to being in this narrow degree one of the most imaginative writers the world has ever seen. Does he not from the beginning cunningly let us into the secret that Crusoe's huge periagua is the hopeless, senseless scheme we are so distressed and delighted at his afterwards finding it to be? We revel in a reiterated 'I told you so'. We sit with heart caught up watching fate's insidious perfidies—the ravaged grapes, the prolific cats, the noble hapless venture out to sea, the immovable roll of sheet lead that we modestly surmise Robinson *might* have thought of hacking into strips. On our own unworthy heads fall the fragmentary and even super-fluous benefactions of that 'Superior Power' which not even the most impious of Defoe's adventurers ever really questioned— Crusoe's 'Mahometan' whiskers, the few grains of barley spared by the rats, the magazine of muskets, the sea-caked barrel of powder, the tobacco pipe (withheld a score of years) in the drowned ship-boy's pocket, the 'refreshing' handker-chiefs, the five black wives for the five white mariners, the mutineers lapped in sleep while their captain roams the shore; the Cavalier's saddle stuffed with gold; Jack's hollow tree in the lonely fields beyond the 'Blind Beggars' at Bethnal Green.

We do not dream of questioning, either, the hints let fall here and there of the subliminal. The highwayman does not surprise us who hears 'very plain' Moll's heart-broken far-away cry, 'Oh, Jemmie, come back, come back!' Nor does Roxana's glimpse of the second-sight, just before, like Lorenzo, the mur-dered jeweller rides out to his doom; nor the oft-repeated veridical dream; nor even the 'line' of piracy on Singleton's tell-tale palm. For when the abnormal visits perfectly normal people it seems merely one of those delightful improbabilities that diversify plain fact. 'How strange and chequered a work of Providence is the life of man!' So strange that it needs little adornment to make of it pure romance.

For it is Defoe's innate, seeming, simplicity, his insatiable in-terest and delight in life, his eager man-to-man appeal to the whole world's teen-year-old children, whether in age or spirit, that are the surest proof of his genius. Youth swept back into that harassed tormented heart which apparently did not so much as begin to dream of Romance until its possessor was all but sixty years old. If ever beauty appears in his work, it is from this clear well-spring. It ebbed hopelessly away from the callous worldliness of *Roxana*, but even in his tedious *Family Instructor*, not very far removed in its ideals from those of *The Complete Tradesman*, in spite of the real touches of character in its natty dialogue, the one fragment that remains in the memory is the opening talk between the little boy and his father. No man can recall his childhood without dwelling on its peculiar sense of solitude. And Defoe, we feel, spent all his wracked and crowded life in solitude—the solitude of an acute, restless personal life besieged by business and care, by 'crowds of fine folks' and mean. 'I can affirm', says Crusoe in his 'Serious Reflections', 'that I enjoy much more solitude in the middle of the greatest collection of mankind in the world, I mean, at London, while I am writing this, than ever I could say I enjoyed in eight-and-twenty years' confinement to a desolate island.' This pervasive sense of inward silence and loneliness steals over the imagination in reading Defoe at his best. How still and close to us is Crusoe's island. There is a sky above us, but we rarely lift our eyes to it; out of utter silence the clamorous host of birds flies up at echo of his gun. The sea stretches around us in its concave immensity, ringing a solitude like that of a picture. It is indeed with a shocked and almost a woeful incredulity that we learn that America itself is in sight when Crusoe ascends his little hill. So too in *Captain Singleton* we push solitarily on in the company of that little band of abstractions, the twenty-seven maroons, beset by unknown fears (and battalions of elephants), through forest and wilderness.

But more hauntingly yet descends silence and solitude upon the reader in *The Journal of the Plague Year*. Defoe's masterly English, compounded of the Bible and the raciest vernacular, is nowhere else so impressive. The 'saddler's' narrative enslaves the mind and seems to shut off all retreat—the first gossip and stir of distrust and foreboding, the cumulative innuendo, the facts and figures that take in their nakedness as sinister a bearing as the far-off waft across the water of a pirate's ancient itself; the thronging, mocking, terror-stricken crowds; the quacks and seers and occultists; the deepening hush broken ever and again by a piercing cry; and then at last the deserted, grass-grown streets, the barred doors, the watchmen and the bell; and the gathering, drifting mist of death settling thickly upon all. A shadowy form seems to stoop over the writer's shoulder, compelling him, though intent only on the bare facts and on his own shadow wandering through the London of his childhood, to record its mysterious presence in his sharp deliberate prose.

Defoe is read 'by schoolboys and kitchenmaids, by sailors', says Mr. Masefield. It is an entranced but not exacting circle, perhaps. And yet it must indeed be an imagination a little over-enriched and belletristic, a little too fastidious, that cannot be content to shut out the greatest awhile and all the Muses, and fly with Jack 'down Old Bedlam into Moorfields' or with Crusoe and Singleton venture out upon the high seas, bound for Man Friday, or the sources of the Nile.

Times Literary Supplement, Nov. 12, 1909

MAPS IN FACT AND FICTION

It is a mournful thought that every explorer, since Adam was exiled from the Garden of Eden and the brighter stars were called by name, has ultimately only succeeded in contracting the human conception of the universe. The world as conceived by Homer was but a small blot on the world known to Ptolemy, and the world of Ptolemy merely a fraction in area of that mapped out by Martin Behaim. And yet the centuries in driving back the frontiers of *terra incognita* have somehow apparently cramped the fancy. For it is in the vaguely dreamed of and in the wholly unknown that the imagination takes its ease and delight. The present generation has experienced the treacherous novelty of having, first, the North Pole and then the South served up with its breakfast. It danced round them for a while as eagerly as children used to dance round a Jack-in-the-Green. But these May days will never dawn again. Does any unknown sea remain into which a yet-to-be-astonished mariner shall be the first to burst? Ought not the civilized world to have saved a few such, as children save a *bonne bouche* or sweethearts the last page of a love-letter? To muse indeed on a piece of water or mountains never seen by mortal eye, blind, can we say, even to its own being, and known only by an inconceivable Creator to be good, is to muse on a mystery past divining. Tomorrow, flight across the Atlantic will make but a three days' journey, a nine days' wonder. And though it would be a dull mind that could find no romance in a modern atlas, that atlas contests with the dictionary the claim to be a record of comparative finality. Neither flowers into guesswork or hearsay. They are concerned with all but finished achievement. There is even less chance (and all hail to Mr. Roosevelt!) of adding a new river or mountain or race to the one than there is of enriching with an endurable neologism the other.

Use and wont, then, as well as rather abject adoration of the practical, make maps of things-as-they-are dullish documents. Nimble spirits may, of course, entertain themselves as pleasantly with Mercator's Projection as with an Ordnance Survey imprint of six inches to the mile, in which one's neighbouring haystack and brook make as fair a show as Baghdad and the Amazons. But the spectacular pens and vivid surmises of the past are things of the past. Utterly out of fashion now are the beautiful old hues and designs, the brilliant banners above the tiny miniature cities, the winds and half winds and quarter winds, in black and green and red, of the portolan skin charts of the fifteenth and sixteenth centuries, with their seas of generous blue and emerald, lavishly edged with gold. And we should hardly even ourselves venture to huddle into the uppermost corner of Europe, as once the map-maker did, an amateur representation of the earthly paradise. Few latter-day travellers, perhaps, would envy Scylax of Cary-anda, the author of the oldest known Greek periplus, his coast-wise voyage of 153 days in circuit of the Mediterranean; but the most prosaic grown-up would rub his eyes in pleasure (mingled with scorn) at a geography chequered with such dream-wide suggestions of infinity as 'Beyond the Pillars of Hercules, which are in Europe, there are many trading stations of the Car-thaginians, also mud, and tides, and open seas.'

It is, indeed, the generous credulity, the childlike wonder, the independence of spirit (all excellently disguised as a passion for accuracy) in the ancient cartographers that are the fascination of their work. One can pore over the Catalan Map, for instance, for hours together, and rise refreshed as with the waters of Hippocrene. Why does the City of Lop, 'leagues south of the route of the caravans which pass from Sarra to Catayo across a great desert', so intrigue the fancy? And the Island of Chis? Has perchance Lord Dunsany trodden the echoing courts of the one, the yellow sands of the other? Why, for quite other than obvious reasons, does Regio Feminarum, tucked securely away in the remote, clear-cut oblong of the Island of Jaua, so cordially 'invite the soul'? Names as outlandish and bizarre throng every gazetteer, but the effect is by comparison sterile.

Whither is fled the visionary gleam?
Where is it now, the glory and the dream?

There are, of course, more succulent sops to the imagination even than these: 'Here reigns K. Stephen, a Christian. In this land lies St. Thomas. Look for the City Butifilis.' We look for the City Butifilis; and there it is. Cook's being our guide; we will pack up tomorrow! Up in the N.E. corner, again, sprawls the princedom of Gog and Magog, securely confined amid delicious mountains, as well as 'shut up by Alexander of Macedon'. Gog must have yearned northwards over those impregnable hills for the islands where abound 'many good Gerfalcons which are taken for the Great Can', and Magog have turned hungry eyes due south towards the '7,548 Islands' in the seas of the Indies 'where grow the spices', where dwell 'naked savages', and southwards still, towards Taprobana, 'last in the East', called by the Tartars Great Cantij, wherein flourish not only cannibals, negroes, etc., but wherein also falls into ceaseless ruin a nameless 'City destroyed by serpents'.

But the Catalan Map is of 1375. Gog and Magog have been reduced to a tavern sign, and the Great Khan's immortality is inextricably bound up with Samuel Taylor Coleridge's. Travellers' tales must grow leaner and leaner. But since there are ghosts in men's bodies, the desire for adventure will never perish. We shall seek other means for travel, dare lands beyond land's end and Thules still more ultimate. Mars shines for conquest. Far, far better—the gradual awakening of a sixth sense may renew and transmogrify the whole habitable globe?

Meanwhile there remains a way out of possible stagnation and ennui that has as yet attracted few adventurers. Neither Columbus nor Cabot, Vasco da Gama nor Vespucci ever set sail for the regions of Romance. Yet romance has always edged into, only to be as pertinaciously banished from, man's record of his earthly voyagings. Castles in Spain may have a poor reputation; yet their ruins, viewed through the perspective of time, wear a winning aspect. And to give to airy nothing a habitation and a name is the office not only of love but also of fiction. The song the sirens sang everybody knows the tune of, though nobody may remember the words. But we can only guess at the sandy trysting-place of Man Friday and Robinson Crusoe, and we are unlikely to explore on Shanks's mare the fabulous island of Monte Cristo. The whole problem, indeed, of the where, the how, and the when of the imaginative novelist is still obscure.

Modern story-tellers for the most part lap their creatures in the luxuries of a real Mayfair, or people with phantasms the streets-in-being of an actual Five Towns. They only thinly disguise their Wessex, their Dartmoor. Chaucer's imaginary pilgrims trod a tangible Watling Street. Scott was a patriot, George Eliot was a *genius loci*. The journey of Little Nell and her grandfather may be traced from London up to Tong. And Borrow, Kingsley, and Dumas could swear pretty straitly by the map. Houses are another matter. And, though by some elusive wizardry we realize that in *that* particular corner of her boudoir our heroine flung herself upon a prie-dieu to weep, that our heedless hero slammed a door to the left, and that the wicked old uncle died in his fourposter with his face to the ivied window, it would often puzzle us to fit in the floors and storeys of an otherwise admirable mansion of the fancy; while to descend from attic to cellar in some dream-houses would be an experience of the purest nightmare. It is a nice question whether a novelist should actually call in an architect before he sets to work, a still nicer whether he should preface his story with a practicable plan—bathroom and porch, pantry and embowered arbour. The indefatigable Watson at times traced Sherlock Holmes's footprints in the snows, as it were, of Scotland Yard; added a twinge of horror to crime by indicating the locale of a corpse with a cross. But then these little conscientiousnesses were rare. No less rare was a clear, precise North-South-East-West sketch to scale of a province, countryside, city, or village that never was on sea or shore. Mr. Conrad has told how a fair and inquiring visitor one workaday morning shattered the whole universe of *Nostromo*. He built it up again, but he did not map it out with compasses and Indian ink. Such a feat is the entertainment and device of a more ingenious, a less grave and creative mind. One can see a Robert Burton absorbedly recording every gulf, morass, creek, and quicksand in the sad and mighty realms of Melancholy; but hardly a Milton, quill in hand, tracing out the frontiers of Paradise. The sport is a childish fantasy, but none the less precious for that.

Precious now and then, at any rate; and even to the tune of £44. For that was the sum squandered only last week on the original of the chart prefixed to *Treasure Island*. Even though it represented the stockinged hoardings of a lifetime, the buyer made a bargain. The map is a little masterpiece. The story goes that it was designed to beguile a youthful stepson. For youth's sake alone the thumbed and perishing chart was sewn up together with Billy Bones's nefarious ledger and sealed with a thimble. So be it, but we know our Louis Stevenson. 'It is about nine miles long and five across, shaped, you might say, like a fat dragon standing up, and had two fine land-locked harbours, and a hill in the centre part marked "The Spy Glass".' 'Methinks it is like a weasel'—but fat dragon will serve. No fancy-itching detail has been overlooked in that 'facsimile struck out by J. Hawkins'. (The original of that is probably in the possession of the heirs of Flint's quarter-master, 'along of his timber leg'.) It has been lovingly done—the rayed compass, the ships in bellying sail, solemn dolphin, spouting whale, and somewhat lamentable sea-nymph, swamp and spring, tide and cove and sounding, and above all, in bright red, in dingy red, in greeny-blue, the scripts of 'J.F.', of 'W.B.' ('this twenty July 1754') and of the bright as fortunate Jim.

'We had run up the trades to get the wind of the island we were after—I am not allowed to be more plain'; for there is still treasure—silver—not yet lifted! It is odd that, in spite of definite description—'. . . General colouring uniform and sad . . . grey melancholy woods and wild stone spires . . . odd outlandish swampy trees . . . the fog had now buried all heaven . . .' —that island remains, in one faraway vision of it at least, ablaze with emerald and sunshine. Was it 'the nutmeg and azalea', 'the poisonous brightness' of the foliage that led fancy astray, or did the brass buttons *thick* on the unctuous, the sly, the murderous, and impossible John Silver's coat cast a reflected and unfading glamour of light upon that 'sweet pretty place'? Jim may write (with artful finish) of 'our dark and bloody sojourn', and in these outspoken days we may cordially admit the bloody. But that dark was surely for ever dissipated by the doubloons and double guineas and moidores and sequins, stamped with the pictures of all a century's kings of Europe, and the shores of Treasure Island (save only where that victim of chuck-farthen and of his brass-hearted shipmates, Ben Gunn, ran doubled-up down the hill) remain radiant with gold and coral, lit not only with a tropical sun, but by the lamp left by Israel Hands still burning in broad daybreak in the cabin of the Hispaniola, and by the wasteful fires of the mutineers. Forty-four pounds! It was a bagatelle for such a memorial of a genius that will for many a long day lure childhood back from the wreckage of the years and once at least kept the austere Dean Church out of bed.

A chart designed by a characteristically evil Chinaman is mentioned though not represented in Mr. Wells's *Treasure of the Forest*. Poe reproduces Captain Kidd's cryptogram (written probably in a solution of regulus of cobalt in spirit of nitre), but, alas! supplies no chart in tints of Legrand's heaven-sent scarabæus. *King Solomon's Mines*, however, is handsomely prefaced by the old Dom José de Silvestra's map, scratched down in his last trickle of blood (before he was frozen cold as mutton) on a fragment of linen (? his shirt) 'in the little cave on the north side of the nipple of the southernmost of the two mountains I have named Sheba's Breasts'. It is written in Portuguese, and the bare route stretches from the River Lukanga to the mountains at the end of King Solomon's Road. 'I know not', writes Alan Quatermain, 'how to describe the glorious panorama which unfolded itself to our enraptured gaze.' And we must take his word for it. But he makes reiterated play with Sheba's Breasts and refers to a scene 'like Paradise'. This is vague, but there is beauty less vaguely paradisical in his record, that of 'the young ladies', 'like arum lilies', for instance, who danced the dance of death before the one-eyed Twala, and 'the snowy loveliness' of Good's bare legs. Detail would not have come amiss regarding 'the five miles round of fertile ground' of the palace at Loo—'unlimited Loo', according to the facetious owner of the legs. But Alan makes up with thrills what he lacks in the picturesque and (with *Treasure Island* in mind) in style.

William Morris's chart of the course of the Sundering Flood is a very different thing. It is the work of an artist—not apparently of Osberne himself—and so outside the story. And the decorative rather than the vividly imaginative was its inspiration. It is, if anything, too definite, if not too rich, and perhaps a little literary and artificially elaborate. We read of dromonds and roundships, but the salt sea wind of the Hispaniola does not pluck at their shrouds. We read of far countries and outlandish folk, of dread and unknown tongues, of dwarfs and landwights, of 'a little cot somewhat kenspeckle'. But Morris is not bent on waking terror or trying our nerves, the little cot *remains*— somewhat kenspeckle. And *The Wood Masterless* is somehow

less woody than poetic. In one thing, too, narrative and chart
are in quarrel. So long as in a series of pictures serene and pure
the little carle, Osberne, meets and talks with Elfhild on the
Bight of the Cloven Knoll, with fifty feet of roaring water sundering each from each, the romantic dream remains unstirred,
unbroken. The arrowing of the boy's gifts across the gulf, those
two loving faces whose nearest approach is in a steadfast gaze—
all this is gay and tender and charming. And Elfhild's 'O thou
beauteous creature, what art thou?' is no less lovely an impulse
than her 'But what else canst thou do, Champion?' is an arch
and womanly piece of naïveté. But chance and circumstance
separate the children. The supernatural machinery creaks a little.
Steelhead is a hard nut to crack. And then, disappointment of
disappointments, when the lovers meet again, Elfhild has long
since crossed the magic waters of Sundering Flood, and by a
ferry! The idea, the symbol has been betrayed. The very essence
of the romance has fainted into air.

Inspired schoolmasters there may be who set their scholars
not the vast cutlet of Africa, sea-fretted Scotland, or the hun-
dreds-and-thousands of the Grecian Archipelago to map out on
paper, but a fantastic country of their own contriving, crammed
with strange beasts and wildernesses, and precipices and virgin
streams and valleys. One such contraption was devised far too
many years ago by a certain small boy now small no longer.
Outlined in cloudy blue, hedged about with tottering, ungainly
print, the shores of his isles—of *Goats*, of *Ba* and *Be*, of *Rags*
and *Riggerbar*—are washed by the tides of the *Graca Ocean*
and the *Sea of Rega* (with the S back side before). 'Here is a
Forest' (green as green), 'Here is the Rem Mountains', 'Here
is a great Castle', run his legends. And an indulged and indul-
gent uncle ventured on the letterpress:

' . . . Now to speak of the Islands that we went in rowboats
to visit before our ship set sail thither (a N.W. point near the
River Dum), the weather remaining calm and fair for three days
and till the fourth morning, first we landed on the *Isle of Butter*
which lieth alongside of the *Isle of Ray*. In this isle is an exceeding steep high Mountian [*sic*] capped with frozen ice that doth
marvellously gleam and twinkle when the sun by day doth fall
upon it, sending forth beams far and near of divers colours like
to a great Lantern. Also at night the moon gloateth upon the

ice and it is like the Opal, for I did look upon it as I lay in my bunk, ashipboard. But to scale this Mountian it were a thing impossible by reason of its steepness and the slipperiness of its perpetual ice. In the *Isle of Butter* is great store of little pebbles that are round and smooth as marbles (that children be accustomed to play with), also in its waters lurketh a little fish called the butter-fish—it is so greasy in the broiling. . . . And hearing strange shrill cries, we lifted our wagging heads and espied a company of dwarfmen, with naked skins grey as the crocus, riding upon shaggy flat-footed beasts after the manner of our mules. But though we threw up our hands and besought them dumbly, our tongues being swollen beyond speech, they galloped away from us. And, when we looked, we counted only seven men left of us, with the boatswain. And I conjecture two men—namely, Benjamin and Robert Small, were taken in their sleep and devoured by these grey people; for such is their barbarous custom to eat man's poor flesh, having dried it in the sun. And we asleep. But Heaven being pitiful to us that remained, we toiled on, the boatswain alone sitting down with courageous face to the west, unable longer to continue, his body being puffed out nigh double through chewing of a root he had found. And he died there looking towards his own country and asking mercy on his sins. . . .'

What, after all, is the great globe itself but undiscovered country to every newcomer? Who even can deny us the privy conviction that we walk and slumber, not, as it might appear, on a silly giddy ball in space, but on an endless sea-ridden plain whose furthermost bourne is breathed of as 'Death'? Our jaded, sated sense of fact is all a fallacy. A green meadow may be El Dorado and all the Indies to a simple and unexacting heart. Thou art—what thou dost gaze upon. To a tortured imagination the homely Thames may wander black as Acheron; to a happier, not Jordan itself is a more miraculous stream. And if, possibly, one sometimes wearies of the old familiar places, of Greenwich time and down-trodden longitudes, how easy to take pencil and brush in hand and idly map out that place where one would be— Life's Courage, Heart's Ease. It would not be necessary to write a book about it. It would fetch not forty-four farthings in open auction. It would be a poor thing, but one's own.

Times Literary Supplement, July 30, 1914

CATHAY AND THE WAY THITHER*

The second volume of *Cathay and the Way Thither* consists of the narrative of the travels of Odoric, a Franciscan friar, born at Villa Nova in Pordenone in 1286. In his early thirties he set out on his wanderings through the Indies, China, and Thibet—Constantinople, Trebizond, Tabriz, Soltania, Persepolis, Baghdad, Malabar, Ceylon, Sumatra, Java, Canton, Nanking, Peking, Lhása, and thence probably by Kabul to Tabriz, to Venice, and so home. At Padua, in May 1330, his brief and racy account of this prodigious pilgrimage was taken down and 'done into homely Latin' by William of Solagna. On his way to Avignon to make his report to the Pope, Odoric fell ill at Pisa. He returned to Udine and died there on the 14th of January 1331. With one accord the whole town rushed to his funeral in the convent church. His body was in danger of complete dismemberment into miraculous souvenirs. Supernatural interposition alone prevented one virago from snipping off an ear with her scissors. On the day following his burial his body was taken up again. The whole country was in a ferment. A noble shrine was prepared; Odoric's formidable array of miracles was formally placed on record; and, hundreds of years afterwards, on the 2nd of July 1755, the beatification of this incredibly way-worn, fearless, and credulous friar, who with his own hands had presented the Grand Cham with a trencher full of apples, was fully sanctioned by Benedict XIV. To this day his body (with the exception of one leg, long since frittered away into reliques) is exposed at Udine on every fourth recurrence of his festival.

In the index to *Astley's Voyages* (1745-7) the saint is thus entered: 'Odoric, Friar, Travels of, iv, 620 a. *A great Liar.*

* *Cathay and the Way Thither*. Translated by Sir Henry Yule. New edition by Henri Cordier. Vol. II. Odoric of Pordenone (The Hakluyt Society).

Ibid.' From this unkindness Odoric has been rescued by Sir Henry Yule, who in 1866 edited his travels for the Hakluyt Society. In spite of incidental infirmities Odoric was a genuine traveller, the first European who distinctly and undoubtedly recorded the name of Sumatra. His accounts of sago in the Archipelago, of leeches in the forests of Ceylon, of fishing with cormorants, of the custom of cramping the feet and extending the nails in China, of blow-pipes and poisoned darts, are peculiar to him among all the European travellers of his age. On the other hand, so skilfully and craftily did that perfidious romancer, Mandeville, steal from his record that Odoric is described by Sir Thomas Herbert merely as 'the travelling companion of our Sir John'.

'Like a humble child', Odoric submitted himself on his death-bed 'to the keys of the church', and so ingenuous is his narrative in its eager curiosity, impressionableness, in its delight in the strange and the marvellous, that to read him is to recall the far-away childish experience of gloating into the lighted windows of an extremely brilliant confectioner's shop. 'Victuals', indeed, figure richly in his remembrance. He bethinks himself of an excellent fruit called *mussi* he enjoyed somewhere, of excellent grown ginger, of a well-dressed and deliciously seasoned goose he fared on at Kansan—as fat as fat can be, and twice the size 'of ours'. He sagaciously adds approximate prices: four good partridges, or an ass-load of rhubarb, or forty-two pounds of dates—all for less than a Venetian groat. He knows how to condense, how to seize on the essential: 'And here they burn the brazil-wood for fuel and in the woods are numbers of wild peacocks.' He knows how to tickle and intrigue the fancy: 'And many other strange things are there which it would be pretty to hear tell'; or 'Marvellous and beastly customs which it is just as well not to write'. He enjoys his fun. Eastward over the Ocean Sea he sailed from the cannibal island of Dondin to the noble province of Manzi (of two thousand great cities); here were bread, wine, rice, flesh, fish and all manner of victuals in plenty, and no beggars: and here, he goes on, 'the men, as to their bodily aspect, are comely enough, but colourless, having beards of long, straggling hairs like mousers—cats, I mean. And as for the women, they are the most beautiful in the world!' How delicious, too, is his hearty burst of laughter at the monk in the shrubbery of grottoes with his buckets full of scraps, and his gong wherewith to summon his thousands of all kinds of apes and monkeys ('with the souls of gentlemen') to their breakfast 'in regular ranks'!

Odoric exults in monarchs with truly regal families of children, 200 or so; and wives to match. 'Great and terrible things' return to his memory like harmless nightmares to the waking mind—the valley of sand, for instance, over against the River of Delights, with its corpses, its face of appalling terror in the rock, its spectral 'makers' of marvellous music, its useless silver, heaped up as it had been fish scales. And how one's pleasure in his wonders—his lamb-cradling melons, his woolly hens—is aided by a dash of scepticism regarding other men's:—'As regards Prester John, not one hundredth part is true of what is told of him as if it were undeniable.' The Great Khan of Cambalech—the Kublai of Xanadu of Marco Polo—is Odoric's set piece, with his fountains and gardens and splendour and divinest rights; above all, with his manner of journeying, drawn in state from one amazing palace to another, by elephants and horses, in a coach of lign-aloes and gold and skins and gems, hawking from out of its windows as he goes, and for guard, an army of horsemen skirring a day's march in front of him, an army of horsemen a day's march behind him, and armies on either hand.

But a fact fully as fascinating and bizarre as anything of Odoric's is related in one of an immense number of learned and curious notes to these travels; namely, that the stately pleasure-dome of Coleridge's dream-poem was not only decreed by the Great Khan, Kublai, but actually built by his Chinese architects to the design of one which he himself had seen in sleep.

Edinburgh Review, April 1914

Poets

JAMES ELROY FLECKER*

To those poets whose fortune it has been to die young, and so at least escape the tragic survival of their own genius, only the last awakening of all has brought what we call fame. Fame, of course, is a relative thing, a spark that has spread into a flame, the enthusiasm of a few multiplying in the minds of many, transient or enduring. To predict it is in the nature of a tribute to one's own standard of taste and judgement—precious enough, to its possessor. In its degree it is some sort of a happy ending to a romantic tale, and the poet who leaves a few lyrics behind him that will outlive the passing fashion of his time has won a fair reward in this curious world, though it is quite certain that no true poet would have toiled any the less enthusiastically with as little active hope of it as of a fortune.

James Elroy Flecker was such a poet. Even in a translation from Catullus, made when he was sixteen, there falls a cadence that makes the sentiment his own:

> *Wherefore to you, my friend, I dedicate*
> *This so indifferent bookling; yet I pray,*
> *Poor as it is—'O goddess of my fate,*
> *Let it outlive the writer's transient day!'*

Much later, he invokes a poet of 'a thousand years hence':

> *O friend unseen, unborn, unknown,*
> *Student of our sweet English tongue,*
> *Read out my words at night, alone:*
> *I was a poet, I was young.*

---

* *Collected Poems of James Elroy Flecker*. Edited, with an Introduction, by J. C. Squire (Martin Secker).

Since I can never see your face
And never shake you by the hand,
I send my soul through time and space
To greet you. You will understand.

One's contemporaries are often hard of hearing; and Flecker is
not yet so well known, perhaps, as are other poets even of our
own day—as Rupert Brooke, for instance, who was a good
many years younger than himself. At present his achievement is
unlikely to attract the industrious commentator, or to become
the esoteric nucleus of a learned society. If it live, it will be
because beauty created in words cannot easily die. It is too rare,
and men treasure it for the sake not only of memory, but of hope.
Flecker's one desire, indeed, was to create 'beauty'; and because he would not, maybe too because he could not follow
other lures, when he wins his desire, he wins all. When he fails
of it, the husk is of little value.

Wherever his spiritual home may have been, Athens or
Samarkand, or some undiscovered isle sea-leagues beyond
Ultima Thule, he was born at Lewisham, and was true Londoner enough in his earlier days to write two ballads, one
'of Hampstead Heath', the other 'of Camden Town'. Neither
of them is a very respectful or attractive tribute. They recall the
smile of which Mr. Squire passes on his remembrance so happily—'a curious blend of the sardonic and the cheerful'. The
ghost of that smile still faintly lingers in the dark, narrow, clear-
eyed, fascinating face of the beautiful portrait in this volume. In
1902—in his eighteenth year—Flecker left Uppingham for
Oxford. He was then, Mr. Frank Savery tells us, 'extraordinarily undeveloped even for an English public school boy'. But
while 'the lights of Balliol' found a lunar month short commons
wherein to distil a solitary Petrarchan sonnet, Flecker at Trinity
was pouring out imitative, decadent verse 'with an appalling
facility'; and, no less profusely, extravagant and audacious talk
at luncheon and dinner parties especially convened for its pro-
vocation. The poems were of a kind which of all kinds may be
most independent of experience—'poems of passion'. The talk
(so at any rate Mr. Savery thought in those young days) was
very witty. Even the precocious poet of passion need not be a
prig, and Flecker took himself lightly enough to call his first

volume by a 'symbolic' title to which he had afterwards to attach
an appropriate poem, *The Bridge of Fire*. One true friend at
least he had at Oxford, we are told, whom he loved deeply, and
who was an enduring influence on himself and his work; and
when in after years in Athens he married a Greek lady, Miss
Helle Skiadaressi, he won another and no less true counsellor.
Otherwise, he went his own way, steadily following his true
vein, and little affected by the writers of his time, though as late
as 1914 he was eager for 'a whack at B. Shaw'. For a few months
he was a master in a school at Hampstead. In 1908 he went up to
Cambridge to study Oriental languages (and thus, it appears,
jilted his first love, Oxford); and in 1910 he went out in the
Consular Service to Constantinople. There he fell ill; and after
many journeyings, Smyrna, Corfu, Beyrout, Lebanon, Switzer-
land, he died of consumption on January 3, 1915.

He had given himself heart and soul from his earliest days to
poetry. It was therefore a special satisfaction to him to know
that his official work had been 'businesslike', that he had thus
helped to shatter the fallacy—which seems so richly to reassure
the unimaginative—that a poet is an unpractical dreamer. Life is
a twofold conflict. We fight (in youth, chiefly) to master circumstance, to exult over it; we fight also to accommodate ourselves to it. We fight in the solitude of the spirit, without hope
of truce or respite, for self-realization; and to win also to some
kind of shelter and security from the dangers and disasters that
threaten us from without. Fortunate people there may be who
are not thus forced to advance with a vigilant enemy ever
menacing their rear. But of those few none can be to the utmost
of his capacity a poet. A poet is born an exile, and an exile he
must die. As such, he never becomes really 'used' to the world
though he is by no means a stranger to it. He knows and loves
and hates it 'of old'. But he is without question a pilgrim. Again
and again he must stand back from the press of habit and convention. He must keep on recapturing solitude, and reiteratedly
begin his task anew. His may not be the Sesame that will fling
open for him the gates of other men's paradises, nor need his
individual integrity make for the precarious stability of that
shifting ideal of conduct (since the sands of the living flow out in
a few generations) which holds together the fabric of society
and civilization, and enforces on humanity the prudent recogni-

tion and acceptance of 'things as they are'. But whether he is a Villon or a Wordsworth, a Milton or an Edgar Allan Poe, he serves to keep age mindful of youth, worldly wisdom in open conflict with faith and enthusiasm, and the living in touch with the dead. 'It is not', in Flecker's words, 'the poet's business to save man's soul, but to make it worth saving.'

He, too, his whole life long, was an exile. Mysteriously woven into his nature and imagination was a passion for all that an untravelled mind means by the East. 'In days long gone', he wrote in *Pavlovna in London*,

> *Have I not danced with gods in garden lands?*
> *I too a wild unsighted atom borne*
> *Deep in the heart of some heroic boy*
>   *Span in the dance ten thousand years ago,*
> *And while his young eyes glittered in the morn*
> *Something of me felt something of his joy,*
>   *And longed to rule a body, and to know.*

That recurrent 'finest story in the world' may not seem even to a Western mind 'all moonshine'. But experience proved that no earthly East was Flecker's true goal. He delighted, with a tense, almost violent excitement, in colour and sensuous beauty, in remote times, in remote places, in names and men and relics outlandish and bizarre. His appetite was always for the strange. But a direct acquaintance with Mohammedanism served only to illuminate Christianity. Greece he loved, and one of his last fragmentary poems is a tribute to its 'glory'.

> *Yet still Victorious Hellas, thou hast heard*
> *Those ancient voices thundering to arms,*
> *Thou nation of an older younger day*
> *Thou has gone forth as with the poet's song.*
> *Surely the spirit of the old oak grove*
> *Rejoiced to hear the cannon round Yannina,*
> *Apollo launched his shaft of terror down*
> *On Salonica . . .*

How strangely these lines, written perhaps not two years ago, fall upon the ear just now! But, though Greece was his devotion, Flecker actually confessed to Mr. Savery that 'he had not greatly liked the East'. As time went on a more personal

element welled into work that had been singularly and deliberately devoid of it. Memory and desire in *Oak and Olive* carry
his thoughts back from Athens to Charing-cross and 'a hall in
Bloomsbury', to Gloucester lanes and Painswick-hill. He was
happiest, as are so many of us, in the place where he was not;
though never may seem the world so fair as on our last earthly
morning. Absence kindled his imagination. But seldom have
romantic dream and actuality, the strange and the familiar, been
so closely reconciled with so generous and balanced an ardour,
as in the poem which he was still working on at the last, *The
Burial in England*. The war broke in upon his isolation and
inflamed his love for the old familiar things. It made him
England's heart and soul; but this in no sense entailed any
sacrifice of his poetic ideal. By a delightful paradox the poet of
that witty fantasia *The Hammam Name*, wherein 'a Turkish
lady' deliriously records the charms of her 'Winsome Torment'
taking his morning bath—'Bitterness was born of beauty; as
for the shampooer, he Fainted, till a jug of water set the Captive Reason free'; the poet also of that delicate, fainting sigh of
languor and loveliness, *Yasmin*, and of 'the Chief Grocer's'
catalogue of Oriental delicatessen, lived long enough to spend
his time and skill, when little time was left to him, on a revised
version of the National Anthem. Popular taste will probably
remain loyal to Henry Carey, but Flecker had learned much of
his craftsmanship in the translation of his favourite Latin and
French poets, and of such translations this out of the English
was unquestionably his boldest enterprise.

But though the later work reveals Flecker as a poet heart and
soul with those thoughts and aspirations which we all hold in
common just now, he was none the less never instinctively a
sociable poet. He was a solitary, and in some men home-sick-
ness is a lifelong malady. Unlike, therefore, the majority of
poets, he did not transform the common into the unfamiliar, nor
burden primrose and skylark with fanciful and tender analogy
and metaphor, nor merely accept from nature and humanity
what poetic imagination may find in them to delight in.
He left all this for the most part unheeded, and pressed on
into the virgin region of fantasy; he laboured to make the
singular unique, the romantic magical, and the rare unparalleled. The beauty he hungered for is indeed past mortal capture

and perilous in pursuit. It cheated or beguiled him on, and ever on. When Lord Arnaldos, gone a-hunting, entreated the sailor of the little ship on the green and shallow sea for God's sake to interpret the song he was singing at the helm, the sailor made answer, 'I only tell my song to those Who sail away with me.' One at least of the merchants in *The Golden Journey* was in quest of impracticable merchandise:

> *We travel not for trafficking alone;*
> *By hotter winds our fiery hearts are fanned:*
> *For lust of knowing what should not be known*
> *We make the Golden Journey to Samarkand,*

and the Watchman in vain endeavours to console the women mournfully indignant at dreams unshackled by 'thoughts of us': 'What would ye, ladies? It was ever thus. Men are unwise and curiously planned,' and voices fainting into the distance chaunt on, 'We make the Golden Journey to Samarkand.' On Iskander, too, and his crew, eighty days after voyaging past the flat Araunian coasts 'Inhabited, at noon, by Ghosts', and three score and ten after seeing the land of Calcobar—where men not only drink blood, but 'dye their beards alizarine'—sink beneath the horizon, storm fell 'and drave them out to that Lone Sea Whose shores are near Eternity'. A Ship of Dreams, silken and silver, an exquisitely fresh and beguiling replica of their cankered, warped, and rotting poop, is sighted, and Aristotle and Plato, who (under a seductive and Oriental *alias*) have been 'impressed' by the Sultan Iskander, are very much at odds concerning her:

> *'And lo! beside that mainmast tree*
> *Two tall and shining forms I see,*
> *And they are what we ought to be,*
> *Yet we are they, and they are we.'*

> *He spake, and some young Zephyr stirred,*
> *The two ships touched: no sound was heard;*
> *The Black Ship crumbled into air;*
> *Only the Phantom Ship was there. . .*

It is an old and tragic, yet consoling parable, and one that Flecker never wearied of enriching and enhancing. The beauty of the world to him was not, as it is to some men, an anodyne, or merely a mystical symbol, but 'a continual intoxication'. Yet out of his passion for the strange came the sense of mystery that was to haunt his later years. Phantasms ('tall stone men') that recall the poems of Blake for an instant gaze out of his verse and are gone. The silent throng about him. A poem called *November Eves*—one of the very few clearly and definitely recorded remembrances of his childhood—is tinged with this 'otherness'. *The Pensive Prisoner* is the tormented expression of an experience that defied even his mature skill and power wholly to reveal:

> *My thoughts came drifting down the Prison where I lay—*
> *Through the Windows of their Wings the stars were shining—*
> *The wings bore me away—the russet Wings and grey*
> *With feathers like the moon-bleached Flowers—I was a God reclining:*
> *Beneath me lay my Body's Chain, and all the Dragons born of Pain*
> *As I burned through the Prison Roof to walk on Pavement Shining . . .*

When thought becomes as instant and close as this, it is reality that dangerously faints into dream. So, too, there is a thin edge to sensibility which even music itself, as distinguished from that of words, can hardly express. *The Blue Noon* is an ecstatic vision—of light and colour, air and space, wherein this solid globe is merely an iridescent bubble that may at any moment vanish away, leaving the consciousness free in a bodiless yet sensuous delight. Even if it be fever and fantasy which admit these experiences, sound sanity, just our everyday selves, can test their truth, and maybe in so doing realize a foretaste of a life beyond the grave. But fear stands in the way, and in *Stillness* the door of the imagination which Flecker had always left lightly ajar for his own escape is forced open by a menacing, unendurable ingression from 'the other side'. Here he can no longer cloak the strange—which, it is prudent to remember, is never far out of calling of the sinister—with a fantastic humour, or elude its gravity with an airy, inconsequent wit, or deck it up, as he sometimes does, to look very much like a solemn and irresponsible nonsense. This extreme revulsion of feeling, however, evokes from him one of the tenderest and loveliest, as well as 'strangest', things in all his poetry:

79

When the words rustle no more,
And the last work's done,
When the bolt lies deep in the door,
And Fire, our Sun,
Falls on the dark-laned meadows of the floor;

When from the clock's last chime to the next chime
Silence beats his drum,
And Space with gaunt grey eyes and her brother Time
Wheeling and whispering come,
She with the mould of form and he with the loom of
rhyme:

Then twittering out in the night my thought-birds flee,
I am emptied of all my dreams:
I only hear Earth turning, only see
Ether's long bankless streams,
And only know I should drown if you laid not your
hand on me.

Like Keats, like Stevenson, Flecker fought a brave fight against an insidious enemy, and, as Mr. Squire remarks emphatically in an Introduction intended only 'to interest the reader and be useful to the critic', but which none the less is a delightful piece of portraiture, warm with a true friendship and illumined with deep and sensitive appreciation, Flecker was never the 'poet of despair'. It is true he once said he was—and 'lean and swarthy' to boot—but that was merely a little self-indulgence common to the youthful and fervent. He wrote *No Coward's Song*:

I am no coward who could seek in fear
A folk-lore solace or sweet Indian tales;
I know dead men are deaf and cannot hear
The singing of a thousand nightingales . . .

But did he know it? Was not the thought merely one of those objective, intimidating hints which the body at times deems it prudent to 'palm off' upon the spirit? 'Yet is not death the great Adventure?' he cried almost jovially on the young English patriots of 1914, many of whom have now faced it, while he himself was to embark but a few weeks after. He was sure what 'True Paradise' would satisfy his longing: 'We poets crave no heav'n but what is ours', a familiar world re-fashioned, without 'Man's and Nature's pain':

> *Grant me earth's treats in Paradise to find*
> *Nor listen to that island-bound St. John.*
> *Who'd have no Sea in Heaven, no Sea to sail upon!*

Notes of exclamation are rare in Flecker's verse, and in a volume that contains *The Old Ships, The Old Warship Ablaze, Santorin,* and *The Ballad of Iskander* this particular one must be given an unusual emphasis. Of the joys of that romantic heart none excelled that of ships and the sea and the 'talkative, bald-headed' mariners that go down upon it. Where else should he discover such beauty and agedness and wonder?

> *It was so old a ship—who knows, who knows?*
> *—And yet so beautiful I watched in vain*
> *To see the mast burst open with a rose,*
> *And the whole deck put on its leaves again.*

It was certainly as much man's imagination as his soul which Flecker was convinced it is the poet's business to make worth saving. His 'single interest', it may be repeated, was 'to create beauty'—a beauty as indisseverable from its form as that of a piece of consummate craftsmanship in stone or metal. The will, alas! must be inherent in the deed. Unlike the majority of English poets, he had an aesthetic theory which he enforced in his practice. It was not less his own because he learned it from the French Parnassians. He disapproved of the customary plump and variegated British nosegay culled more or less at haphazard from the English gardens of verse; his desire was for a poetic attar distilled in the imagination. Such essences are not rare in English lyrics; other poets than Flecker have studied alchemy—Keats, Milton, Herrick, and many more; but Britishers, whether they write in verse or in prose, object to being slaves (or even 'in service') to any particular theory. Still, though a man is born a poet, he must make himself an artist. If poetry, like love and faith, is the first-fruits of an instinctive impulse, art, like chivalry and courtesy and conduct, is a manifestation of character. By sheer, hard, ardent work Flecker proved himself an artist.

Not least of one's interests in this collected edition is to watch his gradual and steady progress, year by year, towards a technical mastery. He sought for the strange and marvellous in life; and so also for the precise yet uncustomary word and phrase that would recreate, embody it. He scorned, says Mr. Squire, 'the pot-shot'. Search for what we may (long enough), it tends to come at last of its own free will. So it was with him. In his earlier work bizarre epithets stick out like gems on a turban. In his later the tissue is uninterrupted, of a piece. Serene and happy in the apparently unlaboured expression of dream, feeling, fantasy, and truth, we no longer exclaim at mere 'felicities'. A hardness and sharpness may be the frigid defect of such work. Conciseness, pure outline, clarity, and a strange detachment like that of some flower, curiously flawless and exotic, burning in the quiet solitude of a wood, are its imperishable virtues. We must not so much ask of such poetry what it does for us, but what it does *to* us. We cannot, so to speak, detach from its ideas, 'beauties', apophthegms, fine feelings, as we mercilessly smoke bees out of a hive. It is not intentionally helpful or instructive or edifying. At its best it is honey of Hymettus in the cell, to be enjoyed not because it is wholesome or nourishing, but because it is delicious. When he died Flecker's imagination was turning homewards, like some high-pooped, 'overpeering' Elizabethan argosy, slow in the water for its burden of apes, spices, ivory and Orient pearl. We can only guess at further voyaging into the might-have-been. Enough that he has transported us—even though such travellers must bear the heavy burden of themselves on their backs, even though the poet himself chaunted a dirge to sweet illusion:

> *Oh shall I never never be home again?*
> *Meadows of England shining in the rain*
> *Spread wide your daisied lawns; your ramparts green*
> *With briar fortify, with blossom screen*
> *Till my far morning—and O streams that slow*
> *And pure and deep through plains and playlands go,*
> *For me your love and all your kingcups store,*
> *And—dark militia of the southern shore,*
> *Old fragrant friends—preserve me the last lines*
> *Of that long saga which you sang me, pines*

When, lonely boy, beneath the chosen tree
I listened, with my eyes upon the sea.
O traitor pines, you sang what life has found
The falsest of fair tales.
Earth blew a far-horn prelude all around,
That native music of her forest home,
While from the sea's blue fields and syren dales
Shadows and light noon-spectres of the foam
Riding the summer gales
On aery viols plucked an idle sound.
Hearing you sing, O trees,
Hearing you murmur, ' There are older seas,
That beat on vaster sands,
Where the wise snailfish move their pearly towers
To carven rocks and sculptured promont'ries,'
Hearing you whisper, ' Lands
Where blaze the unimaginable flowers.'

Times Literary Supplement, Sept. 28, 1916

83

FRANCIS THOMPSON*

From the biography of a man of action we expect to learn what he did; from that of a poet what he was. Of the inmost life of Francis Thompson his own work is the clearest and most infallible, and yet narrow, revelation. His poetry reveals not only what he himself thought and felt most consistently and intensely, but reveals it also in relation to what he considered to be of the deepest moment in life. Few men, few poets even, can have been so much alone as he. And his was often the loneliness of desolation, 'in disgrace with fortune and men's eyes', the solitude of a child shut up in darkness and cold, by an indifferent and worldly stepmother. How pierce into that existence of his, spent on the kerbstone, selling matches in a thronged London street; and that of the night that followed?

None the less his earthly home—with the attic and cellar of which rather than with its 'living' and reception rooms and best guest-chamber, Francis Thompson was most familiar—at least also sheltered kind, ever considerate, ever loyal and loving foster-brothers and sisters. Mr. Everard Meynell makes that clear. Even in his darkest hour it was no chance-sent jinni that put 'golden halfpence' in his way, or, disguised as a Rothschild, paid a florin for a newspaper. It is clear, too, that though anyone who had the good fortune to meet him might as first sight have been struck by what would seem a pathetic figure ('something between a lamplighter and a man of letters', and what a lighter of lamps!) in his great brown cape, independent of all weathers, his disastrous hat, his 'fish-basket' (for review-books) slung over his shoulder—that glimpse would have told only half the story. For, in spite of every conceivable unkindness of self and circumstance, the discoloured features could suddenly light up, the dazed eyes flash, the ready pun would stumble from his lips,

* The Life of Francis Thompson. By Everard Meynell (Burns and Oates).

the readier smile change all his face. His was a laugh, says Mrs.
Meynell, 'readier than a girl's'.

For the ups of life we all of us have to pay with the downs.
And best with ready-money, perhaps. This is certainly true of a
poet whose occasional moods of exaltation, of clearness and
peace (of megalomania, too), may so speedily usher him into
fits of darkness, depression, and intense self-depreciation. The
psychologists have a name for it. Thompson said of himself that
he was born in the shadow of the winter solstice, when the
nights are long. He was not a clubbable man—except at the
heavy hand of fate. He was 'oppressed with fatality', blanched
at the rumour of small-pox, feared even so vague and remote a
bugbear as the Yellow Peril. His 'sole sensuality was not to be
in pain'. And although his biographer—rather unnecessarily
perhaps—decorates three or four lugubrious pages with the
'awful examples' afforded by many of Thompson's contemporary poets, that record does serve to show that Thompson himself was never one of the bad, sad, glad, mad confraternity. He
was an isolated and aloof figure by choice as well as destiny.
His one almost lifelong weakness was the drug that inspired
and exiled De Quincey and may have slightly and etherially
dehumanized Coleridge; and it was a weakness that secured him
for many years—and those of his genius—from the ravages of
consumption. Opium saved and destroyed him.

Mr. Meynell describes himself as 'an inattentive Yahoo of a
friend'. The actual man, none the less, whom he brings us face
to face with in this *Life* is extraordinarily living and real. He has
told his story clearly; has neither evaded the truth, nor fallen, as
a less assured biographer might have fallen, into shallow senti-
mentalities or facile apologetics. Yet even a personal intimacy
of many years' duration never freed Thompson from the effect
of 'a star confined into a tomb'. He was to the end 'as insubstantial as the angel I knew to be at my shoulder'. And personality can reach a further remove yet, for in his own words he
was often sick with the being that inhabited his villainous mud-
hut of a body. He struggled and straggled through life like a
dispossessed hermit crab, looking about everywhere for a new
shell. For months at a time he lived in a condition of acute
mental misery, the sport of dyspepsia and constant colds. 'I
suffer like old Nick.' His absorption in his symptoms was not the

least of his ills. Yet, though the intense flame of his spirit may at times have sunk low, he never for an instant betrayed or lost his allegiance to that inward truth that must and can alone survive all disaster. With the assurance, too, known only to the humblest and most arrogant of all human attributes, genius, he refused 'to vail his crest to Henley, or Robert Bridges, or even William Watson'. (This was in 1893.) 'I absolutely think that my poetry is "greater" than any work by a new poet which has appeared *since Rossetti'*—excepting only Mrs. Meynell's. And he was to earn what we are afraid will always be the most infrequent of tributes that can be paid by any one master to another: 'I am not sure', confided Patmore to his disciple, 'that you may not be a greater poet than I am.'

Such consolations came late. From his earliest childhood he was a pilgrim and a sojourner, 'a stranger to these parts'. He was a dreamer even in his play—a tidy (though it is recorded that he sometimes took his walks abroad without knotting his bootlaces) awkward, good, quiet, shy boy, always poring over books, excellent (according to his masters at Ushaw) at Latin and English, not to be named in the region of mathematics. Time proved that he was unfitted to become a priest. Nor could he submit himself to the grind of learning to be a doctor. Unlike Coleridge, in spite of a gallant effort to succeed, and then only for physical reasons, he failed to become a soldier. Life at home at last became intolerable in circumstances for which we need necessarily blame neither a not unnatural father (paternity *per se* is seldom inclined to the poetic) nor a supernatural son; Francis left Preston. At Manchester he hesitated. 'To stay under happy parental supervision, to work because I must, but to make my delight of the exercise of the imagination', was what he yearned for.

At length he cut himself adrift from his family and relations near and far. With a railway ticket, with an Aeschylus and a Blake in his pocket, and a promise of seven shillings a week to keep body and soul together—a feat of which few men can have been more instinctively incapable—he plunged, in his twenty-sixth year, into 'that infectious web of sewer-rats called London'. He worked at any odd job that offered itself—boot-blacking, book-'collecting', and in a bad week made sixpence. Too weak and anxious, too diffident at last to apply for his pittance, he was drifting, starving and homeless, to his death, when a cobbler of Panton Street broke in upon his phantasmal reverie with a question which, oddly enough, may be less arresting and disquieting if addressed to a millionaire than to a down-and-out: 'Is your soul *saved*?' Mr. Meynell celebrates but at the same time pokes a little Catholic fun at this blundering Protestant, Mr. McMaster, who, after all, received his full change then and thereafter from 'his only failure', Thompson himself.

'What right have you to ask me that question?' was the dreamer's instant retort. It was the right of a very real if officious and dissipated philanthropy. The kindly cobbler—his very trade has a tinge of the Arabian Nights—discovered in the poet a great, though reserved, talker. He lent him his Josephus and his Huxley, and Thompson helped with the shutters. After a visit to Manchester, however, he returned 'as from a bout of drinking'. 'There were accidents'—with the shutters—and once more Thompson drifted out.

His last ha'pence spent on two boxes of matches (to bring in a profit), with only one friend in the world, a 'brave, sad, lovingest tender thing', but an even more desperate outcast than himself, he dropped the MS. of *Paganism Old and New* and some poems into the letter-box of *Merry England*. Six months afterwards Mr. Meynell found that MS. in a pigeon-hole of his editorial desk, and realized at once the author's need and genius. A year afterwards—after vain efforts in the interval to discover him—came a letter out of the depths, dignified, courteous, reticent: '. . . Doubtless, when I received no answer, I ought to have written again. My excuse must be that a flood-tide of misfortune rolled over me, leaving me no leisure to occupy myself with what I regarded as an attempt that had hopelessly failed. Hence my entire, subsequent silence.'

From this point the *Life* is a record of candid and faithful and familiar friendship between editor and chance contributor—one of by no means few in the story of English letters—of a practical sympathy destined to be repaid with a generosity as abundant as it was unique. Thompson was thenceforth never to lack counsel and appreciation; better still, never to want for the work he could do best and with the least stress and fret. He proved, in essentials, the best of all possible reviewers. In what may be called gigantic trifles he was less successful. His one old enemy was the clock. Stars, watched all night from the gusty peace and chill of the Thames Embankment, record eternity, they don't 'tell the time'. His habitual weakness and delight was dissertation. 'On great subjects he was slow and silent; on trifles he became grotesquely tedious.' And the harvest of a whole day's toil at 'the office' might be a tribute to the brilliancy of a fellow-journalist's talk.

His long-drawn letters of apology and explanation concerning some huddle of MS. an hour or a day late, or a volume that had by mischance been sold before it had been cut—never 'cut-up'—are the most amusing and the most endearing things in Mr. Meynell's book. Space has been too freely accorded to contemporary criticisms of Thompson's poetry; and the refutation of what could only have been a malicious or misguided charge of plagiarism against him was hardly worth while. A writer of real account can seldom be a wilful plagiarist—unless he is either a fool or a 'willun'. Unconscious plagiarism is a mishap that few can escape. Authors are suckled by the authors they love, and must of necessity take after their foster-parents. For the generous devotee, hardly less than for the ingenious literary detective, it may be no more than an ingenuous joy to trace a poet's footsteps 'in other men's snow'.

Thompson's first volume of *Poems* was published in 1893. It was followed by *Sister Songs* in 1895. The critics were widely divided. What were 'high, astounding terms' to one school seemed the 'foam and roar of his phraseology' to another. 'An excessive loading both of diction and imagery' was Thompson's description of an obvious defect, and that was abbreviated by the unsympathetic into 'barbarous jargon' and greeted with 'deep-rooted irritability'. But though in the three years following on his death 50,000 copies of *The Hound of Heaven* were sold to a public—of whom a fair proportion, it is likely, could not now afford not to be able to talk about him—his *New Poems* (published in 1897) not only met with a more hostile reception than the preceding volumes, but for the first six months after publication brought the poet in exactly the same number of shillings—this particular sum being one of the few financial records in which the British public is unlikely to take much interest.

Francis Thompson is now assured of being among the English poets, and that was the utmost of Keats's ambition. He will never be 'popular'; his qualities of mind and soul are scarcely less usual than his poetic achievement. His biographer, though here and there the aura of Thompson's style mantles his own, and a certain suggestion of what we may call Catholic clannishness is apparent in his treatment, has done well by his friend. In the light of his biography we can—as far as we can—'understand' Francis Thompson, and at no expense of useless pity. It is easy to make excuses for the frailties of great men; it is less easy to earn the privilege of doing so by becoming their superiors. His was a life of extraordinary contrasts and vicissitudes, but he kept his faith and finished his work in the teeth of the subtlest and most deadly of all adversaries a man can have —himself. To know that he suffered, and how much, will not only give courage to the weary and to the neglected, it will ensure for the lover of his poetry the blest companionship of a singularly solitary human being.

Saturday Westminster Gazette, Nov. 8, 1913

A LAPIDARY*

With one exception the papers collected in this volume were written before 1912. The time which we have lived through since then is not measurable in years. A nightmare has intervened, and we have to piece together a thread violently broken. In 1914 we could have quietly woven these essays into our literary life. Now we follow Mr. Yeats's intricate and rarified prose hesitantly, doubtful to what extent the atmosphere of dream or, rather, the intellectual veil which hangs between our mind and his is the dissipating of that nightmare or an emanation for which he alone is responsible. Here is our 'agate', shaped by a skilled hand, and of an elaborate design. The thoughts expressed are unquestionably 'important', the principles closely applicable to 'life itself'; but never were we less certain what precisely we mean by life, and where exactly, to put it crudely, 'we are'.

This is one passing perplexity. But Mr. Yeats was never in approach an easy writer. He is an ineffable, rather than an affable, expounder. Englishmen he has always seemed to regard as dunces who must be 'larned', as insensitive and incorrigible barbarians. He talks, in tone if not in substance, well over our heads, not as a stranger within the gates (an observer easily indulged or explained away), but as might a rabbi visiting the children of a step-brother who has removed into, and prospered in, Philistia—'finished and finite clods, untroubled by a spark'. That little matters if so be we 'welcome each rebuff', each sting that bids—not go, but stand or kneel. England assuredly would be none the poorer, spiritually, if heed were paid to his counsels, even to his anathemas; though it is doubtful if Ireland would be any the friendlier, or Mr. Yeats the less remote.

That the stars are in his sky it needs no other instrument than

* *The Cutting of an Agate.* By W. B. Yeats (Macmillan).

our sand-blind eyes to discover. That he seems deliberately to attempt to hide his face amid them is regrettable, for our own sake. When Mr. Yeats says of Synge, 'He could not have loved had he not hated, nor honoured had he not scorned,' the accents are so much his own that we do not apply to Synge an aphorism extremely dubious, unless we preclude from the odious and contemptible all men, all nature, and all the gods. The faithful, however ardent in evangelization they may be, do not readily welcome raw recruits into their ranks. To Mr. Yeats the English (or, for that matter, the Irish) heretic is a mortal foe; not merely a child—of wrath, naughty and wilful, it may be, but still a child—that will presently storm itself to sleep and so resemble only its own virtue in repose. Yet he realizes that although humanity may, like an ass, break into a gallop under the whip, its heart is not to be won by violence, nor its love and obedience by the ecstatic abstraction of a carrot dangling unattainable from between its long ears.

'Only that which does not teach, which does not cry out, which does not persuade, which does not condescend, which does not explain is irresistible.' This is a net of ample mesh; and it includes the 'strong silent man', a blind, deaf, tongueless beggar, a briar rose, the soul of goodness, and the Divine 'Mathematician'. But Mr. Yeats does not follow his own counsel. Few men do. He teaches—and castigates the scholar for vaunting himself that he can learn. He cries out on us: always in deliberate and dignified, often in beautiful and moving, at times in a kind of echoing and phantasmal English—a St. John who prefers to remain in the wilderness since his own imagination is its verdant and serene, if occasionally sand-vexed, oasis. He seldom fully explains, preferring to leave his symbols symbolical and his runes esoteric. And so long as he condescends he may convince, but he will never persuade. His book contains many wise things, thoughts and conclusions not pieced together, not deduced, not distilled out of mere knowledge, but which have sprung, as if by the magic of nature, out of experience, out of solitary reverie, out of enthusiasm, and self-sacrifice. He has given himself to his art, and has been rewarded. But from a rare truth, offspring of intuition and of life, he is apt to draw a dubious inference, and perhaps in making his self-surrender he rather too consciously appraised the gift.

He expresses his love of simplicity, yet in these flowers from his secret garden there is always a tinge of the exotic. By an over-close cultivation he seems to have 'made' them beautiful. It is a delight to surprise an author's happiness in some unforeseen felicity or beauty that he has chanced on on his way. But we seldom seem to overhear Mr. Yeats exclaiming not merely 'Why did I say *this*?' but 'Why did *I* say this?' Not that naïveté is a charm that it is not dangerous to indulge too much. But what may be called his keywords sound at times like empty shells, only remotely murmuring of the ocean of human existence, in its odd, rich, teeming, insuppressible, instinctive variety —his 'naked', 'passionate', 'exquisite', 'dangerous', even his 'art', his 'artist', his perilous 'natural', his still more perilous 'life'. His loyalest epithets wear the look of the conscript. His 'Serpent' devours its tail with a certain languor; his 'Phoenix' plays the incendiary with rather too manifest a faith in its ashes. He has ensnared his Beauty, and is a little weary in her possession. He describes symptoms, yet fails to perceive that he is in danger of the malady: 'All art is sensuous, but when a man puts only his contemplative nature and his more vague desires into his art, the sensuous images through which it speaks become broken, fleeting, and uncertain, or are chosen for their distance from general experience, and all grows unsubstantial and fantastic.' The poet, too, who attempts to distil the waters of his inspiration, to enumerate the 'points' of his Pegasus, is bent on the most treacherous of achievements. He may criticize and appreciate the work of other men justly and generously. He may talk of technique to his heart's content. But to enter in and scrutinize his self's self, to 'fix' his secret impulses, to master, and so circumscribe, his own philosophy, may lead not merely to self-satisfaction but to self-security—a giddy equilibrium.

It is a lovely place indeed where dwells Mr. Yeats's imagination, but now and then we find ourselves gracelessly wishing he were not so skilled a cartographer. His poems, though we are at liberty—a liberty he takes himself—to choose between their kinds, rarely play him false as a poet, never as a conscious craftsman. His prose, though it does not exactly cheat him, insists on rather high stakes; and the cards are not all of them 'on the table'. Lovely, again, is his Ireland, however wildly vexed with storms and the dim Hyades, its Trinculos and Calibans.

Yet Prospero somehow succeeds in screening his Miranda from the enamoured glances of the hated stranger. Many a reader of these essays—at heart as sympathetic and remorseful as an Englishman may humbly and tactfully confess himself to be—will be tempted to 'give up' Ireland in a sense which even the most extreme of Sinn Feiners must self-respectingly deplore.

When Mr. Yeats forgets Jerusalem, forgets that he is the only 'adventurer' of his admirable and remote 'discoveries', is no longer concerned with such confessions as 'Without knowing it, I had come to care for nothing but impersonal beauty,' or 'One part of me looked on, mischievous and mocking,' and with such rather solemn little warnings to trespassers as 'When Lionel Johnson and Katharine Tynan (as she was then) and I myself began to reform Irish poetry', he becomes thrice as free, happy, engrossing, and invigorating. He praises nobly and with the clearest discrimination. Without sacrificing one iota of his rare and natural distinction and reserve, he makes Synge live in these praises. When he refers to a fellow-creature whom he loves or is quietly amused at, that fellow-creature is ours. He can so depict himself spinning Gaelic fairy-tales to two delightful nuns that not even Max would need to sharpen a line. His three pages telling how, with 'certain followers of St. Martin' in Paris, he took the Indian hemp, are a sheer joy—vaguely suggesting, queerly enough, a masterpiece as remote from them as Defoe's *Journal of the Plague Year*:

'The poet was wholly above himself, and presently he pointed to one of the street lamps, now brightening in the fading twilight, and cried at the top of his voice, "Why do you look at me with your great eye?" . . . After a while a Martinist ran towards me with a piece of paper, on which he had drawn a circle with a dot in it, and pointing at it with his finger he cried out, "God, God!"'

It was a mere schoolboy who defined a circle as a dot with a line running round it for ever and ever; and another who described ice as 'water that has fallen asleep in the cold'.

'To the Martinist', Mr. Yeats continues, 'some immeasurable mystery had been revealed, and his eyes shone; and at some time or other a lean and shabby man, with rather a distinguished face, showed me his horoscope and pointed with an ecstasy of melancholy at its evil aspects.'

It was a light o' love who finally in the grey of dawn dragged back these dreamers to stepmother Earth. It is far easier, of course, to be amused than to be edified. But Mr. Yeats's edification, his aphorisms, chiselled, recondite, and profound, on art and conduct, poetry, religion, life, are likely to convert only the converted. He etches in his fine prose for a little clan. 'The peering and peeping persons who are but hawkers of stolen goods', the 'scientists', the readers of newspapers, whom he so bitterly detests, if they open his book, will quickly shut it up again and return to their husks and gewgaws. 'There is something of an old wives' tale in fine literature. The makers of it are like an old peasant telling stories.' No doubt. And it is for such stories told with a natural and impromptu gusto and relish, beauty and spirit, that our minds and our hearts long. We have been preached at for four years. And now, not even a change of text can much comfort us, not even a poet in the pulpit, not even if that poet be Mr. Yeats—since from the open window of our old church our eyes stray out towards the half-forgotten historied woods and meadows, the green hills and valleys of the imagination.

Times Literary Supplement, May 1, 1919

THOMAS HARDY'S LYRICS*

If devotion and love are the happiest flowers that can intertwine a poet's laurels, then the wreath upon Mr. Hardy's brows is indeed burdened with sweetness. It is impossible to read him with indifference or in mere admiration. We blow either hot or cold; a fact that may in part explain why, years ago, he was compelled to surrender verse for prose, and long afterwards to forswear the writing of fiction. That dead past has now prudently buried its dead. Today our proud affection may even veil his rarest qualities. In heart as well as in time we stand too close to his work to appraise its complete achievement, to see it in true perspective and in relation to that of the great masters.

In reading again, and in reading steadily through, his lyrical poems we can realize, at any rate, the abundance and variety of his work, its homogeneousness and originality. No other English novelist has, in a chosen context, written prose that in effect, in feeling and atmosphere is nearer to poetry. No other English dramatist has written an historical play which more closely resembles than does *The Dynasts* a vast panoramic fiction, wherein real men and women so strangely reflect the idiosyncrasies of a distinct personality and imagination. So with these poems. They are, one and all, haunted with the presence of their writer. Every line of them—best and worst—is sealed with his own hand. We share an intense solitude of the spirit. We are as close to actual experience as words can bring us.

But even the most lyrical and individual of them is touched with the dramatic. A score of diverse disguises conceal (and betray) the one wearer; and ever to and fro glides the shuttle of wizardry, weaving make-believe out of the actual. More than once Mr. Hardy has warned us that his lyrics are dramatic or impersonative in conception, even when not obviously so.

* *Collected Poems.* By Thomas Hardy (Macmillan).

95

He has bidden us make allowance for widely differing moods and circumstances. He deprecates, that is, an arraignment of himself as A for what another self utters as Z. None the less—Alpha to Omega—all here is his, and all is himself. Nor should the inherent apparent contradictions be cancelled out as in a sum in arithmetic. They are light and colour from the facets of one multi-angled consciousness, that makes a various and chequered beauty of the white ray that is the infinite reality.

The simplest of poets may, it is true, drape himself in more than one domino. Herrick is Ariel in his songs, Caliban in his epigrams; the bacchanalian of the Mermaid and of the Triple Tun at one moment, the pious vicar of Dean Prior the next. But Mr. Hardy in his lyrics not only plays countless parts (from Prospero's to Trinculo's), and will squander on three brief stanzas the nucleus of a novel, but he is untrammelled by the incapacity to make poetry of the commonplace. In the Sala delle Muse, in Rome, he once kept tryst with one (surely a distant cousin of Sue Bridehead's) who was 'an essence of the Nine'—'a pensive smile on her sweet, small, marvellous face'. He lamented his fickleness, his inconstant love for Form also, and Tune, Story, Dance, and Hymn. She consoled him:

> *Nay, wight, thou sway'st not. These are but phases of one;*
> *And that one is I; and I am projected from thee,*
> *One that out of thy brain and heart thou causest to be—*
> *Extern to thee nothing. Grieve not, nor thyself becall,*
> *Woo where thou wilt; and rejoice thou canst love at all.*

So well has he obeyed her that anywhen, anywhere that ghostly face may smile on him in still regard, and make of every working day exactly four-and-twenty timeless hours. Certain themes may recur again and again; but he is not confined to any particular region of thought, experience, or of the imagination. Self-forgotten, he lives in the created. Absorbed in characters of his own making, he none the less fashions them in his own protean image. Never was the tinder of the mind more hospitable to the feeblest of actuality's sparks. The merest glimpse—a boy in a railway carriage with a key hung round his neck, a skeleton parasol, a tapping moth, a cheval glass, a fly bestraddling his midnight manuscript, a candle-lit face, a tottering tombstone, a church clock, a gargoyle, a fiddle, the wind in the chimney, dying daylight—and the poet in him answers as to a decoy. It may be convenient to call him a realist—though what poet, if reality is the habitation of the spirit as well as of the body, can be anything else is a nice question. A more precise term would be realizationist.

But if, apart from mask and domino, his scope, his multifarious range of theme, differentiates Mr. Hardy's lyrical poetry, no less does his treatment of it, the thought with which he complicates and deepens it, and the intensity, less of impulse than of elaboration, with which he constrains it to his will. The poet whose nut-tree bears silver nutmegs and gold pears would only scare his Spanish princess if he plucked for her also crab-apples and sloes. Fruits as tart and acrid abound in Mr. Hardy's orchard; and however gladly we may feast our eyes upon their vivid and sombre clusters, they are as bitter to some stomachs as was the honey-flavoured book to St. John. Lyrical poetry in general makes its own lovely paradise, fresh and sweet with dews of Lethe. Its airs blow rare from the intense inane. Much of Mr. Hardy's poetry limes our wings and tethers us close indeed to a God-forgotten 'tainted ball'. Mutes attired in dead black, their eyes submissive though preternaturally active, their ears exquisitely 'on the *qui vive*', stand on either side of the portals of its philosophy. Poem after poem reiterates that this poor scene of our earthly life is 'a show God ought surely to shut up soon', the 'unweeting dream-work' of some vast Imbecility, that spends eternity in passive reverie or remorse, that framed this planet in jest and abandoned it to hazardry. 'That I made Earth, and life, and man It still repenteth me.' As for Nature—she is nought more pitiful than a sleep-walker. 'Busy in her handsome house known as Space', she has fallen a-drowse; and man's only sure reward for all his hopes and aspirations is that 'storm-tight roof' which 'earth grants all her kind'; his only comfort that, though he must at last fall a prey to the 'iron daggers of distress', twice he cannot die. If this, and scores of kindred maledictions, were the final, unalleviated message to humanity of 'One who, past doubtings all, Waits in Unhope', then the poet in Mr. Hardy would have died in the arms of the philosopher, as might have Heine in those of Schopenhauer. But Mr. Hardy is too imaginative a philosopher to venture a final answer to the great riddle. He asks and asks:

Thy shadow, Earth, from Pole to Central Sea,
Now steals along upon the Moon's meek shine
In even monochrome and curving line
Of imperturbable serenity.

How shall I link such sun-cast symmetry
With the torn troubled form I know as thine,
That profile, placid as a brow divine,
With continents of moil and misery?
And can immense Mortality but throw
So small a shade? . . .

No God, it is true, could loom more phantasmal and remote
from our trivial and agonizing affairs than the 'all-Immanent
Will' that drives us into the world in 'rabble rout', mutters in
slumber, or mocks, or sighs out of his tenebrous abiding-place
in consciousness, at 'the monotonous moil of strained hard-run
Humanity'. But anthropomorphic deities are usually flattering
reflections of their creators. This deity is infinitely less compassionate, tender, magnanimous, and faithful than the poet
whose workmanship he is, and who in every word he writes is
present with us. Wherefore relenting and tenderness often steal
into the limning of this Divine conception, and pity smiles from
the eye-holes of the cold mask of the ironic:

Thou shouldst have learnt that Not to Mend
For Me could mean but Not to Know. . . .

It takes two to make either a quarrel or a friendship. 'Dazed
and puzzled 'twixt the gleam and gloom', the only human hope
is honesty.

Yet would men look at true things,
And unilluded view things,
And count to bear undue things,
The real might mend the seeming,
Facts better their foredeeming,
And Life its disesteeming.

And in *The Spell of the Rose*, another story is told to us:

But I was called from earth—yea, called
Before my rose-bush grew;
And would that now I knew

What feels he of the tree I planted,
And whether, after I was called
To be a ghost, he, as of old,
Gave me his heart anew!

Perhaps now blooms that queen of trees
I set but saw not grow,
And he, beside its glow—
Eyes couched of the mis-vision that blurred me—
Ay, there beside that queen of trees
He sees me as I was, though sees
Too late to tell me so!

That rose-bush is love—'long-suffering, brave . . . sweet, prompt, precious', even though 'cruel as the grave'. Not ours the arrogance to reconcile on his behalf a poet's contradictions. Yet there is a bloom upon this Dead Sea fruit that is more inviting and even more sustaining than the milky juices of that of the mere optimist. Beyond this, simply because the faithful and unflinching presentation of a philosophy, however Spartan, darkened or forlorn it may be, is poetic, it confers light, energy, and even peace on us. *Worse* tidings cannot reach us, nor can Truth wear a colder, harsher, more sardonic grin (and assuredly in the 'Fifteen Glimpses' she displays her dog teeth to some purpose). But we have fallen in love with her ambassador; and like ambassador, the heart argues, like Queen.

Beneath this heaven, indifferent or hostile, Mr. Hardy sets up his stage, the panorama of mortal existence, calls up his characters, peoples his solitude:

Listen: I'll tell the tale,
It may bring faint relief.

Our company, it must be admitted, is not that of 'the winged seraphs': or of alien divinities as lovely as they are inexacting; or of a society urbane, at ease, immune in its Palace of Art. There are not many 'ladies' in this volume—the majority of them are haplessly jilted, or helplessly wed. There are far fewer perfect gentlemen. One such buys an enemy's portrait intent on the joy (of which he is cheated) of destroying it; another is the husband of the unfortunate bride in *A Conversation at Dawn*:

'I'm a practical man, and want no tears;
You've made a fool of me, it appears;
That you don't again
Is a lesson I'll teach you in future years.'

She answered not, lying listlessly
With her dark dry eyes on the coppery sea,
That now and then
Flung its lazy flounce at the neighbouring quay.

A third 'gentleman' affrighted even a wagtail.

In a world indeed wherein, if closely examined, the guise of life is less 'fell' only when it is realized that cold, sickness, gloom, death are but 'subalterns', passively subject to the higher command, class distinctions seem of trivial import, and 'the courtesies of the bland' a mere veneer. It is little wonder then that poor Mrs. Grundy cuts a sorry figure in it; that the conventions and conformities are left to take care of themselves, as they very well can; and that 'Order-keeping's rigorous control' resembles that of a foolish and embittered nurse in a rebellious nursery. Moonshine or noonday, and whether its stage be thronged or deserted, this is a world also, whose borders are astir with the spectral. How could it be otherwise, seeing that of any man's friends so large a number are in the grave? It is here, if anywhere, that literary company looks in on Mr. Hardy, and come to sup with him Emily Brontë and the author of *The Duchess of Malfi*. Barham, too, when the port is on the table, will rap at the door; and neighbour Burton lug in a folio on the Pleasures of Melancholy. His phantoms and revenants are for the most part the wistful evocations of misgiving or regret. Some of them are more lovely, and all are more understandable, even when inclined to the satirical, than when in the real. Many are earthily jovial, 'clay-cadavers', with their mugs and pipes, their lutes and viols, touched by lights of midnight, under willow and yew. And amid their revelries from among the deeper shadows leers out the sinister-grotesque.

Thus freed from the artificial, thus haunted, thus aroused, we share the company of Mr. Hardy's wayfaring men and women, intent on their all-absorbing share in the egregious drama, and part-perfect. Entangled in the webs of circumstance, the majority of them are the prey of their desires, their aspirations or their folly, racked, cheated by mischance, victims of age or affliction, or of a tender and lively charm and innocence that is but a mockery in its transitoriness. Their happiest stories are overcast with the precarious (and at the mercy of an ironic appendix!); but even the most tragic are such as our own experience can ratify, however hastily a self-defensive memory may have strown her poppy.

Like the figure which we discern in the poems that are not obviously impersonative or dramatic, these characters are mysterious, and touched with a kind of strangeness or romance, as indeed all humanity is mysterious when, viewed searchingly, it is off its guard, or when the scales of habit or prejudice have dropped from our eyes. Unobserved, we watch them as closely as in mind we can watch the faces of friends with whom long ago we were in intimate and earnest colloquy; but seldom, indeed, as watches Peeping Tom when the vivisectionist is busy. So passionately intent is Mr. Hardy's 'visionary power' on the naked truth of things in their changing aspects that he seems designedly to reject in his record of them the refinements of art and beauty.

But since beauty and significance are debts which no living imagination can evade paying to reality, his poetry is drenched with them. Even if these figments of humanity were absent from his pages, we might almost guess his portraits from their frames. No other poetry is richer in scene, within doors or without; in landscape—its times and lights and seasons; in Englishness. To present a true account, debit and credit, between Mr. Hardy and his Wessex would make the fame of a literary accountant. But what of that further west of the most passionate of his poems, where 'in chasmal beauty' roars the Atlantic, and swing the surges over sunken Lyonesse?

Yet, for pure melody, the music of this verse is unlikely to redden with envy the cheeks of the Sirens. The style is often crustacean. Occasionally it is 'an irk no local hope beguiles', and as if 'smitten by years-long wryness born of misprision'. The thought, too, may be as densely burdened in its expression as the scar of a tree by the healing saps that have enwarted its surface. But what rare and wondrous clumps of mistletoe bedeck the branches. Stubborn the medium may be, but with what mastery is it compelled to do this craftsman's bidding. Let the practised poet borrow but a score of Mr. Hardy's latinities and vernaculars—hodiernal, receptivity, deicide, a senior-soul-flame, his mindsight, naysaying, eyesome, potent appraisements, smugger, years-haired, forefolk, and the rest, and then invoke his own Muse! Difficulty, seeming impossibility, is the breath of Mr. Hardy's nostrils as a craftsman. He makes our English so much his own that a single quoted line, lifted at random, betrays his workmanship. He forces, hammers poetry into his words; not, like most poets, charms it out of them. He disdains the 'poetical', yet will redeem the veriest commonplace; and will so encrust his chosen theme that it shines the brighter for the roughness and uncouthness of its setting. His argument winds in and out of his congested, complex stanzas, keeping a low pitch, and, by emphasizing rather than by suddenly escaping its monotony, wins his effect.

When indeed life and energy pour their visionings of truth and reality into the mould of form, poetry cannot but be their reward. This imagination, accepting the world even while renouncing the 'Impercipient' that set it in the void, redeems its mischances, and of the sorriest disaster makes a memory for our comfort and understanding. Charm, grace, delicacy seem idle terms in the presence of this genius. Bare, uncompromising, mocking, pitiful, and utterly human. Mr. Hardy has gone his way, aloof, impassioned, watching life, living it, sharing it with man and nature; and, above all, loving its seared, suffering, heroic face that smiles on at grief, and is indomitable in happiness in a world that seemingly cheats to destroy.

A poem entitled *In the Seventies*, having for motto 'Qui deridetur ab amico suo sicut ego', tells, in retrospect, of the starry thoughts that in those far days shed their magic light on this poet's 'worktimes' and his 'soundless hours of rest'; tells, too, of 'the vision';

> *In the seventies nought could darken or destroy it,*
> *Locked in me.*
> *Though as delicate as lamp-worm's lucency;*
> *Neither mist nor murk could weaken or alloy it*
> *In the seventies!—could not darken or destroy it,*
> *Locked in me.*

Upwards of forty years have passed since that day, and all but a fraction of the work in this volume is of the last two or three decades. Mr. Hardy, once and for all, set up as a poet, then, at an age when Shakespeare left our mortal stage. This book, for that reason alone, is an unprecedented achievement. Apart from that, to read steadily through it—and what severer test of lyrical poetry could be devised?—is to win to the consciousness, not of any superficial consistency, but assuredly of a 'harmony of colouring'; not, however keen the joy manifest 'in the making', of an art become habitual, but of a shadowy unity and design. In the seventies Mr. Hardy could not have foreseen that full design, nor can he have consciously traced it out. But laborious days and an unfaltering constancy have set free those starry thoughts, that secret wondrous vision, and have thrown open one of the most hospitable doors in English literature in welcome to all.

Times Literary Supplement, Nov. 27, 1919

THE POETRY OF BARNES*

Every reader dreams as fondly sometimes of the might-have-been in literature as the forlorn lover dreams of the might-have-been in his retrospect of life. If only Charon could occasionally smuggle back an MS. across the shadows of Acheron—Sir Thomas Browne's edition of Donne; Webster's early Lyrics; the Reminiscences of Christopher Marlowe! This little volume has forestalled one such vain longing. It has for once become a reality: a selection of William Barnes's poems made by Thomas Hardy. It is one of those signally appropriate coincidences that even Chance could not better.

In his introduction Mr. Hardy speaks of the slow but inevitable dying-out of the Dorset dialect, to many 'an unlamented language that need leave behind it no grammar of its secrets and no key to its tomb'. But the death of a language—as childhood soon desperately learns—is but the wicket-gate that opens into immortality. Dead languages are the only languages beyond the canker of time, as they are—if Erse be but a splendid exception —beyond its enrichment. But even regarding so little a language as a dialect, while it enshrines the beautiful and calm thought and feeling of such a poet as Barnes, and so much of the dialogue of Mr. Hardy himself, the fact that as time goes on it is destined to echo less and less in living speech is not so mournful as it else would have been.

If anything, perhaps Mr. Hardy makes too much of the difficulties likely to beset the general, even the cockney, reader of Barnes's poetry. Much of its strangeness is due to but slight differences in spelling. Words in it that positively require a glossary are as rare almost as they are precious; and though 'the qualifying face-play and the gestures which so largely figure in

---

* *Select Poems of William Barnes.* Chosen and edited by Thomas Hardy (Oxford Library of Prose and Poetry. Frowde).

the speech of husbandmen' must be beyond the born Londoner's realization, and though the sound of the words on the inward ear of the reader bears probably a far from close resemblance to the sound of the words as spoken, he still may divine something of their charm. Besides this, there is in dialect a refuge from the commonplace. The mind enters, as it were, into a secret understanding with the poet through his language; it sets at once the key. Literary English seldom cries so keen a challenge to the imagination. And so far as mere sound is concerned the Dorset dialect has, we think, and not merely for the genius of Barnes, a small but real advantage over classical English. There is a beautiful and slow graveness in his verse which it may not be fancy to suppose is in part due to its frequent 'v's' and 'z's', and the conversion of the rather jingling 'ing' of the participle into the Dorset 'en'. The soft drawl of the prolonged vowel-sounds and the use of the auxiliaries 'be' and 'do' serve to enhance this effect. If, for example, we pronounce the words in the first verse of the Old Hundredth Dorset-fashion, we shall realize what in so doing is gained—and what is lost. The rustic congregation evoked in the fancy changes its aspect; the little country church itself ages and perhaps grows darker; there is no *organ* accompaniment; we are deep in the country; the birds are singing.

The few poems written by Barnes in other than dialect show clearly the debt it was his good fortune to owe to his beloved Dorset. This is truly virgin English. It comes upon the ear like the distant lowing of oxen, the cawing of rooks. It is chequered with light and shade like a sunny orchard, and has the encrustations of time and the unearthly earthiness of an old churchyard, with its stones and lichen and grasses.

The chief difficulty for the lover of Barnes is to speak temperately in admiration of his poetry, which is no more to be analysed than is anything else in the world that is beyond the conscious manufacture of man. To attempt to prove its loveliness, its evasive presence in its words, its quick conspiracy with the heart, its truth, would be merely to endanger one's own delight in it and to fail to convince anyone not convinced already. It is invariably and markedly individual. The same voice sounds in every poem as that which haunts *To Me.*

'Even if Barnes often used the dramatic form of peasant speakers as a pretext for the expression of his own mind and experiences . . . it enabled him to elude in his verse those dreams and speculations that cannot leave alone the mystery of things—possibly an unworthy mystery and disappointing if solved, though one that has a harrowing fascination for many poets.'

This is a highly characteristic aside from the author of *The Dynasts*; and so far as Barnes is concerned, it would be difficult to show, except perhaps in his humorous verse, any vital distinction of personality in the poems. They all portray the same equable, tender, and all-loving nature. Each in turn reveals the same intuition, the same uninquisitiveness, the same quiet, effortless, yet studious form of expression. Barnes certainly does not speculate in his poems. *Locksley Hall* is as far from his chosen themes as are *Bishop Blougram's Apology* and *Holy Willie's Prayer*. But would he have written in a different vein had he written in his own person, without any disguising and restricting medium? He seems to have deliberately chosen for the subject of poetry only what he deemed most suitable and fitting for poetry. His depth is the clear but profound depth of simplicity. 'Lwonesomeness' is his natural place of observation. The beauty of faithful sorrow for the lost, a childlike tenderness for children, and for men whose evening casts back a colour on the east whence shone their daybreak, the magnanimity of refusing to peer too closely, and of seeking out in his fellow-creatures only what he most hoped for in himself—these are among the rare elements of the spirit that haunts his poetry. And in complete harmony with these was, of course, his style. Is there a single 'purple passage'—or heedless one either—in the whole of his works?

The simple intuition Barnes displayed so effortlessly and unassumingly is that of a man who glances up in reverie and saturates the small thing seen with the quiet dream and emotion out of which he saw it.

> *I thought her like the rwose that flung*
> *His sweetness vrom his darken'd ball—*

that is the heartfelt comparison he makes in *The Rwose in the Dark*, to describe his 'true-love' sitting with him in the moonless gloom of an open window.

> *I went hwome in the dead o' the night*
> *When the vields wer all empty o' vo'k,*

An' the tuns at their cool-winded height
Wer all dark, an' all cwold 'ithout smoke.

So he reveals the forlorn chimneys of *The Widow's House,*

An' orcha'd apples red half-round
Have all a-happer'd down.

And as if out of the strange silence in which the poet worked
an invisible hand had dropped lightly a fresh flower on his
paper—so his inspirations seem to come:

Oh! the moon, wi' his peäle lighted skies,
Have his sorrowless sleepers below,
But by day to the zun they must rise. . .

Vor lovely wer the looks her feäce
Held up avore the western sky . . .

Although they do not stand out, either in theme or thought or
workmanship, conspicuously one from another, nor ever *sparkle,*
there is scarcely a poem of Barnes's which does not harbour
quiet and pacifying affection and tender insight. His poems are
simply real and beautiful in their setting as a child's eyes are
beautiful in its face. And with a word, a hint, he confides in us
what life—now and always—meant to him. As for what he
omits, does not heed or mention—perhaps that is an even surer
test of true poetry. We go in under the porch of his homely
dialect, and we leave behind us nearly all we talk about, much of
what we think, much even of what we hope for, in the roaring
and dusty street of experience whose echo seems scarcely ever
to have disillusioned or even disquieted his sorrow or his joy.

Times Literary Supplement, Feb. 11, 1909

THE POETRY OF ROBERT BRIDGES

Not long ago English poetry enjoyed a brief but genial summer in the British Press. Poets who for the most part spend their days in a pensive seclusion, chequered by an occasional venture into print, were openly invited to sun themselves in publicity, and here and there a conceivable claimant to the vacant Laureateship was cajoled into casting his vote for an improbable rival. It was, indeed, a matter that most concerned the poets themselves, and the dedication of E.M.'s recent anthology of verse by living poets proved at least that in this unanimity was not so forlorn a hope as it might have seemed. That volume offered a modest but sincere homage to Mr. Robert Bridges. And it may be said as truly of Mr. Bridges as of Edmund Spenser, that he is a poet's poet.

This is not merely a tribute to a consummate artist, it implies the recognition also that Mr. Bridges's devotion to his art has been in the service of an ideal unalloyed with other, though not necessarily meaner enthusiasms. His work is not only incontestably his own and no other man's, but its aim has always been essentially poetry, and only indirectly ethical, didactic, circumstantial. This probably accounts for the fact that his admirers until the other day were comparatively few, that his name was rather a touchstone and assurance to his fellow-craftsmen than a household word or a party battle-cry.

The Oxford Edition of his poetical works contains all his verse with the sole exception of his dramas. It is comparatively small in content. But the writing of verse easily becomes a dangerous habit. Complete editions serve too often merely for an imposing monument. We see the mound of busy dust; we catch only a fleeting glimpse of the mole. The conscious artist avoids such a defeat. He learns to distinguish one kind of impulse from another. Like Herrick, he bids his book make haste away:

108

> *Lest wrapped from hence, I see thee lie*
> *Torn for the use of pastery;*
> *Or see thy injured leaves serve well*
> *To make loose gowns for mackerel . . .*

and when the Good Demon has forsaken him awhile he does not force his mood, but is content alone to sit and 'over-read' what he has writ. To Mr. Bridges this patience is not merely the outcome of wisdom acquired from experience; it is an innate quality of mind. A deliberate reticence, a sedulous restraint, a hatred of revelations, are its constant marks. It is never in danger of a loose insincerity, bombast, mere prettiness. Its tendency is rather towards the impersonal and academic. It may become austere almost to the point of aridity. A trace of Augustan formality edges at times into the verse; 'rival amorous vows Amaze the scented air'; an acrostic on the revered name of Purcell diversifies the exquisitely told tale of *Eros and Psyche*. But though inspiration occasionally flags or fails it, the tinder, as it were, is always there; it is the spark that is wanting. This is only another way of saying that Mr. Bridges is that too-rare combination of excellences—a scholar as well as a poet. Whatever his interest centres on, whether music, or hymnody, English speech, prosody, or technical criticism, his method and treatment are always close and thorough, and his conclusions are never extravagant. In an age of crazes and caprice, of curiosity, ostentation, and publicity, he has consistently stood aloof—but not as a mere spectator. He is beyond any of his contemporaries—and forerunners, too—the poet of discipline, of a serene assurance, of an unfretful though by no means passive endurance of what a divine destiny may send and life commit to:

> *Far sooner I would choose*
> *The life of brutes that bask,*
> *Than set myself a task,*
> *Which inborn powers refuse:*
> *And rather far enjoy*
> *The body, than invent*
> *A duty, to destroy*
> *The case which nature sent;*
> *A country life I praise,*

> *And lead, because I find*
> *The philosophic mind*
> *Can take no middle ways;*
> *She will not leave her love*
> *To mix with men, her art*
> *Is all to strive above*
> *The crowd, or stand apart. . .*

or again:

> *Think not that thou canst all things know, nor deem*
> *Such knowledge happiness . . .*
> > *but what 'tis joy to learn*
> *Or use to know, that may'st thou ask of right—*

therefore:

> *O soul, be patient: thou shalt find*
> *A little matter mend all this;*
> *Some strain of music to thy mind,*
> *Some praise for skill not spent amiss.*

A tranquil ease and mastery invariably characterize his work, an assured play of mind, a slightly astringent irony. No smoke, no fire, says the proverb; but this close artist kept even his chimney out of sight. His consistent example is a counsel of excellence. It would, moreover, be as futile to expect of him the incandescence of a Donne as to go epic-hunting in the gardens of the *Hesperides*.

More than half of this volume consists of 'shorter poems', and to these may be added the sonnet-sequence of *The Growth of Love*. It is as a writer of lyrics that Mr. Bridges will live; though for the artist sufficient unto the moment is the immortality thereof. 'Go', he bids his work 'of today', 'Go, find thy friends, if there be one to love thee; Casting thee forth, my child, I rise above thee.' Whether it lives on or is forgotten is no matter.

Flowers fade, music falters into silence:

> *. . . Die, song, die like a breath,*
> *And wither as a bloom;*
> *Fear not a flowery death,*
> *Dread not an airy tomb!*

> *Fly with delight, fly hence!*
> *'Twas thine love's tender sense*
> *To feast; now on thy bier*
> *Beauty shall shed a tear.*

Fate, like the robins in the wood, may strew these poems over with leaves from other poets awhile. How delightful a surprise in that case is in store for the Mr. Bullen of the twenty-second century.

The lyric may be a mere snatch of music, a thought loosed from a cage of words, an amazingly rare and happy moment in flower. Many faultless examples of all these kinds are here: 'Thou did'st delight mine eyes,' 'I love all beauteous things,' 'My spirit sang all day,' 'Angel spirits of sleep'. It may present a quiet, clear description of the world, touched, like a cloud at evening with rose, by the warm light of feeling; as in *The Downs* or *Winter Nightfall*, or *A Passer-By*, or *London Snow*. It may be filled almost beyond the conveyance in words with an intensity of delight.

> *I saw the Virgin-mother clad in green,*
> *Walking the sprinkled meadows at sundown*
> *While yet the moon's cold flame was hung between*
> *The day and night.*

Melody and echo, rhythmical elusiveness, can suggest the silence, clarity, and unearthliness of dream:

> *Angel spirits of sleep,*
> *White-robed, with silver hair,*
> *In your meadows fair,*
> *Where the willows weep,*
> *And the sad moonbeam*
> *On the gliding stream*
> *Writes her scattered dream:*
>
> *Angel spirits of sleep,*
> *Dancing to the weir*
> *In the hollow roar*
> *Of its waters deep;*
> *Know ye how men say*

That ye haunt no more
Isle and grassy shore
With your moonlit play;
That ye dance not here,
White-robed spirits of sleep,
All the summer night
Threading dances light?

And vision may suddenly transcend the faculty of sight:

. . . The woodland willow stands a lonely bush
Of nebulous gold;
There the Spring-goddess cowers in faint attire
Of frightened fire.

And in such poems as *The Affliction of Richard, Pater Filio, I never shall love snow again,* a heart desperately charged with grief and perplexity may still express itself in words that reveal more clearly even than these its faith and trust and courage. But though the initial spontaneity of Mr. Bridges's lyrics is never entirely hidden, it much more clearly shows itself to be a kind of distillation of reflection and reverie. And this is true although —beyond perhaps that of any other English poet—his verse is free from regret or melancholy or sadness or reproach. And there falls across his page no Shadow of Despair. Sorrow— whatever the analogy may be worth—seems generally a deeper thing than joy. Darkness a more substantial thing than light. It is, at any rate, humanly speaking, easier to express the disappointments and defeats, the melancholy, disaster and gloom of life than its sheer happiness, its moments of purest peace and rare content. All the world's sea-traffic skirts the isle where sing the Sirens; and the heart that is broken, or at least has been carelessly handled, makes the most plangent and appealing lyre. Mr. Bridges is first a poet of an almost matchless craftsmanship, whose primary theme is love—love itself, not the quite admirable though somewhat over-domesticated love of some of the Victorian poets, nor the no-less-exacting bitter desire of others. And next he is the poet of happiness—not of mirth, gaiety, joviality, Bacchic abandon, but that of a mood, or, rather, a state of being, in which mind and heart are at one, a balance between joy and solemnity such as delights and solaces us in the music of Handel, as beauty and its reflection are at one when a child, stooping over some green, quiet, sky-reflecting pool, stays rapt in the contemplation of the half-dreaming picture it meets there in the water.

Saturday Westminster Gazette, Aug. 30, 1913

EDWARD THOMAS

An Annual of New Poetry* contains the work of many poets already well known. There are lyrics by John Drinkwater, W. H. Davies, and Gordon Bottomley; narrative poems by Sturge Moore, Wilfrid Gibson, R. C. Trevelyan, and Robert Frost. They are one and all characteristic of their writers. For this reason alone such a collection would be sure of a welcome. But its chief good fortune, both for its contributors and for lovers of poetry, rests in the fact that it contains also the first published work in verse of a writer who long ago won the fullest recognition from all who delight in literature, for the beauty, delicacy, and imaginativeness of his prose. Eighteen of these poems, signed by the pseudonym 'Edward Eastaway', are by Edward Thomas, the news of whose death in action reached his friends early in Easter week.

Habit is, of course, a writer's most treacherous foe. But it is not by taking thought that he can safely leave a familiar self, or impulse, or technique, or even range of subject behind him. Better write no more than merely strive to be original. From this kind of effort—though not from the effort to master a new form—these poems are wholly free. They are unlike anything which keeps them company here, and they are more closely his own than almost anything else that Thomas did. He could not but be conscious of this. If he had lived, he might still have wished to remain hidden behind his pseudonym, though such secrets are apt to creep about. Why share everything? He had discovered a new vein, if not a new bent; a new form of expression. It set free a renewal of delight and desire. It was one of the richest gifts, and the last, that life could give him. And he gave that life for England.

Such breakings away are rare. Edward Thomas must have

* *An Annual of New Poetry* (Constable).

114

been a critic of rhymes in his nursery. How much generous help and encouragement many living poets owe to his counsel only themselves could say. To his candour, too. For the true cause, he believed, is better served by an uncompromising 'Trespassers will be prosecuted' than by an amiable 'All are welcome'. Until he became a soldier, and so found a fresh and vivid interest, it had been his fate, day in, day out, to write for a living. To a temperament so independent and so self-critical this experience was at times little short of purgatory. A few of his books, his *Richard Jefferies*, his *Heart of England* and *Tales of Rest and Unrest*, for instance, came freely and from the heart. Others of them, however conscientious in workmanship, and rich in his qualities, were forced and distasteful. For though reading and writing were almost as natural to him as walking and talking, books were for him a fulfilment of life, never a substitute for it; and to those who love him, he meant, beyond most men, a great deal more than his books. Never lived a man more resolute in fidelity to what he himself held dear in the world; and dearest to him were the simplicity, grace, freshness, livingness of what springs of its own nature, clear and sweet as a wellspring out of the earth, and, as impulsively, out of a man's heart and mind and imagination.

No devotion can be free from strong prejudice when it is the outcome of a sensitiveness so quick to recoil. 'Singularly moved To love the lovely that is not beloved', he could not endure compromise. Everything which frets and cages and constrains the spirits and bodies of living creatures he hated, and he fought against all that darkens life, denaturalizes, and makes it ugly. Servility, pretentiousness, tyranny, pedantry, officialism, snobbery, dogmatism—such things were to him as evil a blight in human affairs as red tape, corrugated iron, and barbed wire.

All old things—not merely 'old-fashioned' or antique, and certainly not quaint—all old things he delighted in, with no restless desire to question why: people, houses, manners, ways, customs, songs, books, wisdom, learning, beliefs, loyalties. And to care as he did for them was to be found friend unchanging to all that moves in freedom in air or earth or water, and to enjoy every mortal thing that a man can make with his hands, from a flint arrow to an apple pie, from a Suffolk church to a sound cheese, a hedge-cut walking-stick, and a Cox's orange pippin.

115

Virtues attracted him more even than the virtuous, and the instinctive more than the acquired. He delighted in 'characters', both in life and in letters. 'Causes' he was apt to scrutinize a little whimsically and of 'cries' he listened for the echo. Important people and things are, of course, 'important', but elusive detached observers are apt to smile at apocryphal mountains, and be no less amused at their mice.

The word 'England' meant for him its loveliness and oldness, its centuries of quiet labour, its villages and solitudes, its truest, simplest people; and his was a patriotism therefore that needed neither to be tainted by hatred nor heated by war. His interests, indeed, were not confined to the newspaper, not political, nor what is usually meant by social. (He managed even to live without novels—a war economy that might give even Mr. Bathurst pause). His last tribute to a man would be that he was respectable, to a woman that she was a lady. It was not Providence, he believed, who had set the human race this kind of handicap. There are idle cults and busy cults, art cults, religious cults, and the cults called Bohemian. Thomas was outside them all—at any rate in his later years. To live in content a 'simple life' was perhaps what he desired most of the world, but no man can have less respected the cant phrase.

Friend of friends—and of many friends—that he was, he could not but be in spirit a solitary. He looked it, too: the slow gestures, the grave, quiet smile of eye and mouth, with a gleam of irony at times, or a slanting, faun-like raillery, the quiet, deliberate, beautiful voice, the bony, powerful hands, the long, slow stride which even the drill sergeant only just succeeded in making intermittent. For that stride had carried him along the high roads and by-lanes and field-paths, the rides and bridle-paths and forest ways of every southern and western county in England:

> *They are lonely*
> *While we sleep, lonelier*
> *For lack of the traveller*
> *Who is now a dream only. . . .*

Fleet Street will remember that rare figure, but not so well or so long as the unseen eyes in brake and thicket, nor as Peasblossom and Mustardseed, who used to drop acorns and oak-apples on his head as he passed by.

That country solitude came in with him at the door even of an ugly little house in the suburbs, and shamed one's own noisier mind. And one friend, at least, felt always something of a cockney in his company, and ink-dyed at that. He wanted to feel and be at peace and to remember rather than to think and to plan; to keep living things whole and just themselves rather than to dissect them or huddle them up in categories; to brood rather than to speculate or even to dream. Such natures are prone to melancholy—a distress unforeseen that descends out of the unknown, and like a cold, dark cloud betrays hope and assurance. Earthly existence may seem then nothing but a cage, of God or Man; and they are subject to reactions bitter and intolerant as well as tender, wise, and loving. He muses:

> *What does it mean? Tired, angry, and ill at ease,*
> *No man, woman, or child alive could please*
> *Me now. And yet I almost dare to laugh*
> *Because I sit and frame an epitaph—*
> *'Here lies all that no one loved of him*
> *And that loved no one.' Then in a trice that whim*
> *Has wearied. But though I am like a river*
> *At fall of evening while it seems that never*
> *Has the sun lighted it or warmed it, while*
> *Cross breezes cut the surface to a file,*
> *This heart, some fraction of me, happily*
> *Floats through the window even now to a tree*
> *Down in the misting, dim-lit, quiet vale,*
> *Not like a peewit that returns to wail*
> *For something it has lost, but like a dove*
> *That slants unswerving to its home and love.*
> *There I find my rest, and through the dusk air*
> *Flies what yet lives in me. Beauty is there.*

So, nearly every one of these poems shares, yet keeps a secret, of mood or feeling. They carry the mind away into the solitude of far-off memories, of the half-forgotten, even of 'things I have forgot that I forget', places where no one else has been, where dwells the beautiful 'Unknown', who, maybe, 'may not exist'. And the present can be so saturated with memories that it becomes a kind of mirage of the past. There is little company—trees, a butterfly, aspen, thorn, a sedge-warbler, a child.

Where haunt the small brown birds
Wisely reiterating endlessly
What no man learnt yet, in or out of school.

The words he used are precise: 'water'; now 'running frizzled over gravel', now a 'shining pane' in the middle of a wood, now 'combing the dark-green hair' of its weeds; 'bright, thin grass', or a 'mist like chaos surging back'. They are there for their own sake, of course, but chiefly because the things they represent have been lived with and loved so long that their names are themselves. Mere observation will detect the salient sharply enough; but only a passive, half-conscious reverie will at last win to and share in the life itself. Most poems are final and isolated, as it were, in their own form. In these there is a kind of endlessness in the experience they tell of, and in its expression the desire only to convey it without friction or emphasis, from consciousness to consciousness, as in the first of the morning one tells to one's self a dream. It is this, one feels— apart from the artist's joy of discovery and experiment—that was the writer's secret happiness in them. Unforced, unsought, 'unnecessary', they came straight out of himself, from the furthest, yet nearest, verge of experience; and his last poem, *Lights Out*, tells of the secret crossing:

> *I have come to the borders of sleep,*
> *The unfathomable deep*
> *Forest, where all must lose*
> *Their way, however straight*
> *Or winding, soon or late;*
> *They cannot choose.*
>
> *Many a road and track*
> *That since the dawn's first crack*
> *Up to the present brink*
> *Deceived the travellers,*
> *Suddenly now blurs,*
> *And in they sink.*
>
> *Here love ends—*
> *Despair, ambition ends;*
> *All pleasure and all trouble,*

Although most sweet or bitter,
Here ends, in sleep that is sweeter
Than tasks most noble. . . .

Saturday Westminster Gazette, April 28, 1917

*   *   *

We turn from his clear, abstemious, unemphatic prose to the verse of the *Poems*,* and it is as if a wind had suddenly come out of the south, setting the waters free. Thomas had been criticizing other men's poetry for twenty years, and all these years had been steadily storing up his own. It is a poetry that not only breaks away from poetic convention, into a verse in which the rhymes are the faintest of echoes, the metre at times scarcely distinguishable, and the form as insubstantial as a ghost's, but much of it is 'about' what most poets leave unremarked, or, at any rate, unrecorded. We listen to a kind of monologue, like that of one of his own nightingales softly practising over its song, as though in utmost secrecy we were overhearing a man talking quietly to himself, or to some friend strangely silent and understanding, pouring out his reveries, ruminations, remembrances. Yet these are not remembrances only of what has happened in the past, but of what is almost insupportably real and near and present, taking the aspect of the past on the eve of a long farewell:

> *The past is the only dead thing that smells sweet,*
> *The only sweet thing that is not also fleet.*
>   *I'm bound away for ever,*
>   *Away somewhere, away for ever;*

on a journey 'that tempts me on to something sweeter than love'. In no other poetry, unless perhaps in Vaughan's or Clare's, is there so profound a solitude. And, in spite of melancholy, of a grief for beauty more intense than delight, in spite of a sorrowful dwelling on the fleeting, vivid, salience of things which one may never see again, there is a wellspring of happiness.

* *Poems* by Edward Thomas (Edward Eastaway) (Selwyn and Blount).

*Yet naught did my despair
But sweeten the strange sweetness, while through the wild air
All day long I heard a distant cuckoo calling
And, soft as dulcimers, sounds of near water falling,
And, softer and remote as if in history,
Rumours of what had touched my friends, my foes, or me.*

As in reverie, and as if out of an enormous distance, the eye sees with astonishing clearness and discrimination the things of actuality close to it, so in these poems there is this distance of time and of space and this exactitude. 'The earth outspread, like meadow of the future, I possessed'—it is not the language of hyperbole but of truth to the rarest of experiences. Over everything, too, in these poems broods age. The names of a dozen English villages are held sweet on the tongue, for a while, as if the very sound of them might surrender a hidden secret, as if they were a talisman, a rune, an incantation.

*Yes. I remember Adlestrop—
The name, because one afternoon
Of heat the express train drew up there
Unwontedly. It was late June.*

*The steam hissed. Someone cleared his throat.
No one left and no one came
On the bare platform. What I saw
Was Adlestrop—only the name*

*And willows, willow-herb, and grass,
And meadowsweet, and haycocks dry,
No whit less still and lonely fair
Than the high cloudlets in the sky.*

*And for that minute a blackbird sang
Close by, and round him, mistier,
Farther and farther, all the birds
Of Oxfordshire and Gloucestershire.*

Some time in life 'the express train' for most of us draws up at Adlestrop. If so, please heaven, the immortal moment bringing the peace, understanding, and reconciliation which are the recurrent theme of these poems, is ours.

In Edward Thomas's prose one is conscious of a born lover of words, using them with all care, circumspection, assurance, and delight. But here is the stranger delight of a man who has suddenly stumbled on a power, a freedom, till now unperceived. 'Choose me, you English words,' he pleads, almost in the same accent, with the same tenderness, as in one of the very few love songs in this volume, *Will you come?* He is half bewildered with this opportunity of expressing what would otherwise have remained unsaid; and life, too, had as suddenly opened out, revealing the unforeseen. He must test and find his way, gradually mastering both the experience and the expression of it:

> *Look at the old house,*
> *Outmoded, dignified,*
> *Dark and untenanted,*
> *With grass growing instead*
> *Of the footsteps of life. . . .*
> *I am something like that;*
> *Only I am not dead,*
> *Still breathing and interested*
> *In the house that is not dark. . . .*

We feel that no friend on earth could ever have known him so truly and closely as the unseen friend with whom he is communing here, out of a darkness and grief well-nigh unendurable, out of a happiness, too, almost past bearing. 'If we could see all, all might be good.' It is like the saying of a child comforting an elder, as *The Trumpet* is the saying of a man, out of the wisdom of the heart and of the imagination:

> *While you are listening*
> *To the clear horn,*
> *Forget, men, everything*
> *On this earth newborn,*
> *Except that it is lovelier*
> *Than any mysteries.*
> *Open your eyes to the air*
> *That has washed the eyes of the stars*
> *Through all the dewy night:*
> *Up, with the light,*
> *To the old wars;*
> *Arise, arise!*

There falls at last in *Lights Out* the solitude that lies between two worlds, two realities, in which either is like a scene in a dream:

> *There is not any book*
> *Nor face of dearest look*
> *That I would not turn from now*
> *To go into the unknown*
> *I must enter and leave alone*
> *I know not how.*
>
> *The tall forest towers:*
> *Its cloudy foliage lowers*
> *Ahead, shelf above shelf;*
> *Its silence I hear and obey*
> *That I may lose my way*
> *And myself.*

'Such a poem', Thomas says, in *The Tenth Muse*, of one of Carew's songs, 'shows how little need the lyric has of the best that is thought and said in the world. It is made of materials that are worth nothing and yet is itself beyond price.' That is an old paradox. Of his own verse the materials may more often transcend the form. What is uncustomary, especially in art and in literature, must slowly win its way. So may it be with these poems! But whether they have few readers or many, they are among the rarest fruits of these strange years.

Times Literary Supplement, Oct. 18, 1917

GEORGIAN POETRY*

To prove that English poetry is 'now again putting on a new strength and beauty', that we are even perhaps at the beginning of another great poetic age, is the aim of a little anthology, recently published, entitled *Georgian Poetry*. Some day, if fate smile kindly on the promise of his venture, the initials of its 'onlie begetter', E.M., may become the nucleus of as animated and academic a controversy as has raged round those of 'William Himself'. *Georgian Poetry* is a collection of verse drawn entirely from publications of the last two years, and presents the work of writers who, either before 1911 had published nothing, or who have since then gained some accession of power. With the single exception of Mr. Sturge Moore, it excludes poets of established and incontrovertible reputation, and it is dedicated with all gratitude and devotion to Mr. Robert Bridges. That titanic achievement, for instance, *The Dynasts*, is not here! Upwards of a hundred and seventy names are mentioned in *The Literary Year-Book* under the heading of poetry. Nor is this list exhaustive. Such writers as Mr. Ralph Hodgson, Mr. Vivian Locke Ellis, and Mr. John Freeman, were eligible for this volume, and no woman's work is included in it. This is only to say that E.M. has ample forces in reserve. Still, a volume which comprises thirty-six poems by seventeen poets who have published between them fifty-five volumes of verse, should be sufficiently representative for his purpose.

If, however, *Georgian Poetry* is justified of its challenge, what does that justification imply? English poets do not readily marshal themselves into schools, nor strive for anything but a personal cause. Whence comes this unanimous impulse to write (and to publish) poetry in an age of journalism? Has the fountain of Hippocrene suddenly showered wild 'drafts of spray'

---

* *Georgian Poetry*, 1911–1912 (The Poetry Bookshop).

upon this emerald isle; did Pegasus, a generation ago, venture, wildly treading its green pastures, among the mares? If English poetry is indeed renewing its youth, does the phenomenon imply a promise of even wider significance: the stirring and awakening of the whole national imagination, a widening desire to escape

> *from that which sinks each individual man*
> *Into the common dream?*

Hope may falter, though it need not sink, when it is discovered that some of the poets included here must have been practising their art under three rulers. It is nine years since Mr. Sturge Moore published that masterpiece, *The Rout of the Amazons*. Here we have a further example of an art never content to repeat its first triumphs—the First Scene of the classically pure and ripe *Sicilian Idyll*. Mr. Masefield, too, has long since proved himself, what need not always imply a contradiction in terms, a 'popular poet'. What some critics would consider the flower of his work appeared in 1902. His *Biography* is the last of a series of remarkably original and vivid, but somewhat unequal narrative poems. Mr. Chesterton, still happily young in years, is old in fame. Only to this degree is E.M.'s anthology in any substantive sense Victorian.

But in any attempt to appraise this volume with the jealous eyes of posterity not only must we be sure that poetry distinctly of our own day is here, but some kind of parallel is necessary. What kind of volume, for example, would have been put together by the poets, then under forty and over twenty, who were writing in 1611–12?—Dekker, Browne, Donne, Carew, Beaumont, Drummond, Heywood, Jonson, Massinger, Ford, Fletcher, Quarles—when Shakespeare was forty-eight, Milton was three, and Shirley, Herbert, and Herrick were still in their teens. By 1712 the stage was dark and deserted; Pope and Gay were thirty-four. Another crucial date—skipping the two years of Keats's *Poems*, of *Alastor*, *The Revolt of Islam*, *Childe Harold*, *Christabel*, and *Kubla Khan*—would be 1865–6, when *Atalanta in Calydon*, *Enoch Arden*, *Dramatis Personæ*, *The Prince's Progress*, were published, when Morris, Gabriel and Christina Rossetti, Canon Dixon and T. E. Brown were still in their thirties, and Matthew Arnold's *New Poems* may have been in proof. Such comparisons are only comparisons, but as such, searching enough.

Every age necessarily needs and seeks its own poetry. And, as has been said of man and wife, nation and ruler, every age has bestowed upon it the poetry it deserves—though this is not a genial comment to make on the eighteenth century. But true poetry is never the peculiar possession of any particular race or period. It varies superficially and in differing environments, it flags, and is renewed; but in essentials it does not change. As each new poet, then, responds to one of the rarest and deepest of all impulses, he is bound to follow and at the same time slightly to stray from the one clear tradition. As rhythm is to metre, so is his divergence into originality to the poetry of his great predecessors. In every individual poet in this volume, as in its contents as a whole, if its achievement is to justify the claim of its editor, we must look for both these features. The test, we think, is easily survived. These poets are at least legitimate. A wholesome independence is manifest, together with as wholesome an exuberance and bravado. Their faults are the faults of youth. They have gone 'exploring'; have chosen their own path and filled their hands with wild flowers, many of which by noon-day will have withered and been thrown away. But there is no anarchic challenge of old ideals, no obvious tendency towards any particular *ism*. The general trend of the work is lyrical—with a dramatic undercurrent. If Coleridge's assertion, that poets of promise usually choose themes remote from their own personal life, be a sound one, then promise is here in abundance. The range of subject is remarkably wide. Mr. Lascelles Abercrombie, in *The Sale of St. Thomas*, pictures the saint anxiously setting forth on his legendary mission to Melankara and King Gondophares in worldwide search of a carpenter to build him a satanic palace made of souls. Mr. Gordon Bottomley's poems are entitled *The End of the World* and *Babel*. Mr. Flecker contributes *Joseph and Mary* and the pagan *Queen's Song*; Mr. Edmund Beale Sargant, the lovely wizard, *Cuckoo Wood*. Mr. James Stephens roars with joy with Mad Patsy in *The Poppyfield* and in *The Lonely God* returns to the Garden of Eden. Mr. Ronald Ross stands solitary upon a peak in Darien. Mr. Wilfrid Gibson is away in the heather under sunned and starry skies in *The Hare*. Mr. Robert Trevelyan contributes an exquisitely modulated and tender little dirge. Mr. William Davies flits on the wings of Ariel back to childhood and tells over again a ne'er-do-well mariner's fabulous tales of the sea. Mr. Chesterton sings *The Song of Elf*. And Mr. Rupert Brooke views existence from the 'cool, curving world' which enshrines *The Fish*, and lives again 'an immortal moment', spent in the extremely mortal environment of *Dining-room Tea*.

If, for all other qualities essential to lyrical poetry—intensity of vision, imagination, architectonicé, metrical craft, economy of means, music and finish—*Georgian Poetry* be compared with such a volume as *The Oxford Book of English Verse*, the ordeal is drastic but not discouraging. Simple, sensuous, passionate— the old formula is inescapable. And again, viewed roughly as a whole, it is clear that what is more or less undilutedly 'Georgian' in this anthology tends less towards simplicity than elaboration and complexity; that it is undeniably sensuous, though it exhibits not less clearly symptoms of genuine 'fundamental brainwork'; and that its passion reveals itself in a desire for beauty, and for a truth, not objectively and consciously moral or philosophic, but imaginative and creative. Those who seek in poetry ethical solace and edification, or demand of it a reasoned criticism of life, are unlikely to be won over. There is a strikingly modern, but none the less poetic, 'moral' to *The Sale of St. Thomas*:

> *Now, Thomas, know thy sin. It was not fear;*
> *Easily may a man crouch down for fear,*
> *And yet rise up on firmer knees, and face*
> *The hailing storm of the world with graver courage.*
> *But prudence, prudence is the deadly sin. . .*
> *Keep thy desire closed in the room of light*
> *The labouring fires of thy mind have made,*
> *And thou shalt find the vision of thy spirit*
> *Pitifully dazzled to so shrunk a ken,*
> *There are no spacious puissances about it.*
> *But send desire often forth to scan*
> *The immense night which is thy greater soul;*
> *Knowing the possible, see thou try beyond it*
> *Into impossible things, unlikely ends;*
> *And thou shalt find thy knowledgeable desire*

Grow large as all the regions of thy soul,
Whose firmament doth cover the whole of Being,
And of created purpose reach the ends.

But with the exception of Mr. Drinkwater, whose *Fires of God* is a profound questioning of heart, a lofty, somewhat too eloquent hymn to the glory of the world, to the courage, hope, and aspirations of humanity, the aim of these poets is as alien from that of *The Prelude* as it is from that of *Prometheus Unbound*, of *Don Juan*, or of the *Essay on Man*. They borrow inspiration neither from books nor from science, unless it be the science of psychology, or the Proceedings of the Society for Psychical Research. To express his love, desire, dream, grief or rapture, his sense of an age-long solitude beset by a cloud of witnesses, to bear record, if it may be for a little longer than mortal life permits, to his experience of a strange, absorbing, baffling world, in the briefest and truest terms within his power —this in some sort is every poet's aim. He may write not always because he can, and better do so only when he feels he must: Noah, after all, did not reject the piercing tiny entreaty of the wren·when he welcomed the nightingale to the shadowy roostings of his ark. And since the expression of beauty beats on the mind like a purifying flame, and any lucid imaginative truth of presentation bears hidden within it the secret of life, and kindles the desire to possess life more abundantly, from these pages, too, cannot be absent what it would be rather disheartening and restrictive to call their 'lesson'.

There is, at any rate, no attempt to say pretty and acceptable things; no bait to tickle and catch small fry. 'Muse' and 'lyre' are left hushed and unevoked. The love that rhymes with grove nowhere wastes its sweetness. But in its stead we have the turbulent, arrogant rapture of Mr. Brooke's *Dust* and *Town and Country*; the delicate and lucent visionariness of Mr. Harold Monro's *Child of Dawn*; the dense, brooding desire that in the broken stanzas of Mr. D. H. Lawrence's *Snapdragon* almost dazes and nauseates the reader with its desperate, naked excess. Page after page of this volume will prove that it is not an unexacting standard of thought, feeling, and technique which these writers share. In a word, unquestionable *seriousness*, as distinguished from what another generation rather solemnly and

127

chillingly called 'high seriousness', is the sincere mark and claim of this anthology.

It is, it may be hoped, only a fine loyalty to the past that induces most historians of English literature to disparage their own times. What student of modern criticism has not been professorially assured that poetry nowadays is 'Every dead thing'? A little enthusiasm for the work of one's contemporaries does no mischief to the secure immortals. *Georgian Poetry*, even after it has been subjected to the discipline of a sound and conservative criticism, should at least momentarily shake the confidence of such pessimism.

As regards individual poets, space will admit only of the briefest comment and quotation. Mr. James Stephens contributes two poems. It is the conception and atmosphere of *The Lonely God*, rather than its theme, which give it strength and originality. Mr. Stephens is inclined to allow his Celtic imagination to run away with him, and his verse falls occasionally into the florid and rhetorical. Like many a theologian before him, he has made God in his own image.

> *So Eden was deserted, and at eve*
> *Into the quiet place God came to grieve.*

In the still twilight He paces the dews of the garden, brooding on His might and majesty and 'solitude unspeakable', considering His creation—Man. 'It is not good for man to be alone.' In the fruition of time He foresees:

> *The perfect woman of his perfect race*
> *Shall sit beside Me in the highest place*
> *And be My Goddess, Queen, Companion, Wife. . . .*

He stoops to the beehive hut wherein Adam and Eve sit happy and at fearful peace in each other's company, sharing their common doom. He takes up the dusty garland with which Eve has been crowned:

> *So the Mighty Guest*
> *Rent, took, and placed the blossoms in his Breast.*
> *'This', said He gently, 'I shall show My queen*
> *When she has grown to Me in space serene,*
> *And say 'twas worn by Eve.' So, smiling fair,*
> *He spread abroad His wings upon the air.*

In the Cool of the Evening is a less anthropomorphic pendant
to the longer poem:

> *I thought I heard Him calling. Did you hear*
> *A sound, a little sound? My curious ear*
> *Is dinned with flying noises, and the tree*
> *Goes—whisper, whisper, whisper silently*
> *Till all its whispers spread into the sound*
> *Of a dull roar. Lie closer to the ground,*
> *The shade is deep and He may pass us by.*
> *We are so very small, and His great eye,*
> *Customed to starry majesties, may gaze*
> *Too wide to spy us hiding in this maze;*
> *Ah, misery! the sun has not yet gone*
> *And we are naked: He will look upon*
> *Our crouching shame, may make us stand upright*
> *Burning in terror—O that it were night!*
> *He may not come . . . what? listen, listen, now—*
> *He is here! Lie closer . . . Adam, where art thou?*

The happiest poetry wins from its readers not only admiration but a warm and familiar regard for its writer. So it is with
Mr. Davies's work. Clear as a well-spring, even its art seems to
be (yet how can it be?) an outcome of the purest intuition. Mr.
Davies loves instinctively all simple things. He gives us back
the eager absorbed eyes of childhood. Never before in a poem
do birds seem to have hopped down from line to line; or bees to
have 'stood upon their heads' in pollen, or the moon

> *behind the clouds' dark bars,*
> *Searched for her stolen flocks of stars.*

They do all this with ease in these delightful lyrics. Nothing is
forced. A romantic Elizabethan conceit, a romantic credulity,
slips as naturally into his speech as does the exquisite cadence
in the last two lines of his *Kingfisher*:

> *It was the Rainbow gave thee birth,*
> *And left thee all her lovely hues;*
> *And, as her mother's name was Tears,*
> *So runs it in thy blood to choose*
> *For haunts the lonely pools, and keep*
> *In company with trees that weep.*

K   129

Go you and, with such glorious hues,
Live with proud Peacocks in green parks;
On lawns as smooth as shining glass,
Let every feather show its marks;
Get thee on boughs and clap thy wings
Before the windows of proud kings.

Nay, lovely Bird, thou art not vain;
Thou hast no proud, ambitious mind;
I also love a quiet place
That's green, away from all mankind;
A lonely pool, and let a tree
Sigh with her bosom over me.

Mr. Gibson owes nothing to Crabbe or to Goldsmith, but shares their sympathy with those who (like poets) do hard work for small pay. He never rants; he puts bare things barely. His verse is supple; its ease, the outcome of craft and labour. *The Hare* is full of light, movement, and abandon; though its supernatural element is symbolically a little over-ingenious. *Geraniums* is the shortest, but not the least characteristic, of his poems here. 'Broken with lust and drink, blear-eyed and ill', an old woman comes nid-nodding from under her dark arch to barter a nosegay for a night's lodging. And this is how Mr. Gibson escapes a facile moral:

And yet tomorrow will these blooms be dead
With all their lively beauty; and tomorrow
May end the light lusts and the heavy sorrow
Of that old body with the nodding head.
The last oath muttered, the last pint drained deep,
She'll sink, as Cleopatra sank, to sleep;
Nor need to barter blossoms for a bed.

Reference has already been made to Mr. Abercrombie's *Sale of St. Thomas*. Flaubert's St. Anthony himself never woke from a dream of more fabulous and sinister bizarrerie, nor Mandeville imagined more exotic marvels, nor Purchas's pilgrims explored a stranger world than are described in this poem. The verse blazes with radiance, jets, leaps, dins, insinuates with every turn and twist of the narrative. Quaking with the 'huddled man' upon the quay, the reader listens to the cynical Captain's recital of the terror and cruelties that await his timid hyper-imaginative passenger's entry into unknown India, with its flies and apes, its gongs, horns, and enormities. The verse breaks into the wildest fantasy. With a sardonic humour the poet gloats over the pictures that at the same time appal and enthral him; yet he never loses his grasp. The poem is admirably constructed and kept in tone, and comes to a dramatic and serene conclusion.

There are many influences perceptible in this volume; but that of Donne—Donne in his headlong, rebellious youth—is traceable only in the work of Mr. Rupert Brooke. He is more self-centred than the rest, more analytical and intellectual. He is also more impatient of tradition, and defiant of the dictates of poetic Grundyism. His verse keeps unusually close to actual experience and is yet imaginatively in focus. He rails at dull sublunary 'fools', and, like Mr. Abercrombie, cannot resist the fascination of what repels him. He is at once the youngest and the most promising of his contemporaries. And his are among the curiously few love-poems in the collection. The following extract is from the poem entitled *Dust*:

> *When the white flame in us is gone,*
> *And we that lost the world's delight*
> *Stiffen in darkness, left alone*
> *To crumble in our separate night;*
>
> *When your swift hair is quiet in death,*
> *And through the lips corruption thrust*
> *Has stilled the labour of my breath—*
> *When we are dust, when we are dust!—*
>
> *Not dead, not undesirous yet,*
> *Still sentient, still unsatisfied,*
> *We'll ride the air, and shine, and flit,*
> *Around the places where we died.*
>
> *And dance as dust before the sun,*
> *And light of foot, and unconfined,*
> *Hurry from road to road, and run*
> *About the errands of the wind.*

And every mote, on earth or air,
*   Will speed and gleam, down later days,*
And like a secret pilgrim fare
*   By eager and invisible ways.*

Nor ever rest, nor ever lie,
*   Till, beyond thinking, out of view,*
One mote of all the dust that's I
*   Shall meet one atom that was you.*

There remains Mr. Gordon Bottomley to be mentioned. Quiet as swiftly falling, drifting, thickening snow is the verse that depicts the cold, dark 'End of the World', etched in with little familiar pictures of life amidst its desolation:

The dawn now seemed neglected in the grey
Where mountains were unbuilt, and shadowless trees
Rootlessly paused or hung upon the air . . .

A gigantic phantom figure strides out of sight,

But if he seemed too tall to be a man
It was that men had been so long unseen,
Or shapes loom larger through a moving snow.

Night darkens; earth and air congeal.

The air was crumbling. There was no more sky.

And at last Death himself, flaked with the same dazzling whiteness, enters where love and fear sit half insanely awaiting the end:

She said, ' O, do not sleep,
Heart, heart of mine, keep near me. No, no; sleep.
I will not lift his fallen, quiet eyelids,
Although I know he would awaken then—
He closed them thus but now of his own will.
He can stay with me while I do not lift them.'

It is a poem that absorbs and haunts the imagination. Like 'Babel', where, daring the solitudes of heaven,

Man with his bricks was building, building yet,
Where dawn and midnight mingled and woke no birds,

where Nimroud stands up 'conceiving he shall live to conquer god', and men's tongues crumble into the inarticulate, it transports consciousness out of the tangible world. It is the poetry of magic and strangeness; indefinable, inexplicable; the farthest venture beyond the confines of time and space recorded in the pages of E.M.'s anthology.

Edinburgh Review, April 1913

W. H. DAVIES

*F*oliage is Mr. William Davies's sixth volume of poems. The pure vein is still unexhausted, the impulse as clear and fresh though not quite so spontaneous as ever. Birds, the wind, a country cheek warmed with its own roses on a snowy winter's night, ships at sea, the poor and homeless, a child's fair, heavy hair—these are still his delight and ours. We no more weary of their repetition than one wearies of the cuckoo heard in June. Once again, too, Mr. Davies spends a little super-fluous pity on 'poor kings', pours a somewhat unimaginative scorn on rich dukes, 'graces the frantic thyrse', and twice, for certain, expresses his despisal in delicious verse of ladies whose wanton luxury it is to bathe in milk. But who else can do all that with so disarming a simpleness, without pomposity or any sug-gestion of bands and a black gown? With a tender, instinctively wise heart he tells his truth and does not litter and spoil his verse with needless lumber of the intellect. His art is simply second nature. He delights and at the same time shames his reader, who never in all his born days, or at any rate never since that he was a little tiny boy, saw anything quite so sharply and only its beautiful self, and, even if he had, couldn't to save his life have remade and recorded it in a music of words. He dares a simplicity which ornament would obscure, remints the very Maundy Money of poetry into gold:

> *The Lark that in heaven dim*
> *Can match a rainy hour*
> *With his own music's shower,*
> *Can make me sing like him—*
> *Heigh ho! The rain!*
>
> *Sing—when a Nightingale*
> *Pours forth her own sweet soul*
> *To hear dread thunder roll*

Into a tearful tale—
Heigh ho! The rain!

Sing—when a Sparrow's seen
Trying to lie at rest
By pressing his warm breast
To leaves so wet and green—
Heigh ho! The rain!

How could the world be made more wholly one's own carved, magic, cherry stone than by the tender, unfettered ease of:

Sweet Stay-at-Home, sweet Well-content,
Thou knowest of no strange continent:
Thou hast not felt thy bosom keep
A gentle motion with the deep;
Thou hast not sailed in Indian seas,
Where scent comes forth in every breeze.
Thou hast not seen the rich grape grow
For miles, as far as eyes can go;
Thou hast not seen a summer's night
When maids could sew by a worm's light;
Nor the North Sea in spring send out
Bright hues that like birds flit about
In solid cages of white ice—
Sweet Stay-at-Home, sweet Love-one-place. . .

Times Literary Supplement, Nov. 6, 1913

*   *   *

Mr. Davies's new book is called *Child Lovers,** but its real title is *And Other Poems.* He bade *Farewell to Poesy* in 1910, but she ran after him with *Songs of Joy,* and they have met again and again under the dappling shadow and sunshine of *Foliage,* vocal with wholly indigenous 'Birds of Paradise'. Apart from her clear smooth cheek, her small, sweet, round voice, it is easy to say what there is not in Mr. Davies's work—or, rather, play. It has a Caroline grace and ease, but no 'elegance'. It expresses no more mystery, or criticism of life, than a buttercup or a gold-finch, since it shines and sings and rejoices in response only to its own impulse. Mr. Davies can paint an almost Hogarthian

* *Child Lovers and other Poems.* By William H. Davies (Fifield).

135

picture of actuality in *The Inquest*, but his fellow-jurymen would
have hesitated to declare his rider, and it would have scandalized
the coroner:

> *And I could see that child's one eye*
> *Which seemed to laugh and say with glee:*
> *'What caused my death you'll never know—*
> *Perhaps my mother murdered me.'*

Mr. Davies rarely says anything but for that thing's sake, and
seldom in a syllable more than enough for his purpose, whether
he tells of May finding him inexplicably mute, 'My lips, like
gills in deep-sea homes, Beat time, and still no music comes'; of
'The white cascade, that's both a bird and star That has a ten-
mile voice and shines as far'; or of the winter song of the robin:

> *How sweet! like those sad tunes*
> *In homes where grief's not known;*
> *Or that a blind girl sings*
> *When she is left alone.*

One is apt—and how easy!—to call such things simple, but they
are simple only in the sense that an essence is simple. Was it
merely a happy five minutes or a complete, strange, sensitive
lifetime that went to the making of *This Night*?

> *This night, as I sit here alone,*
> *And brood on what is dead and gone,*
> *The owl that's in this Highgate Wood,*
> *Had found his fellow in my mood;*
> *To every star as it doth rise—*
> *Oh-o-o! Oh-o-o! he shivering cries.*
> *And, looking at the Moon this night,*
> *There's that dark shadow in her light.*
> *Ah! Life and Death, my fairest one,*
> *Thy lover is a skeleton!*
> *'And why is that?' I question—'why?'*
> *Oh-o-o! Oh-o-o! the owl doth cry.*

We use the word originality, too, as if, like Oxford marmalade,
it were a delectable addition to a literary breakfast. But life
cannot be neatly potted like that. The very Self in every man is
all original. Now and then comes one who, like Mr. Davies, can

be at times not only that naked self but also can express it. He sets down in infant English 'The Cow stares o'er the field,' or in a croon to a sick child this old, old truism:

> *And when our babies sleep their last,*
> *Like agèd dames or men,*
> *They need nor mother's lullaby*
> *Nor any rocking then,*

and somehow death and the cow are such as we have only once really seen before—that is, for the first time. It is either poetry or nothing; and first we must accept Mr. Davies's mood, his quiet, happy, and serious outlook. He fails when he writes heedlessly, merely as he has written before, or with his eye straying towards the sophisticated. But the wonder is that after so much writing of verse he still can not only cry, 'Come, thou sweet Wonder . . . Come to my heavy rain of care And make it weigh like dew'; but that his call is heard.

Times Literary Supplement, June 8, 1916

TENNYSON

For those whom the gods love a hundred years affords ample time, not only for their life's achievement, but also for a lull, a brief reflective silence in which posterity may hope to count up its gains and to express its gratitude without bias or caprice. But so clear and fresh and contemporary in the minds of even the younger generation are the poetry and presence of Tennyson that it is almost with a sense of incredulity we turn to the hundredth celebration of his birthday. When, therefore, the question inevitably arises as to the degree in which the work of those many devoted years has withstood the corrosion of the last few, two perplexing difficulties at least must be encountered.

English poetry, it may be definitely asserted, has floated out beyond the Tennysonian tradition. *The Dawn in Britain*, *The Dynasts*, *The Rout of the Amazons*—it is not necessary to go further afield, or to cross the Irish Sea for illustration—such work as this, in conception as in execution, is little influenced by, if not actually antagonistic to, the ideals of the Victorian age. Art has its stepping stones, and each may bring humanity according to its present needs a little nearer to the further shore. But what concerns us now is not whether the conscious aim and the half-conscious impulse of modern poetry are towards a rarer, fuller, and more enduring ideal, but that they are undeniably in a different direction. The reverberations, moreover, of the applause which greeted each new volume of Tennyson's— applause that was ever loyally in danger of quenching judgment in enthusiasm—cannot but baffle the lover of poetry who would walk circumspectly, and endeavour to appraise his complete accomplishment without sentiment for the immediate past, or too lively and sanguine a prejudice for the present.

Tennyson, by good or ill fortune, was a marked figure from

his earliest years. He moved in young manhood like a queen bee dispensing her priceless benefactions amid a charmed circle of diligent and scrupulous attendants. His son's biography, the testimony of influential friends, nearly every one of whom succeeded in making his mark on his own generation, present a many-sided and yet perfectly conceivable image of so closely and lovingly observed a personality. The wistful and sincere regret—'I wish I had been A.T.'s Boswell'—is pregnant comment enough, coming from such a critic of life and literature as Edward FitzGerald. 'He uttered by far the finest prose sayings of any man I have ever met' is a weighty corroboration. Even Carlyle, that master of the acid summary, apart from a characteristic jeer at the poetical dung-heap, talked of Tennyson goodnaturedly as 'the spoiled Lifeguardsman'. Peculiarly impressive, rough-hewn, downright manliness was the outstanding feature of this humorous 'grumpy' poet, who left his hair to the chance barbering of his candle; who answered a flattering and formidable invitation to breakfast with contemporary demigods with a brusque, 'I should hate it, Duchess'; who, eager to shine his brightest, could think of nothing but beer to talk about to Robertson of Brighton; who chanted his 'hollow oes and aes' with 'a voice like the sound of a far sea or of a pinewood', out of a cloud of tobacco smoke, to any old crony that would listen to the poems scribbled down in that historical butcher's book.

In almost direct contradistinction to these traits are others not so conspicuous but even, perhaps, more significant: his extreme sensitiveness ('I *am* thin-skinned,' he once owned frankly, drawing up his sleeve to exhibit the two-inch ravages of a fleabite, as proof that it was more than a merely metaphorical confession); his intense love of that solitude within solitude—introspective, brooding reverie; his chafing against the least show of hostility, even the 'pen-punctures of those parasitic animalcules of the Press', the critics; his 'moods of misery unutterable'. These conflicting characteristics form a tangled combination of qualities which might have made only for depth and reach were not the conviction borne in on us that its less precious elements are more conspicuous in his work as a whole. Boswell's Johnson, only in part concealed in *Rasselas*, is actively present in *The Lives of the Poets*. Is, we wonder, the Tennyson whom FitzGerald would surely have portrayed as easily detectable in anything like the same measure throughout that life-time's elaborate self-expression? But poetry is the outcome of an environment as well as of a personality. In his early days, and when under the malign influence of the 'indolent reviewer', Tennyson longed, we know, for the quiet and workaday life of a Lincolnshire yeoman, passing rich on £400 a year. A light fierce enough, however kindly, beat on Farringford. Tennyson detested—even exaggerated, but would conceiv-ably have missed—the close and trying attentions that his renown and popularity entailed. Whether the narrow and en-forced seclusion of obscurity, of narrow means, of few and humble friends, but free from the artificial cares of the too much and the too many, and from the disquietude of a name and character and domesticity almost public property—whether such an environment would have enriched or diminished his imperish-able achievement it is tempting but vain to surmise. The mere profession of poetry is by no means an irresistible invitation to the Muses. Tennyson, none the less, deliberately set himself out to become the national poet, to write for the general under-standing and appreciation, and without any extreme defection admirably succeeded. What part of his work will eventually sur-vive the perils and privileges of such a career, what part of it carries the capricious but inextinguishable lamp of genius beneath the mantle of a classic art are questions the critics of a hundred years hence may answer without presumption, unani-mously, and with ease.

If we turn, however, to the earlier and what may at last prove the most enduring fraction of his work—to those two volumes whose date, 1842, comes as patly to the tongue as that which brought the Conqueror sweeping across the Channel—it may at least be possible to distinguish the qualities that will tend to endanger and those which may at last ensure Tennyson's final appeal. Through its whole range, and in all its diversity, Tenny-son's work was singularly of a piece. The imprint of his con-densed, deliberate, fastidious style is on every page of his work from the soliloquy which, when a boy of fourteen, he put in the mouth of the devil, eighty-six years ago:

There is a clock in Pandemonium,
Hard by the burning throne of my great grandsire,

The slow vibrations of whose pendulum,
With click-clack alternation to and fro,
Sound ' Ever, Never' thro' the courts of Hell,
Piercing the wrung ears of the damn'd that writhe
Upon their beds of flame. . .

throughout the prize poem on *The Battle of Armageddon*, im-
mortalized as *Timbuctoo*; far on to that stanza which is the very
consummation of his gifts, and one of the most gravely beautiful
in English poetry:

But such a tide as moving seems asleep,
Too full for sound and foam,
When that which drew from out the boundless deep
Turns again home.

The same attachment to a definite experience, the same precision of presentation, apart from many other more technical
resemblances, are obvious qualities in these far-scattered quota-
tions. Every facet of the poet's art shines out somewhere in
these two early volumes, in examples of his three main forms of
verse, the purely lyrical, the narrative, and the dramatic. The
narrative, which in its many varieties of method combined practically all these forms, became his favourite device. Yet, in spite
of the latitude, the over-plus, and the decoration that verse
admits, it is questionable whether Tennyson was endowed with
the gifts that go to the equipment of the born story-teller. He
had little of that essential but, even in minds much less well
endowed than his own, not very rare faculty, invention. There
are at least half-a-dozen poems of the 1842 period alone which
are threaded on the rather jejune and dispiriting theme, the
mésalliance. It is usually Mammon, too, that shuffles the cards.
Other themes and subjects he acquired and elaborated, but in
actual incident seldom enriched. Even with so simple a nucleus
as this he rarely succeeds in telling his story well. His endings
are often psychologically, and in some of the lyrics poetically,
the weakest parts of the whole. He studied and analysed
men and women, but he cannot perfectly put them together
again; life has flown. His gaze is set and keen, but intuition
and sympathy prove its but feeble allies. His characters do not
shake themselves free, cast off all likeness to, all control of,

their creator and with a bold, unfaltering sweep of gesture stalk out of the void, with an energy and a mastery that set the reader wondering if he himself has ever really lived. Nor, on the other hand, have they the power of hinting by subtle and accumulating innuendo that reality itself is nothing else but a disturbed and fragmentary dream. Nearly all Tennyson's men and women are bodiless, skilful pictures, or a voice that accompanies so many minutely observed and recorded mental and bodily traits and features. We see with extraordinary distinctness a Will Waterproof, a Farmer Allen, a fat-faced curate Edward Bull, a Maud, a Northern Farmer, a Grandmother, a Guinevere, even a Hallam; but do they haunt us uncalled for, unannounced? Do they ever evoke in us that hidden self which seldom stirs but never sleeps beneath life's restless consciousness? Do we stumble on the secrets of our hearts in theirs? Even in such a masterly piece as *A Dream of Fair Women* how chill and meagre are the uttered words:

> *I had great beauty: ask thou not my name:*
> *No one can be more wise than destiny.*
> *Many drew swords and died. Where'er I came*
> *I brought calamity.*

Was this the face that launch'd a thousand ships, and burnt the topless towers of Ilium? There is indeed so often a strain of the 'yeoman' who scolded 'Lady Clara Vere de Vere', or of the stricken hero of *Maud*, in all Tennyson's treatment of women. A haunting suggestion of mock modesty hangs over passages even where modesty herself consents a while to hold her tongue. He detested priggishness; he could speak out bluntly enough in prose, he could splash over the shallow tub of mere conventionalism, and was a man of a broad, wholesome humour; and yet in his narrative poems how rare and niggardly is the pinch of Rabelaisian salt which could so wonderfully have seasoned that tantalizing niceness, that laborious simplicity; how vainly we listen sometimes for even the rumble of a voice against which Mrs. Grundy shall dutifully and punctiliously stop at least one ear! Poetry, true, deep element of normal humanity that it is, languishes in life's best parlour, forbidden the freedom of the house.

It is when we turn to Tennyson's lifelong and passionate

adoration of nature that all such criticism seems graceless and beside the point. 'What is Master Awlfred always a-praying for?' inquired the cook, who had heard him clanging his verses as he paced to and fro at Somersby. If it was for the power of conveying to the world something of his worship of beauty, and zeal for its perfect expression, it was a prayer abundantly answered. He even stumbles sometimes simply by reason of his ardour for the last exquisite finish, the golden hair's-breadth of felicity. He drops the nosegay of the poem in stooping for the bud of a half line, or crystallizes what should be free and fluent with a too precise, an overburdened epithet. The verse is sometimes as sharp and clear and as durable as marble. Yet he does not, as do so many poets, depict and transmute the scene. Even in a simile he will take his reader bodily up, as it were, and set him there in the midst:

> *She woke: the babble of the stream*
> *Fell, and, without, the steady glare*
> *Shrank one sick willow sere and small.*
> *The river-bed was dusty-white;*
> *And all the furnace of the light*
> *Struck up against the blinding wall.*

and succeeds even in lines packed with 'literariness'—

> *Thridding the sombre boskage of the wood,*
> *Toward the morning-star.*

It is merely a platitude to repeat now that he is the master of the 'magic' word—how eagerly sought and, unless at the inspiration of the moment, how slow and arduous a quest!— unless to add that nowhere else is evident quite such a magic after so eager a search—

> *Still on the tower stood the vane,*
> *A black yew gloom'd the stagnant air*

> *. . . I linger'd there*
> *Till every daisy slept, and Love's white star*
> *Beam'd thro' the thicken'd cedar in the dusk.*

Who, too, cannot remember a score of such intimate and happy touches as the rabbit's 'harmless face', the 'blue fly' singing on the pane, the 'crackling frost', the 'woodbine spices', 'the horns of Elfland'? Such things as these have long ceased to be a poet's pictures, and have become our own enchanted memories. It is difficult even in these hard and Spartan days to keep back our tears simply for the beauty revealed in such poems as *The May Queen* and the *Morte d'Arthur*.

> *When the flowers come again, mother, beneath the waning light*
> *You'll never see me more in the long gray fields at night;*
> *When from the dry dark wold the summer airs blow cool*
> *On the oat-grass and the sword-grass, and the bulrush in the pool.*

There is scarcely a lyric but has for its charm not a simple passionate thought, not a mystic allusiveness or a profound human emotion, but some one supremely beautiful or significant fragment or aspect of nature. However near and dear his companion, Tennyson always, his son has recorded, withdrew himself into solitude to muse upon what most deeply affected him in the day's journey. Out of that 'never less alone than when alone' came the happy harvest fields, the ship in *Tears, Idle Tears*, the shadow in *St. Agnes' Eve*, the city in *Will*, the wrinkled sea in *The Eagle*, and, again, that miraculous glimpse of the sea in the last four lines of *The Captain*. The verse blows salt on our lips, with its roar and hollow crying; and its sea-birds wheel in an abysm of air between eye and printed page. Where too beside, unless in Milton, arches such space and burns and glitters such splendour of moon and sun, of Orion and the Hyades, in a mere leash of words? All else in his earthly life, so far, at any rate, as his poetry is concerned, seems of secondary import. 'Beauty' is the unfailing impulse of his genius, the springing fountain amid the ocean of countless other earthly experiences. Science was little more than the diligent and curious servant to his love of nature: his thought a medium in which to float its undisquieting, imperplexing beauty. Poets there are whose vision of the world is as far withdrawn as was the Lady of Shalott's; they weave the mirror's magic sights into the web of fantasy: Tennyson from the windows of his eyes, 'dark, powerful, and serene', looked down direct on Camelot.

Inspiration comes and goes. Let a man toil or tarry in patience, poetry will not be cajoled, or circumvented, or suffer compulsion; and a lifetime's devotion may be remembered at last only for the outcome of one supreme moment. We may each, according to his own bypath of thought, or feeling, or imagination, set store by this or that above all else in our English poets—Chaucer's true charity, Donne's intensity, Shelley's rapture, Keats's loveliness, Coleridge's magic, Wordsworth's depth of tenderness, arbitrary and piecemeal though these distinctions may be. Still remain the virgin riches of a world that would suffice for theme and inspiration though every man that breathes was born to rhyme. And even from so distant and confined a fragment of Tennyson's work as it has been practicable to touch on here the uniqueness of his achievement stands out clear and unassailable—his impeccable truth of observation, his never-waning love of beauty, his devotion to an ideal of art from which in that long, concentrated and conspicuous life he never heedlessly deviated. These are among the distinctive qualities that have set Tennyson among the great poets of his time, and by virtue also of a certain dignity and simplicity of character established his name in history as one of the great traditions of Victorian England.

Times Literary Supplement, Aug. 5, 1909

VAUGHAN*

A great national crisis, though it draws men together into a mutual brotherhood, isolates the individual. It drives inward every mind that is capable of thought to the discovery of what it holds most dear, to the discernment of what is of lasting value as compared with what is fleeting or makeshift. Imaginative genius, by its very nature solitary and aloof, is at such times made still more solitary. Its possessor may give his all, and we know how noble and complete such a sacrifice may be, to the common cause. But to give that genius itself is not always within his power. It may for a while be overwhelmed, or it may follow its own impulse the more strongly by reason of the conflict and opposition of circumstance. And though a comprehensive mind here and there may be capable of lifting itself above the tumult and of surveying the present with as equal and tranquil a scrutiny as mortals in general can bestow upon the past, the man of a rare, but less universal consciousness, while remaining true to the ideals which he shares with his fellows, goes his own way. And not until the hurly-burly and the strife are over can the world realize what strange flowers may grow on stony ground.

Vaughan was such a man. He came to maturity at a time when England was divided against itself. He knew the years, as he said, and what coarse entertainment they afforded to poetry. His first poems, as 'ingenious' and ingenuous as they were imitative, were published in 1646, four years after the *Religio Medici*, and nine years after the death of Jonson and the composition of *Lycidas*. He was then twenty-four, had been called home to Wales by an anxious father, from London and the law, and was

* *The Works of Henry Vaughan*. Edited by Leonard Cyril Martin. 2 vols. (Oxford: Clarendon Press).

146

soon to begin successful practice as a doctor in Brecon. 1646 was also the year of Crashaw's *Steps to the Temple* and *Delights of the Muses*, published immediately before he went to France. Cowley's *Mistress* appeared in 1647, Herrick's *Hesperides* and *Noble Numbers* in 1648; *Lucasta* in 1649. And a year afterwards followed the first part of *Silex Scintillans*.

Mr. Martin's labours as an editor have been exacting but fairly straightforward. His main object has been to supply an accurate text and, secondarily, to throw fresh light on the poet's literary affinities. There are no manuscripts, and though Vaughan's poems are sometimes obscure in their personal references, and often derivative, the most beautiful of them are fetched no farther than from his imagination, and offer not a fraction of the difficulties squandered by Donne. As Pope said of Crashaw, 'I take this poet to have writ like a gentleman—that is, at leisure hours, and more to keep out of idleness than to establish a reputation,' naïvely adding that, therefore, 'nothing regular or just can be expected from him'. What biographical facts Vaughan's poems reveal are usually vague. We know that he was twice married, that he had five children, and lost by death a dearly loved younger brother. By family tradition he was a Royalist; but though he mourned friends sacrificed to the cause, he did not, like his brother Thomas, the alchemist, fight for the King. He was, however, a sharp partisan and, so far as his enemies in Church and State were concerned, does not appear to have sought for the soul of goodness in things evil. His age, he reiterates, was degenerate. Bad men had made a bad world worse. But though such a poem as his *King Disguis'd* on that 'Royal Riddle, the Hieroglyphic' Charles, is sincere enough in intention, it has a gilding of rhetoric and a flourish of conceits that clearly disclose an effort to be equal to a great occasion:

> *A King and no King! Is he gone from us,*
> *And stoln alive into his Coffin thus?*
> *This was to ravish Death, and so prevent*
> *The Rebells treason and their punishment.*
> *He would not have them damn'd, and therefore he*
> *Himself deposed his own Majesty.*
> *Wolves did pursue him, and to fly the Ill*
> *He wanders (Royal Saint!) in sheepskin still.*

Poor, obscure shelter! if that shelter be
Obscure, which harbours so much Majesty.
Hence prophane Eyes! the mysterie's so deep,
Like Esdras books, the vulgar must not see't. . . .

Vaughan, indeed, was by nature a recluse. He loved to ponder
away, 'mild, dewie nights and sunshine dayes' beside his Usk,
far better than to brood or embark on any tide in the affairs of
men. He lived to justify a divine right that is not the sole
prerogative of kings:

For each Birth of thy Muse to after-times
Shall expiate for all this Ages Crimes:

so foretold the matchless and youthful Orinda of a poet whose
'charming rigour' would some day teach the world 'there's no
pleasure but in serious things'.

That strikes us, even today, as an austere gospel for a man
under thirty. But it was his. 'I shall hold it no paradoxe to
affirme, there are no pleasures in this World.' What is it but 'a
Wildernesse? a darksome, intricate wood full of *Ambushes* and
dangers; a Forrest where spiritual hunters, principalities and
powers spread their nets and compasse it about.' Vaughan was
heaven's own antithesis of a pessimist. He did not affirm that
there are no pleasures, only that this world's are treacherous.
He suffered remorse for what had been the proof of this. But
even in the dedication of his first fancies he assures such refined
spirits as 'outwing these dull Times, and soare above the
drudgerie of durty Intelligence' that here they would cheer
them at 'a Flame, bright only in its owne Innocence. . . . The
fire at highest is but Platonick, and the Commotion within these
limits, excludes Danger.' And in this first poem he invites his
friend R.W. (afterwards to fall at the battle of Rowton Heath)
not to the clusters of the Triple Tun, but to the Elysian Fields,
to the holy meads, where great Ben would be found and ill-
starred Randolph. In a song to Amoret, he speculates on what
fresher youth, if he himself were dead, might grace the arms left
empty. That rival, he realizes, might be of a blood as chaste as
April's mildest tear, or rich and landed and beautiful, but even so
mighty an Amorist as this could not give her such 'endless holy
fire' as his. Indeed, the only satisfaction he foresees for the

threadbare, goldless genealogy of poets is not a pension or a sinecure from a grateful Stuart, but in a better world the attainment of a 'native and celestial scope' again.

And there is in *A Rhapsodis* a delightful piece of unconscious self-portraiture. He describes himself, like any other wanton young blood of poesy, sitting with his cronies in the Globe Tavern 'where rich Tobacco and quick tapers shine'. He admires, then jeers at the painted walls and ceiling, at the base brush that has set up the full moon's face for nothing better than a 'landmarke to the tipling trade'; then goes on to speculate on what vanities they would encounter, *if* they should do the town —'Catchpoles, whores, and Carts in ev'ry street. . . . Riotous sinfull plush, and tell-tale spurs', 'bawdy, ruffled silks'; and ends with the exhortation to drink deep—to Caesar and to Sylla, so that the jovial company may retire 'possessours of more soules'. It isn't a frantically Bacchanalian interior. But though Vaughan's lines on 'a piece so full of sweets and bliss' as the country beauty, Fida, prove that his eyes had dwelt long enough on a pretty face and figure to enable him to enter the lists with Robin Herrick, it is only the light of fancy that plays on these demure pages. There is no danger. If he, indeed, loved Amoret or Etesia, these verses do not pulse to his 'fierce wild bloud', nor tell how much, or why. It is rather such a poem as *The Charnel-House* that is first touched with imagination, with that gravity, penetration, ardour of thought, and that facet of humour glittering edgewise across the thought, which mark Vaughan's true poetry—that vein, indeed, which he told his honoured cousin, Aubrey, when the latter had condescended 'to reflect upon such low and forgotten things' as his brother Thomas and himself, is called in the Welsh bards Awen, signifying 'as much as Raptus, or a poetic furor'.

> *Leane, bloudless shamble, where I can descrie*
> *Fragments of men, Rags of Anatomie, . . .*
> *How thou arrests my sense? How with the sight*
>   *My* Winter'd *bloud growes stiffe to all delight? . . .*
> *Have I obey'd the* Powers *of a face,*
> *A beauty able to undoe the Race*
> *Of easie man? I look but here, and strait*
> *I am Inform'd, the lovely Counterfeit*
> *Was but a smoother Clay. . . .*

But the grudging Sun
Calls home his beams, and warns me to be gone,
Day leaves me in a double night, and I
Must bid farewell to my sad library. . . .

Platonic or not, in his preface to *Silex Scintillans*, castigating the cant-termed vicious 'wits' of his time, whose energies remind him of the sun busy upon a dunghill, Vaughan frowns on his first innocent, smiling Amoretti. This least of many converts, as he describes himself, to the true practical piety of the blessed man, George Herbert, makes public confession: 'I myself have for many years together, languished of this very *sickness*; and it is no long time since I have recovered. But (blessed be God for it!) I have by his saving assistance supprest my *greatest follies. . . .*'

Vaughan had been very near to death; and to be turned back from that door gives a strange and crooked look to the street of life. And yet those greatest follies—if we may judge from the 'innoxious'—can but have proved this saint to have been human, and, therefore, a sinner. To see the good cast down into evil is a sight for the rejoicing of none but devils; to know that a tender and stricken heart has beaten to the drums and fiddles of Vanity Fair, and still remembers their heady tunes, is to give even the least and worst of us a better hope. The pious are not always the most persuasive exemplars of a godly life. Even in the wise and gentle Herbert there is at times too placid and prim a tone. He is then merely sententious and 'edifying'; and unworldly in a sense that does not imply the unearthly. As Professor Saintsbury once said, Herbert, with all his beauty and simplicity, is among sacred 'where the late Mr. Longfellow was among profane poets'. He has been the precious solace of many hearts. He wrote a handful of the serenest lyrics in English verse, but his influence upon Vaughan's work as a poet was by no means wholly good.

Vaughan had a more subtle, a more impulsive and passionate nature. Many of his poems, too, are meditative musings of self with self, a kind of lyrical reverie. He can be arid, persists in mere ingenuities (a magnifying glass, a book, a kalendar, a grave, rust, candied fruits, green branches, all go to the imagery of one tender lament and regret), and he often wastes and dilutes a fine onset. But he knew that poetry is not just a matter of preparing the tinder.

> O! 'tis an easie thing
>   To write and sing;
> But to write true, unfeigned verse
> Is very hard! Oh God, disperse
> These weights, and give my spirit leave
> To act as well as to conceive!
>   O my God, hear my cry;
>   Or let me dye!—

His poems are nearly all of them in the nature of parables; they convey precepts. But they are, too, 'private ejaculations'. They are infinitely winning because they have for impulse and admonishment not the sinful reader, but the poet himself. And their earthly story is certainly not less beautiful than their heavenly meaning. They reveal a purity of the senses, an innocence of the eyes, known to us only in childhood, that 'Angell-infancy', 'our first faire bud', whose memory 'dazled' even Vaughan—caught back perhaps at the moment of waking from some crystal-clear and haunting dream. With an urbane, an almost wistful, bonhomie he invites his reader into his own solitude—

> The air was all in spice
>   And every bush
> A garland wore. . . .

> It was high-spring, and all the way
> Primros'd and hung with shade. . . .

He transfigures the most ordinary allusion with at once the simplest and wildest of longings, and so condenses expression that for an instant its meaning eludes the mind:

> O that I were where I but see!
> Is all the note within my Bush.

which recalls and fulfils the lovely-cadenced stanza in the poem beginning 'They are all gone into the world of light!'

151

He that hath found some fledg'd bird's nest, may know
At first sight, if the bird be flown;
But what fair Well or Grove he sings in now,
That is to him unknown.

And to the most solitary heights of poetry he transports us with
the quietest of confidences, 'I saw Eternity the other night.'
One word, one phrase—neither far-fetched nor heightened—is
often all his magic, as when he writes of flowers 'opprest with
dew', of the 'Slow Isicle' hanging at the 'stiffe thatch', of the
budding rose of daybreak and the 'Pilgrim-Sunne', of how of
death we make 'a mere mistake', of the Saints who show their
light like candles 'and light us to bed', of God 'keeping close
house Above the morning-starre', and prays—

Grant I may not like puddle lie
In a corrupt security. . . .

Or it is as if we overheard the thoughts—'the roving exstasie'
—of a traveller on a perilous and lonely journey—

Stars are of mighty use: The night
Is dark, and long;
The Rode foul, and where one goes right,
Six may go wrong.
One twinkling ray
Shot o'r some cloud,
May clear much way
And guide a croud.

But though this may seem all an accident of happy ease, the
close intensity of observation it implies is often revealed. In *The
Lampe*, for instance, Vaughan almost scientifically explains how
the very instrument at his side uses its waste oil; he tells with
exquisite fidelity how he has heard and watched—

Some drowsie silk-worme creepe
From that long sleepe,
And in weake, infant hummings chime, and knell
About her silent Cell
Untill at last full with the vital Ray
She wing'd away.

The leaden arduous passage of time to one in sorrow could not
be more poignantly expressed than in these few words:

> *Silence and stealth of dayes! 'tis now*
> *Since thou art gone*
> *Twelve hundred houres . . .*

nor more surely proved a fallacy of diuturnity than in this, the
soul's rebuke of the body—

> *Ah! go; th'art weake, and sleepie, Heav'n*
> *Is a plain watch, and without figures winds*
> *All ages up; who drew this Circle even*
> *He fils it; Dayes and hours are* Blinds
> *Yet take this with thee; The last gasp of time*
> *Is thy first breath, and mans* Eternal Prime.

Earthly life to such an imagination was but a thing of masques
and shadows, and we all only apparitions. The business of a pilgrim, he said, is to seek his country. And every experience
which he records is charged through and through with this one
mystical significance. Darkness was horror to such eyes, though
the dead and silent night for the solitary be 'the day of spirits'
and though—

> *There is in God (some say)*
> *A deep but dazzling darkness.*

Glowworm, candle, lamp, the beams and clouds of dawn, the
stars, the sun—light was to him a never-ending rapture and
inspiration. His poems are drenched with it, but rarely dyed
with colour. Even in the cock he praises the sunny seed which
the Father of Lights has confined into this bird, and his Eagle
'gets to the Moon and pores with scorn upon her duller face'.
The absence of light is to him the dread and menace of Hell:
'Those furious and unquenchable burnings . . . though they be
of such an insuperable *intense heat*, as to work upon *spirits* and
the most subtile Essences, yet do they give no light at all, but
burn blacker than *pitch*. . . .' The other extreme, equally
abhorred of the soul, is death. But death, though truly the wages
of sin, was to Vaughan simply and doubtlessly the fulfilment of
life's one happy promise, and the corruption of the grave was
neither revolting nor fascinating. He asks God to watch over

and at the same time to forgive such a falling away of the empty
house, 'which I sometimes liv'd in'.

> *It is (in truth!) a ruin'd peece*
> *Not worth thy Eyes,*
> *And scarce a room, but wind and rain*
> *Beat through, and stain,*

and joy shines in his penitence like tears in the eyes of a child
smiling in its mother's forgiveness. As simply, he looks forward to the Day of Judgment, as if to a release from a long and
desperate task, to a day of life, of light, of love.

Men may be convinced that the world—in spite of its beauty
and beguilement—is a bad place to be in, by grief, by disillusionment, by the fantasy and transiency of things rare and dear, by
weariness of self, by contempt of others, by the blind resent-
ments of insanity. When Vaughan pines for a country far beyond
the stars, it would be as vain to argue that this is false or distorted doctrine as to adjure a linnet to be content in a cage. Two
weapons he asked for the defeat of the enemy—a living faith, a
heart of flesh. In him imagination and faith were at one. The
one sets the other burning. He did not turn aside from the ordinary morning to write his poetry. He did not cultivate a beautiful
seclusion. His poetry is merely a record of the reallest and most
intimate things of a workaday life. Its supreme things are never
prepared for. They are as intrinsic a part of it as is the sudden all-
changing light of greeting in a sensitive face. It is as impossible
to discredit such witness as it is impossible to discredit the
happiness, or grief, or rapt inklings of a child. But although
Vaughan had indeed returned to the childhood which he coveted
and longed for again, though there is a kind of courtesy and
indulgence in his poems, and again and again the homely
abstractedness of one accustomed to live alone and to be a little
shut away from strangers, there is, too, a manhood of a rare
strength and inflexibility. A seraph, no less than a villain, may
smile and smile, and be a seraph. This loftiness is never absent
from his poetry. In his utmost humility and self-sacrifice he is
still of a high lineage, the servant of an unearthly prince; and
pride in one's office is as formidable a quality as pride of self
would be a feebleness. Because that mind was devout and that
heart so sensitive, because always unusualness has a tinge of the

eccentric and even of the grotesque, his beauty, his radiance, his strange far-flying thought, are not surrendered to a chance acquaintanceship. And even love of such a man can only fill the little vessel that brings to it its own small content.

Times Literary Supplement, July 15, 1915

DONNE*

It is alike the despair and the solace of human existence that
we can divine little more from the world of men or books
or of solitude than what we bring to them. We are limited
by the straitness, by the unity in diversity, the diversity in
unity, of our senses. The mind is a mirror that can reflect no
more of reality than its clearness and circumference can command. It is experience that searches us, rather than we who
search experience. Beauty itself depends for its being, less on
that which reveals it than on him who perceives it. The best
things—if in a sense it is true that the best is not only highest
good but what is rarest—can, therefore, never be really popular.
And so, as Ben Jonson wrote to Lucy, Countess of Bedford, in
one of his *Epigrams*, published in 1616, and prefixed to the 1650
edition of the works of John Donne: 'Rare poems ask rare
friends.' Even regarding the Satires, Jonson argued that since
the majority of mankind is the subject of them, few can appreciate them without offence; and those few must be of the best.
And, turning from Donne's *Egeria* to the poet himself, he scornfully dismisses 'those that for claps doe write':

A man should seek great glory, and not broad.

That will always, as things go, be Donne's fate as a poet—
great glory, but not broad. He captures an ardent, almost
impassioned few; but has little share in the admiration of the
many. He is too bare and direct, and he is too obscure and
abstruse. He is at the same time too little and too much a poet.
Jonson, indeed, though he enthusiastically acknowledged him
as 'the first poet in the world for some things', also remarked in

---

* *The Poems of John Donne*. Edited from the old editions and numerous manu-
scripts, with introductions and commentary by Herbert J. G. Grierson, M.A.,
Chalmers Professor of English Literature in the University of Aberdeen (Oxford:
Clarendon Press).

convivial confidence to Drummond, that 'Donne himself, for not being understood, would perish'. It is undeniable that the full appreciation of his work, even by his devotees, needs not only all the research, scholarship, acute analysis, and sustained and penetrating diligence and thought that Professor Grierson has given to this new and surely definitive edition: it needs also some temperamental affinity, a certain openness of mind, and freedom from prejudice. To some extent, too, even in regard to the work of Donne's headlong, hedonistic youth, such appreciation is a question of age. Life, fortunately, does not empty her whole cornucopia of delights on man's devoted head in one generous gesture. She refuses to let him ever irretrievably 'come of age'. She reserves joys for maturity, joys for antiquity. And Donne—though he may bedazzle the young—is among those intended for life's meridian—when we look before and after and are compelled to realize that thenceforth, though what little wisdom we may have may ripen, it will ripen at the expense of the tree.

It is possible, of course, to dwell and marvel and delight in him, to blunder on through the difficulties, putting one's own free interpretation on his meaning, without seeking or desiring the aid of notes and references. Poetry, initially, should be so read. But even if Mr. Grierson were not concerned with textual corruptions and misreadings, Donne's poetry is only enriched, much of it even is actually retrieved, by the sagacity which such an editor can bring to bear upon it. For, as Mr. Grierson explains, 'the text and canon of Donne's poems present an editor in one form or another with all the chief problems which confront the editor of a classical or medieval author.' His attempt has been to face these problems and to overcome them. Practical experience revealed their presence. One cannot, as Mr. Grierson was compelled to discover, explain what one does not understand. A close scrutiny of previous editions assured him that all of them, including those of Grosart and of Mr. Chambers, were in certain respects either inaccurate or misleading, or had been unsystematically prepared. Not until his task was nearly completed did Mr. Grierson discover in the Grolier Club edition— an edition published in America, revised by Lowell and edited by Professor Norton and Mrs. Burnett—a partial anticipation of his own considered scheme. That scheme was to return to

what after careful examination proved to be the most trust-
worthy of the five editions published during the seventeenth
century—the edition of 1633. In this, all the poems—with the
exception of three which appeared in Donne's lifetime, and of
those which were added later—were published for the first time.

But before arriving at this conclusion, and in order to present
the full canon of Donne's poems and of such as have been rightly
or wrongly attributed to him, not only a searching examination,
but in some instances a complete collation of upwards of forty
manuscript versions of the poems was necessary. Mr. Grierson's primary achievement, then, is a text as near accuracy as
mortal care can bring it, together with a page-by-page citation
of the smallest variations in the several readings. From Mr.
Gosse's invaluable Westmorland MS. nine poems have been
added, and one from the Burley MS.

But all this irksome and unostentatious work is only a fraction
of Mr. Grierson's devoted service on behalf of his author. No
less than three comprehensive introductions are concerned with
Donne's poetry, with text and canon. In the first of these Mr.
Grierson analyses Donne's wit—that 'wonder-inciting vigour,
intenseness, and peculiarity', as Coleridge described it; or, in
the words of De Quincey, 'the last sublimation of dialectical
subtlety and address with the most impassioned majesty'. He
discusses the absence of description in Donne's poetry, his
melancholy and scepticism, his worldly ambition, steadfast
effort and (after the death of his wife) profound, self-plaguing
penitence. He explains the by no means inexplicable extremes of
sensuality and spiritual exaltation revealed in his love poetry.
But although in so doing he expresses a warm and discerning
appreciation, the general tone of his essay—to those readers at
least who find it impossible to keep their admiration of Donne
on this side idolatry—will suggest something in the nature of
an apology. He seems to be addressing an audience inclined to
be hostile, or at least neutral, rather than sympathetic. And his
references, for comparison, to Tennyson, Burns, and Mr.
Bridges are neither very apt nor happy.

On the other hand, the serious student of Donne will be
enthusiastically grateful for every one of Mr. Grierson's two
hundred and seventy-five pages of Commentary. Without the
least parade, acrimony, or contentiousness, and with the readiest

modesty, he cheerfully faces countless and at times almost insuperable difficulties, and elucidates nearly all of them. Such a commentary, apart from its being an indispensable appendix to the poems, may be read and enjoyed at leisure as an *olla podrida* of curious and far-fetched knowledge and scholarship, and a kind of natural history of Elizabethan ideas.

The finest achievement of most lyrical poets—Keats, Coleridge, Herrick, Blake, Shelley—seems to be something apart and aloof from their mere workaday selves. It is the outcome of rare, heightened moments, of an elusive and, to a certain degree, alien impulse. We speak of inspiration and so imply an instrument attuned. We speak of art and so imply a direct choice and rejection. And such poetry, alike for writer and reader, is the fruit of a golden pause in life, when time's chariot-wheels are at rest, and the heart no longer tolls *memento mori*, or whispers a feverish *carpe diem*, but beats for a while to an immortal rhythm. Existence is simplified in this intensified and isolated moment. Life is no longer a riddle but a dream.

Donne's poetry is different. He is the poet not of escape from, but into, the depths and mysteries of personality. It is his personality that enslaves us. 'By our first strange and fatall interview', we are once and for all made captive. He can be almost as intolerably coarse as Swift, as ecstatic as Shelley, as imaginative as Sir Thomas Browne, as nimble and insolent as Mercutio, as thought-ridden as Hamlet, as solemn as the *Dies Irae*, as paradoxical as a latter-day moralist. He may overwhelm a lyric with learning, juggle with the erudite ideas of 'wrangling schooles', be affectedly and fantastically intellectual, tediously labyrinthine. 'Subtile to plague himself' he was; but however straitened the view we catch of him, he is always in some indefinable and virtual fashion the man—John Donne. And it is from out of the midst of his obscurity, in the hugger-mugger, as it were, of his alembics and retorts, that we are suddenly dazzled and enthralled by a sheer incandescence of thought and feeling—the attar of his poetry. Donne 'perplexes the mind of the fair sex', said Dr. Johnson. None the less, except it be Browning, far more of a sentimentalist, in spite of his philosophical gallantry, than Donne, to no other poet do women—apart from the 'fair sex'—owe a rarer debt: for his insight, exquisite tenderness, and masculine understanding. No man ever

159

'deeper digg'd loves Myne' than Donne, nor retrieved from it a stranger treasure. Who that has really read him does not know 'by heart', *The undertaking, Sweetest love, I do not goe, The Funerall, The Exstacie, A Nocturnall, A Valediction: of weeping,* the Anniversaries, the best of the Elegies; the wonderful onset of *Aire and Angels,* of *Loves Deitie, The Legacie, A Feaver,* of *The good-morrow*?

Throughout his life the same bare, emotional directness is apparent; from *The Canonization*—'For Godsake hold your tongue, and let me love'—to the *Holy Sonnets*:

> *Thou hast made me, And shall thy worke decay?*
> *Repaire me now, for now mine end doth haste,*
> *I runne to death, and death meets me as fast,*
> *And all my pleasures are like yesterday;*
> *I dare not move my dimme eyes any way,*
> *Despaire behind, and death before doth cast*
> *Such terrour, and my feeble flesh doth waste*
> *By sinne in it, which, it t'wards hell doth weigh;*
> *Onely thou art above, and when towards thee*
> *By thy leave I can looke, I rise againe;*
> *But our old subtle foe so tempteth me,*
> *That not one houre my selfe I can sustaine;*
> *Thy Grace may wing me to prevent his art,*
> *And thou like Adamant draw mine iron heart.*

Reading him, we do not throw off the world; we are not, as by a miracle, made innocent and happy. 'Witty depravity', the sharpest actuality, extremes of exultation and despair, passion and disillusionment, love, death, the grave, corruption—all this is the material of his verse—a verse that breaks into beauty and music the moment feeling and thought are clear and free. Everything that we have—mind, body, soul—he invites to his intimacy.

> *A naked thinking heart, that makes no show,*

is his demand; a reader 'mad with much heart', rather than 'ideott with none'; but he exercises also all our mature, modern complexity, for 'man is a lumpe, where all beasts kneaded bee.' 'Made one anothers hermitage', we share with him a tense, vigilant, silence in some withdrawn chamber of our minds,

as men who through a Cipres see
The rising sun.

'Forget this rotten world!' he cries; what 'fragmentary rub-bidge' it all is!

And unto thee
Let thine own times as an old story be.

The house of life, darkened, haunted, is above and around us. Brightest lover and friend, like clear-illumined ghosts, offer their wordless company. Passionately realized, or dimmed in ecstatic brooding, long they have been away,

long, long, yet none
Offers to tell us who it is that's gone.

For us in this solitude with him, at any moment a further door may quietly open, and Death, like a groom, will bring a 'taper to the outward room'. 'The last busie day' done, we shall 'ebbe out with them, who homeward goe': and then, 'good morrow to our waking soules'. Only the best of life is in most poets; all man's inward life is in Donne—from his reckless, squandered youth, the youth of the long sensual face, with its high, sloping forehead, wide, dreaming, searching, interrogative eyes, to the shroud-swathed, 'ruinous Anatomie' of the Droeshout engraving. And his poetry has conferred upon him, so far as this world is concerned, life's only real immortality.

Edinburgh Review, April 1913

M

SIR JOHN SUCKLING*

Suckling was that rather unusual kind of poet—a very ordinary man. He wrote scarcely a line that is beyond the thought, or the sentiment, or the experience of the majority of his social equals. But he wrote many so frank and unpretentious, of things so clearly seen, and of trivial feelings so takingly expressed, that his name is all but proof against oblivion. His life, however, was by no means ordinary. Few poets have had to contend against the dangers and difficulties of wealth. Suckling was as renowned for his vast fortune as for the way he spent it—gaming so wantonly, says Aubrey, that his trust was precarious with the shopkeepers even for sixpence. One feat at least of his prodigality we know of, that of decking-up, at the handsome cost of £12,000, a squadron of popinjays for Charles I against the Scots, that, either from natural fear or anxious for their fine clothes, at sight of the enemy ran away:

> *The colonell sent for him back agen,*
> *To quarter him in the van-a,*
> *But Sir John did swear he would not come there,*
> *To be killed the very first man-a.*

Suckling, indeed, gained many reputations, more or less worthwhile. He not only wrote that delicate little lyric of extremely unromantic sentiment, *Why so pale and wan, fond lover?* but was, says Pope (in his gnat-like fashion), 'an immoral man, as well as debauched'. He was renowned for his wit and gallantry, was the best 'bowler' in England, and invented the game of cribbage. He borrowed from, and ruined in the conveyance, Donne. He presented a play with scenery at his own expense, with two fifth acts—one, loyal and bloodless, for Court use; one

---

* *The Works of Sir John Suckling.* Edited by A. Hamilton Thompson, M.A. (Routledge).

elaborately sanguinary for the sake of dramatic finish. He sat down at an inn and scribbled off *An Account of Religion by Reason*, that very faintly recalls here and there the *Religio Medici*. Even the manner of his early death was striking, for he either, according to the best-attested evidence, poisoned himself after his flight to France, when the Army plot for freeing Strafford had been exploded, or died 'by the malice of a man-servant' who had concealed a razor or a pen-knife in his boot. He spoke Latin at five, lived all his days a bachelor, with an entirely plastic bachelor heart, had 'a brisque round eie', a reddish face and 'red nose (ill liver), his hayre a kind of sand colour', a beard that 'turned up naturally', and he was painted by Vandyke. Moreover, he dressed his gayest—and it must have been very gay—when he was most dejected. It is not surprising, then, that even on his own showing,

> *He loved not the Muses so well as his sport;*
> *And prized black eyes, or a lucky hit*
> *At bowls, above all the trophies of wit.*

None the less, the Muses resented his indifference no more, apparently, than did his numerous lady-loves. His little triumphs in poetry are all but considerable ones. If they are not exactly 'Fragmenta Aurea', *Out upon it! I have lov'd; I prithee send me back my heart;* and *Honest lover whosoever*, have the un-fading charm of a kind of genial heedlessness, an easy finish, and so instantly take the fancy that one scarcely realizes what a renegade it is who has wheedled himself into the company of poets infinitely his betters, and essentially different from himself.

The universally renowned *Ballad of a Wedding* is printed in this volume without its usual alluring asterisks. There is, we may venture to say, very little in the stanzas that are generally omitted that could much imperil the modesty of a student of our newspapers. Suckling is coarse, but he does not leer. He often writes rather too much 'like gentlemen talk', but is rarely sickly or suggestive. What he says he at least says out, and sometimes with a kind of rank but boyish humour. The 'house with stairs', the 'little mice', the wedding ring 'too wide a peck' are un-forgettable, and have scarcely any rival in their own kind unless it is the delightful stanza that keeps them company:

Her cheeks so rare a white was on,
No daisy makes comparison
(Who sees them is undone);
For streaks of red were mingled there,
Such as are on a Katherine pear
(The side that's next the sun).

Such dainty bubbles go a long way to redeeming the sediment in the rest of the poem—and even perhaps so far as to forgive their writer a perfectly intelligible dread of the bagpipes! It is curious, after all this, that Suckling should have written such incredibly dull letters, affectedly, almost witlessly worldly-wise, repeating stale jests on widows, and dishing up the shallow philosophy of his lyrics in the stickiest prose. Even here he is immensely complaisant over his 'hawk's-eye' for a woman, and probably, therefore, met with no little success. It is not quite so unexpected to find him seriously concerned over his almost unreadable plays. But though *Aglaura* is feebly constructed, Suckling has studied his predecessors (as well as hit upon the best in Donne), and his blank verse is often quiet and sweet and rhythmical. He could deck his *Sad One* with so fine a simile as:

On me the whole court gaz'd, as at
Some comet set in Cassiopeia's chair;

could be as slashing as, 'But I will find him out, and kick his soul to hell. I'll do't'; and as fantastically Elizabethan as,

Her hair's so preciously fair and soft,
That, were she fall'n into some river, and
In danger, one would make a conscience
To save her life, for fear of spoiling it—

every syllable a 'beat'. But for the most part the plays are interesting only as very dim reflections of a Shakespeare who had quitted the stage about twenty-one years before the first of them, *Aglaura*, was written. And for that reason, we think, among others even better, this volume of *The Works*, which might as truthfully be styled *The Recreations of Sir Thomas Suckling*, has justified Mr. A. Hamilton Thompson of his care in editing it, and of his interesting Introduction.

Saturday Westminster Gazette, May 7, 1910

THOMAS CAMPION*

Campion's is not the least enviable of fates for a poet. The fact that he charmed all who were worth charming in his own generation, that he suffered almost complete eclipse for a while, and then, centuries after, blossomed yet more freely in the grave, gives an aroma to his lyrics which not even an unfailing remembrance can bestow. It was one of the greatest of Mr. Bullen's well-merited privileges, so recently as 1887, to stumble on this lawyer and doctor who was also a musician and a poet. And now, for the first time, Mr. Percival Vivian has collected into one volume all the work either in prose or verse that is known with certainty to be his, together with a few poems that may on internal and indirect evidence be fairly attributed to him. Mr. Vivian claims also in his Introduction to have definitely settled what precise parents shall have the credit of the poet's production; not, that is, Thomas Campion and Anastace, his wife, of Witham, Essex, as has been hitherto asserted; but John Campion, of Anstey, in Herts., and Lucy, the widow of Roger Trigg and daughter of Laurence Searle, one of the Serjeants-at-Arms in attendance upon the Sovereign. This being the case, the poet was 'borne upon Ash Weddensday, being the twelfth day of February, An. Rg. Eliz. nono (1567), and cristened at St. Andrewes Church, in Houlborne'. His father was admitted to the Middle Temple, enjoyed the post and privileges, probably obtained with his wife's money, of a Cursitor of the Chancery Court, and died young in October 1576. His widow for a third husband accepted less than a year afterwards Augustine Steward, who in 1575 had had a lively passage of arms with Dr. Cox, the Bishop of Ely, who forthright accused him of having 'in mine Absence entered into mine House, and broken up my Chapel Doors. And whereas in the

* *Campion's Works.* Edited by Percival Vivian (Frowde).

165

Heat of Summer, for two or three Days in the Time of Thunder my woman had set her Milk pans in a cold place of the Chapel, he spurned them down with his foot.' And his language, it seems, matched his manners. The poet's mother died in March 1579–80. Steward married again ten months afterwards another widow, and the poet was packed off to Peterhouse, Cambridge; his name, followed a little while after by that of his step-brother, Thomas Sisley, being entered in the Buttery Books for the first time on May 13, 1581. For the two scholars' 'weakely diete' their father assigned 5s.; he allowed in the dark months of winter 'a pound of candell betwen them every fortnight'; two quires of paper quarterly; also 2 dubletes, 2 payres of hose, 4 payres of netherstockes, 2 shirts, and 6 payre of shoes every year each, which seems at first sight an intolerable deal of shoes for so reasonable a supply of hose.

Of Campion's career at Cambridge Mr. Vivian can give no record; but on April 27, 1586, he was admitted to Gray's Inn. Thenceforward his biography follows the generally accepted facts. All this precise history, Mr. Vivian tells us in his Preface, is based upon a clue afforded by Egerton MS. 2599 in the British Museum; and the fact already ascertained by Mr. Bullen that the poet was a member of Gray's Inn. Mr. Vivian must be cordially congratulated on his enterprise and diligence, although perhaps it is too early yet to add also his triumph. Champions of Anastace's Thomas may yet appear. Poets still in the land of the living should, at any rate, take at least one lesson to heart— to keep their family records clear, and beware of remote and prosaic cousins sharing their own Christian names.

Campion's later life was busy and studious and of many interests. The frontispiece to this volume reproduces his evidence, with his signature attached, concerning his innocent connexion with the long-spun-out murder of Sir Thomas Overbury in the Tower—by means of rosacre, white arsenic, tarts and jellies containing corrosive sublimate, and finally, all these having proved unavailing, with a poisoned clyster. It was for the 'Nuptialls' between the instigators of this miserable revenge, the Earl of Somerset, then Viscount Rochester, and the Countess of Essex, that no fewer than three poets set their wits to work— Campion, Donne, and Ben Jonson.

Campion's actual works as here set forth make up a book of

over three hundred pages. But by far the greater portion of it is devoted to his Latin epigrams and elegies, his Essay on Counterpoint, and his medley of *Observations in the Art of English Poesie*, of which it may be said with certainty that had his own art been based solely on his science he would never have survived his age. His masques, even apart from their songs, still make excellent reading. Pageant devisers in those days no less than in ours had teasing difficulties to contend with, as an explanatory and pathetic little note in the Hayes masque will show: 'Either by the simplicity, negligence, or conspiracy of the painter, the passing away of the trees was somewhat hazarded; the patterne of them the same day hauing been showne with much admiration.' Which is atoned for by another note, in another masque, to the song:

> *Aduance your Chorall notions now,*
> *You music-louing lights.*

'According to the humour of this Song, the Starres mooued in an exceeding strange and delightfull maner, and I suppose fewe haue euer seene more neate artifice, then Master Innigoe Jones shewed in contriuing their Motion.'

But it is, of course, in Campion's lyrics, written for the most part to his own music, and published in his various *Bookes of Ayres*, that his genius shines most clearly. No other poems in the language have quite their bird-like exquisite movement. They vibrate with a frail delicate music that sings and dies away, and reawakes, like the voice of a bird in the shadowy moonlight of a wood. Campion delights too in the calm, mellow sunlight of early morning, in pale pure colour, and in a kind of dreamlike peace and serenity. All the loveliest of his songs, *Follow thy faire Sunne, vnhappy shadowe, Follow your Saint, follow with accents sweet, Neuer weather-beaten Saile,* and *Kinde are her answeres,* are haunted by a wistful but unrepining melancholy, happy in expressing itself in words whose music is not the least essential part of their meaning. Some of his lines have a curiously modern ring, such as:

> *'Tis now flow'ry May,*
> *But eu'n in cold December,*
> *When all these leaues are blowne away,*
> *This place shall I remember.*

167

or:

> Come, chearfull day, part of my life, to mee:
> For while thou viewst me with thy fading light,
> Part of my life doth still depart with thee,
> And I still onward haste to my last night.

Even Herrick, who owed not a little to his influence, has not a grace so fine and unalloyed, though he was perhaps a more diligent and conscious artist.

Saturday Westminster Gazette, Jan. 8, 1910

METAPHOR*

Mr. Jennings's Essay is brief, not because it is cursory and superficial, but because it keeps close only to the essentials of his subject. He has packed into a few illuminating pages not only a scientific analysis and a historical survey of metaphor and its uses, but has also enriched his study with a conception, both imaginative and philosophical, of his theme, and in so doing has left many beckoning by-paths clearly in sight of the adventurous reader which he may explore at leisure. The poet who reads him will have the gratification of being justified of his own instinctive intuition, the critic of strengthening his judgment; and both should enjoy a piece of writing often as beautiful in thought as it is lucid in expression.

Metaphor itself lies closely hidden at the very roots of language. 'Under the microscope of the etymologist' the most desiccated terms of intellectual speech reveal their sensuous and metaphorical origin. 'That skull had a tongue in it, and could sing once.' This 'radical' order of metaphor is not Mr. Jennings's concern, though he cites Max Müller among his authorities, and in order to begin at the beginning of his subject returns to the fountain-head of clear conceptions, Aristotle, his *Poetic* and his *Rhetoric*. From Aristotle Mr. Jennings proceeds to Quintilian and Longinus, and so at length to Coleridge, who out of the abundance of his acute and creative mind scattered quickening ideas as freely as an oak scatters acorns. For the most part the older inquirers treated the question analytically. They were at best vivisectionists. Mr. Jennings's aim is rather synthetic and constructive. Why is poetry so rich with metaphor? Why do imaginative minds not only delight in it, but pine in its absence? It is because metaphor is the creative factor in language no less than in literature and life. If not, indeed, the

* *Metaphor in Poetry*. By J. G. Jennings (Blackie).

169

'spirit of poetry', it is its 'atmosphere', without which it could neither move nor breathe 'with joy'. In prose ('which, in its purity, takes everything abstractedly') metaphor may be an explanatory, elucidatory and rationalistic element, for in prose man reasons about himself and the world. In poetry, as naturally as in a child or a lover, it springs from emotion, from feeling. Far from being a mere ornament or floriation, a flutter of fancy, or an ingenious flourish, it is a rich imaginative exercise of the whole poetic mind in contemplation of that complexity in unity which is alike the delight, the wonder, and the mystery of all human experience in the world. All things bear an intrinsic resemblance to one another, since all are compounded of the same elements; and metaphor is the revelation of such resemblances. 'How like a winter hath thine absence been'; 'Send home my long-strayed eyes to me'; 'With how sad steps, O moon'; 'And I awoke and found me here, on the cold hill's side'—so this metaphoricalness haunts poetry, the idiom of its language, the fabric of its dream. It reveals the presence of the one in the many; it folds all things again in the changeless security of the one.

A fine prose will bear the closest rational scrutiny. Its every word stands for the full and exact meaning of that word, is as true to its root as to the last fine flower which continuous cultivation has brought it to bear. In a true poem as strictly logical a scrutiny will find no organic flaw, but prose is compounded of thought, poetry of intense vision, of a vision and intensity beyond the reason wholly to explore. There we must *see* as well as think, give heart, life, insight as well as mind. Poetry, as it were, translates beauty, loveliness, sorrow, delight into words; a poem is therefore not only charged with metaphor, it is itself a metaphor, and we through word and metaphor must re-create that loveliness or mood, must pierce back to the visionary reality of what they tell.

It is because 'the depreciation of Tennyson that one now so frequently encounters is largely due', Mr. Jennings thinks, to a dull and inactive reading of his poems that he himself in this essay has chosen *In Memoriam* for an illustration of his theory. Yet his appendix, in spite of its closeness of study, insight, and enthusiasm, is more open to question than that theory itself. One may question even the perfect appropriateness of the two fragments he has chosen as a kind of touchstone for his essay:

> *Short swallow-flights of song, that dip*
> *Their wings in tears, and skim away.*

> *The glory of the sum of things*
> *Will flash along the chords and go.*

They are beautiful, but there is a slight *apparent* artifice in that beauty. The 'fusion' of which Coleridge speaks is not quite complete. The comparison in each as a comparison is a little far-fetched, conscious; the image all but obliterates that which it is intended to reveal.

But,

> *Take, O, take those lips away,*
> *That so sweetly were forsworn,*
> *And those eyes, the break of day,*
> *Lights that do mislead the morn!*
> *But my kisses bring again,*
> *Seals of love but sealed in vain:*

here the fusion is absolute. The metaphor is as much one with that it colours, enriches, illuminates, as is the rainbow in a drop of dew.

Or again, take Keats's—

> *His soul shall taste the sadness of her might*
> *And be among her cloudy trophies hung. . . .*

In what region of wake and dream are we here, how shall we sever metaphor from the naked statement, how dissociate the picture from that which it depicts, how disentangle the mood and feeling expressed from the vision? So in the purest poetry the image is lost in the thing in itself, and that is as it were but a translucent veil between two realities.

Times Literary Supplement, March 2, 1916

DOGGEREL

Pegasus, being a creature of sensitiveness and caprice, frets at times at his golden bridle, refuses to mount into the intense inane. A stubborn scurry of wings ensues, a clatter of hoofs upon stones, the sound perhaps of a strong man 'struggling with a word'; and the term for that particular cacophony is doggerel. Mine host on the road to Canterbury, more than five centuries ago, was deceived in his fellow pilgrim of the 'elvish' countenance. He fumed in his saddle until the fifth stanza of the second 'fit' of Sir Thopas:

> *Sir Thopas was a doghty swayn;*
> *Whit was his face as payndemayn,*
> *His lippes rede as rose;*
> *His rode is lyk scarlet in grayn,*
> *And I yow telle in good certayn*
> *He hadde a semely nose.*

And then his contempt for this 'drasty speche' could contain itself no longer: 'Na moore of this, for Goddes dignitie!' he cried. ' "This may wel be rym dogerel," quod he. "It is the beste rym I ken,"' was the meek reply. But there are two kinds of rym dogerel. Doggerel—in the summary definition of the Oxford Dictionary—may be an epithet applied to comic or burlesque verse, usually in irregular rhythm, or to a verse mean, trivial, or undignified. The fastidious critic takes small pleasure in either variety. He chafes at 'a pitiful defence of poor poetry'. It would enlarge his sphere of legitimate pleasure, however, even deepen his capacity of appreciation of true poetry, if he could be happy with either. Take a little volume published only the other day:

> *'Thank God!' says she, as brave Lonnaire,*
> *With deftness and a cunning rare*

Grips hold and quickly hauls himself
Upon the raft like some strange elf.
'Thank God!' says she—'Great God!'—and then—
Oh! how can this be writ by pen?—
Aghast she stands, her frenzied stare
Is fixed upon the brave Lonnaire.
'Thank God!' repeats the glad Lonnaire,
'That I am with you here to share
The dangers of this ocean wild;
For I will save both you and child.
Cheer up! and fear me not, for I
Will land you both soon high and dry!'

What wonder 'holy wedlock' turned the key 'upon an earthly
mystery'! Hardly a week passes but some such flower of fancy
fades unseen—

> *Loved I in my distant boyhood*
> *For the blood is hot in Spring;*
> *I endorse the poet's theory,*
> *Woman's love's a fatal thing.*

Sentiments thus expressed give us to feel, perhaps, in Sidney's
phrase, 'how many headaches a passionate life bringeth us to'.
'And when the music sweet had died away, I murmured much
and longed to leave my clay.' Unfortunately poetry is not merely
a matter of good intentions, or even of high seriousness. But still
of this order of doggerel it is not flattery to affirm that it is bad
poetry, not merely bad verse. It is an efflorescence of the feelings, not of the intellect. Within its hope lie all the joys and
graces of true poetry. Its snow-clad peaks are at least in sight.
Actually it need but be yeasty prose cut up into lengths with a
rhyme here and there at the end of them. Potentially it may be
anything. It rests with the fickle Muse: 'The spirit of Poësie is
silver shod, And it is partly me, and wholly God,' as another
modern modestly expresses it. It may fitfully smoulder with
imagination. Its velocity, as the elder Disraeli said of that rude
railing rhymer, the 'beastly Skelton'—'its velocity may have
a carol of its own.' It may fall, as Skelton frequently does, into a
cadence worthy of that exquisite musician, Thomas Campion.
And, 'however rudely raine beaten, rusty and moughte eaten',

it is certain to have some 'pyth'. But whether it be the achievement of an over-ripe culture, or the crude, hobbledehoy tooraloora-lido jargon of that once renowned and now all but effete ballad-monger, Jack Bull, the worse it is the better it is.

Samuel Butler was a master of the other kind of doggerel; but the blind, solemn naïveté, the beatific idiocy, sentimentality, and bathos of unintentional doggerel was out of his reach. And

> *Who would not give all else for two p*
> *Ennyworth only of beautiful Soup?* . . .

Damning the dull fiend a thousand times (and without Herrick's patience, who, when impulse failed, simply 'over-read' what he had writ), Butler was often tempted to forswear all rhymes, simply because he was an artist and could not endure a 'dull epithet'. The true doggrelizer is placidly, seraphically unaware that his epithets are dull. He lisps in numbers from a native infirmity. But the arch and skilful pseudo-doggrelist is hardly less at the mercy of mere inspiration, for no rational being can sit down at any moment and pour out rich, unctuous, galumptious doggerel worthy of the name. He will need to submit himself to a vigilant (and arduous) absence of mind. He must endeavour not to conceal art, but the premeditated lack of it. He must take infinite pains to take none. In short, he must—like the creator of the Yonghy Bonghy Bo—be a child of genius and positively crammed with ideas—'Saith the poet of Nonsense, Thoughts into my head do come Thick as flies upon a plum.' He just 'breaks out':

> *Why, or when, or which, or what*
> *Or who, or where, is the Akhond of Swat,—óh* WHÂT
> *Is the Akhond of Swat.*

> *Is he tall or short or dark or fair?*
> *Does he sit on a throne, or a sofa or chair,—or* SQUAT?
> *The Akhond of Swat.*

> *Does he live upon Turnip, tea, or tripe?*
> *Does he like his shawls to be marked with a stripe,—or a*
> SPOT?
> *The Akhond of Swat.*

And so on till the rhyme gives out—but not the well-spring, that crystal, perennial geyser of 'Ajoskyboskybaysoness'. But Lears and Carrolls are as unusual fruits upon the tree of life as Blakes and Shelleys. Not less instantly than the magic of Coleridge their nonsense enchants the mind out of the arid rut of the ordinary into a world of freedom and delight. They spirit us back, not into an irrevocable past, but into the ever-present, ever-new, and limitless realm of childhood, where dwells that best of all the Messrs. Anon—the poet who squandered a rare imagination and romance on that supreme doggerel, the Nursery Rhymes. A poet so artless that he never even whispered how artful he truly was, and so selfless as to leave himself utterly out of his work. Merely a blaze on a thick-leaved wayside tree in the starlit and solitary Woods of Fantasy, and he is gone:

> ' *How many miles to Babylon?* '
> ' *Threescore and ten.* '
> '*Can I get there by candle-light?* '
> ' *Ay, and back again.* '

That candle shines only in dream, only in dream that Babylon rears its terrifically distant uncrumbling walls. But this is inspired doggerel. The more self-conscious and reasonable we are the less our impulse is likely to be to fall under the spell and take our natural ease in this shining region of moonshine, with Puck and Bottom for company, and the March Hare in the bracken. Great wits only distantly allied to this midsummer order of madness have done their ingenious best to doggrelize. Swift, with the love of Stella in his heart, could jot down offhand whimsical lovable verses, half-serious, half-jocose. 'Accept for once some serious lines,' he says, and is immediately his unlaboured natural self a while. But his rhyming bouts with Sheridan and the rest (39 monstrous efforts to ring the changes on music—Jew sick; hue sick, etc.) blotted off against time, farced with puns which too often make merely dull and coarse things intolerable by a thin veneer of wit, are lifeless by comparison with true doggerel, whether ingenuous or intentional. Even 'their King's Majesties Water-poet and Queen's Waterman' John Taylor— a vain, confirmed and, it must be confessed, rather tedious doggreller, was nearer orthodoxy:

> *Thus do I make a hotch-potch of Nonsense*
> *In dark enigmas and strange sense upon sense:*
> *It is not foolish all, nor is it wise all,*
> *Nor is it true in all, nor is it lies all.*

Water-poet's or Swift's, such doggerel is feebleness itself compared with Skelton's. He grew remorseful, it is true, for a very real kind of good works, 'suppleyng to Fame', in a penitent moment, to 'scrape out the scrollis, Apollo to rase out of her ragman rollis'. But give his doggerel its just pause and gravity, it can be as beautiful as it is serious:

> *I haue well espyde*
> *No man may him hyde*
> *From Deth holow eyed . . .*
> *To whom, then, shall we sew,*
> *For to have rescew,*
> *But to swete Jesu,*
> *On vs then for to rew?*
> *O goodly chyld*
> *Of Mary mylde,*
> *Then be our shylde!*

His light-hearted tenderness, his humanity, that kind of innocent, merrily immodest humour of his, and an occasional obscenity that should be free of offence to men and women who know what it is to be women and men—all this is at its best in the fresh aromatic *Garlande of Laurell* with mayden Isabell, merry Margarete, and maistres Marjery for theme, and above all in the delicious *Phyllip Sparowe*:

> *It had a veluet cap,*
> *And wold syt vpon my lap,*
> *And seke after small wormes,*
> *And somtyme white bred crommes;*
> *And many times and ofte*
> *Betwene my brestes softe*
> *It wolde lye and rest;*
> *It was propre and prest.*
> *Somtyme he wolde gaspe*
> *Whan he sawe a waspe;*

A fly or a gnat,
He wolde flye at that;
And prytely he wold pant
Whan he saw an ant;
Lorde, how he wolde pry
After the butterfly!
Lorde, how he wolde hop
After the gressop!
And whan I sayd, Phyp, Phyp,
Than he wold lepe and skyp,
And take me by the lyp.
Alas, it wyll me slo
That Phillyp is gone me fro!
Si in i qui ta tes,
Alas, I was euyll at ease!
De pro fun dis cla ma vi,
Whan I sawe my sparowe dye!

It is not easy to decide into which of Dr. Murray's classes of
doggerel Skelton's should be consigned. He shines and smokes,
clearly and dingily, in both. He never took obvious pains,
though he could heap up learning, whip in macaronics, and pack
with mordant satire his ragged rhymes. As soon, indeed, as
pronounced finish and polish and too much taking of thought
become manifest, honest doggerel puts off its dusty shoes, is
asked into the best parlour for sherry and biscuits, promptly
expires, and is beatified and frenchified into *vers de société*. But
though as deep a gulf is fixed between doggerel and so-called
occasional verse as between 'verse' and poetry, a few fortunate
authors have enjoyed an occasional turn on the tight-rope
between them. A topsy-turvyfication of talent and an auspicious
moment are all that is necessary. Or:

The poet divine, that cannot reach wine,
Because that his money doth many times fail,
Will hit on the Vein to make a good strain,
If he be but inspired with a Pot of Good Ale.

There is the rich, grotesque, and at times sinister treasury of
Barham's helter skelter quizzicalities to rifle:

Mamma means to enclose
Two white 'wipes' for your nose;
As your purse may be run rather hard.
I shall also attack her
To augment your exchequer
With a Sovereign, stuck in a card.

That is a royal way of speaking 'roughly to your little boy', and
one thoroughly after the heart of that universal tipster Thackeray, who could also indulge an arch and succulent talent: 'The
Pope he is a happy man, His palace is the Vatican, And there he
sits and drains his can . . .' The whole rhyme approaches a little
too near the dainty 'triolet and Round O', whereas the button
of Billy's shimmie in the ballad of Gorging Jack and Guzzling
Jimmy, is a positive bull's eye. Ruskin, too, who (somewhat
long-windedly) considered 'the meritorious rhythmic cadence
of *Dame Wiggins of Lee* as not, in its way, imitable', boldly sup-
plemented that cantering classic, and delighted in pig rhymes
'made to amuse Joan'.

If little pigs when evening dapples,
With fading cloud her autumn sky,—
Set out in search of Norman Chapels,
And find, instead, where cliffs are high,
Half-way from Amiens to Etaples,
A castle full of pears and apples,
On donjon floors laid out to dry;
—Green jargonelles, and apples tenny—
And find their price is five a penny,
If little pigs, then, buy too many,
Spare to those little pigs a sigh.

And yet it is clear—even in the company of Thackeray and
Ruskin—that the air has become a little rarefied. We are
indoors. The words are set in almost too delightful proportion.
Ink is about. The ready and serious writer is only on a minute's
holiday; he is only whispering Pegasus in the ear; while true
doggerel may be the grave devotion of a wasted lifetime. Even
Gilbert, even Hood, Calverley, Lowell, an occasional Ancient or
Modern Hymn (alas!) and even Mr. Belloc—though his was the
ill-fated aunt in Yucatan, his the unbreathable gnu—even Mr.
Belloc has other fish to fry:

'My value,' William Blood *began,*
'Is ludicrously small.
I think I am the vilest man
That treads this earthly ball;
My head is weak, my heart is cold,
I'm ugly, vicious, vulgar, old,
Unhealthy, short, and fat.
I cannot speak, I cannot work,
I have the temper of a Turk,
And cowardly at that.'

The Modern Traveller is doggerel right enough; but it is satirical and so cannot be positively *frabjous*. And after all, back to the old black-letter broadsides we must go—doggerel both kernel and husk, milk and rough together—leaving the laureates and the stylists and satirists in the lurch, if we are really to revel in a doggerel bare, naked and unadorned. Their very titles have a kind of Englishness, a verdure, a raciness and music, past imitation: *Love in a Maze,* or *the Young Man put to his Dumps; The Fox Chace,* or *the Huntsman's Harmony; All you that cry O hone, O hone, Come now and sing O hone with me; Faire fall all good Tokens; The Bride's Good-morrow; A Pretty Ballad of the Lord of Lorn; The Lamentation of* George Strangwidge; *Death's Loud Allarum,* or *Death's Dance: To be sung to a Pleasant New Tune, call'd Oh no, no, no, not yet;* or *The Meddow brow:*

If death would come and show his face, as he dare shew his power,
And sit at many a rich man's place both every day and houre!—

and suchlike hearty sentiments. Shakespeare poked fun enough at these old doggrelizers, but he'd learnt them and their trade by heart. What could surpass the winning unpretentiousness of Hamlet's ballad of the Judge of Israel—'Am I not i' the right, old Jephthah?'

. . . It came to pass, the wars was o'er,
And he returned with victory;
His dear and only daughter first of all
Came to meet her father foremostly:
And all the way,
She did play

179

On tabret and pipe,
Full many a stripe,
With note so high,
For joy that her father is come so nigh. . . .

But the old doggreler could be poet true when his wits, metre, and rhymes gave him the chance. Conciseness, distance, real vision are in this stanza from *The Patient Countess*:

Once hunted he untill the chace,
Long fasting, and the heat
Did house him in a peakish graunge
Within a forest great.

What a stroke is 'peakish'! Or take the lorn and frenzied lover, tossing on his bed: 'One while he spred his armes him fro, one while he spred them nye'; or summer woods: 'It is merrye walking in the fayre forest, To heare the small birdes singe'; or the jocund page in *The Child of Elle*.

Over the border we must go for true glamourie and witch-craft; but the English minstrels knew well what onset means: 'Princes that be prowde in prese', 'Sweet *England's* pride is gone, *welladay! welladay,*' 'Come, Love, let's walke into the Springe,' 'As ferre as men ride or gane', or

You Batchelors that brave it so gallant in the street,
With Muske and with Rose water, Smelling all so sweet,
With Shooes of Spanish leather, so feately to your feet
Behold me a married man!

We shall never perhaps recapture this old strain. The magic woodway forked. And one turning leads the pilgrim, via *Vilikins and his Dinah, The Ratcatcher's Daughter, The One Horse Chay*, and breadths of humour more natural than nice, to the worst fustian of the music-hall; the other to the at times too-too fastidious and faultless verse of yesteryear. Possibly if our newest and young-est poets would forget their art, the nice reviewer, and the stupidity of the 'public' a while, they might re-discover this queer old fascinating Eldorado; they might lure back this blunt workaday world, flesh, and devil into their verses—the world they are apt to ignore, the flesh they tend to exoticize, the devil they rarely raise. If but one ardent and gifted minor bard would suffer martyrdom in a cause of such real virtue and efficacy! Doggerel that proves a rich feast in the reading must be amazingly good fun in the writing. And the artless doggrelist would win an inalienable reward.

Times Literary Supplement, August 21, 1913

Various

THE SPIRIT OF MAN*

In a preface, grave in judgment and wise in counsel, Mr. Bridges explains the conception and aim of his anthology.* It has been made during the war, and is for the purpose of a defence and stronghold in times of trouble. Those who are fighting for England's cause—'the fairest earthly fame, the fame of Freedom'—may need it less than others. In action there may be rest from thought, when mind and heart are at one. But on those of us who are not soldiers the influence of the war broods like the memory of a nightmare. As Lowell wrote, 'We rather seemed the dead, that stayed behind,' and the trumpets may ring in our ears with but a feeble exultation. Morning after morning consciousness wakens to that memory, only to find it a condition of reality. It corrodes thought, veils the future, and has almost obliterated the past which, when it was ours, we so often failed to recognize as the happy present. All this is a reaction against the strain of attention and anxiety—need not mean any slackening of principle or of persistency. But some remedy must be sought against inevitable moods of gloom, weariness, and misgiving; some solace for the grief and bitterness of personal loss. And they can be found, as Mr. Bridges says, only by holding true to our faith in God and in goodness, only if we believe that life at length will redeem itself and that truth will prevail.

The war was not of England's making.

'The signs of the time cannot all be distinctly seen, nor can we read them dispassionately; but two things stand out clearly, and they are above question or debate. The first is that Prussia's scheme for the destruction of her neighbours was long-laid;

* *The Spirit of Man*: An Anthology in English and French from the Philosophers and Poets. Made by the Poet Laureate in 1915 (Longmans).

185

. . . the second is that she will shrink from no crime that may further its execution.'

How far the whole of Germany has consciously shared, and is deliberately sharing, in that responsibility, we can still only surmise. What is certain is that all that gives man's life on earth graciousness, stability, love, and hope has been betrayed by 'the apostasy of a great people', whom we once accounted 'an honest and virtuous folk'. Even now the overwhelming significance of all this baffles and eludes the mind. Beneath the babel of rumour, boasting, and recrimination there is an unfathomable silence; until that is broken it is vain to question.

The one supreme danger is the loss of sanity and balance. We too have 'our national follies and sins'. To deny or to cloak them would be cowardice, to brood over them a waste of spirit. Life for most people is not at any time material ease, life that is worthy of the name is for every man a bitter conflict. In that war of the spirit there is no truce or respite. But to learn is hard for those who are old in the world. This much mere experience may have taught us, '*Prosperity* doth best discover Vice, but *Adversity* doth best discover Virtue'; and the virtue of adversity is fortitude. Everywhere, in secret, and openly before men's eyes, that virtue, like the life of spring in the woods, is stirring.

'We are still free and true at heart. . . can take hope in contrition, and in the brave endurance of sufferings . . . take joy in the thought that our country is called of God to stand for the truth of man's hope, and that it has not shrunk from the call.'

To reveal that hope, to bring together every kind of witness to human constancy in face of the world's changeableness, to the vision that pierces its glare no less than its darkness, to earth's loveliness, and to God's all-understanding loving kindness, has been the purpose of this anthology.

It is, then, the record of the journey—an arduous one, whatever its own rewards—of 'one mind at one time' through the minds and imagination of others. Childhood and Death, Nature and Romance, Faith and Conduct, Philosophies and Humanities, Social Virtue and Freedom—over the whole of human experience it ranges, and that experience as it has been expressed in the words of the world's philosophers and poets. To follow anywhere merely the page-headings of this anthology is to taste of its delight, and to realize something, too, of the care and insight that have been put to its service; 'mountain music, visionary flowers, shadow worlds, tawny trees, the Phoenix, the Charioteer, nocturnal notes, celestial light, man's heritage, childhood, the rainbow, Heaven's shadows. . .' so the legend runs. Its one impulse and implication is the belief that 'spirituality is the basis and foundation of human life . . . rather than the apex or final attainment of it'. No strict logical argument is pursued—even if that had been possible it would only have obstructed the rarer influences of such a book. But there is a sequence of context, a sequence not mechanical nor obvious nor painfully elaborate, but one that wanders and returns upon itself—through a valley between the hills and the sea.

The reader, then, is 'invited to bathe rather than to fish in these waters'. Only invited; he may dream on the pleasant banks if he so please, may dip and dabble, but this book has other uses as well as the precious indulgence of an idle hour. Even if he plunges in he will soon have to return to his workaday clothes again, and he may be disappointed to find himself very much the same manner of man that he was. 'Go where thou wilt,' says one of Mr. Bridges's sages, 'to Benares or to Mathura; if thy soul is a stranger to thee, the whole world is unhomely.' If, indeed, we were a tenth as wise and as imaginative and lively as the books we have read, the world would be Paradise enough, for ourselves and for our neighbours. But though these waters may not positively restore health to the sick in mind and strength to the weary in spirit, they will cleanse and revive.

This anthology, moreover, will live on in memory. The impression it leaves behind it is something other than that of the mere confused sum of its parts. Its influence is a peculiarly personal one. No venture is easier or pleasanter than that of wandering in the gardens of literature and binding together a nosegay of immortelles. Mere diligence, and a none too attentive diligence, may go far and fare richly, without venturing out of bounds. Discretion in such matters is a more prudent counsellor than charity. An anthology that shows originality as well as catholicity of taste, some more vivifying motive than mere subject-matter, that aims at a certain standard of form and completeness of effect, is a rare thing. But there is a vigilance here, a certain poise and precision, deliberation, and subtlety, which prove that *The Spirit of Man* is the work of one mind, and of that mind in the ripeness of its judgment. A more or less mechanical form has become plastic. A picture has been painted with the pigments of scores of imaginations, and lo!—it is a portrait. What, then, are the qualities and features that differentiate this from other books of its kind?

Some are clear and may seem, but cumulatively are not, trivial; some are elusive. In the first place, the titles of poems and the names of authors are banished to an index. 'It is an idle and pernicious habit to ask for information on any question before bringing one's own judgment to bear upon it.' But that is not the whole of the matter. For when a magician weaves a spell it is unwise of him to interrupt it with the matter-of-fact names of his authorities. An occasional interpretation, or rather explanation, illuminates the margin, but for the most part the reader need only attentively regard what he reads 'to be at perfect ease'. If difficulties confront him, let him wrestle with them; if they prove insuperable, he can turn to the index for enlightenment. There is a marker in the book for this purpose, and even instruction how to use it! Help is freely given, but not indulgently. Digression into aesthetic appreciation—which sometimes enlightens and sometimes frets the reader in *The Golden Treasury*—is rare, and, whenever present, terse. Punctuation has been altered when accuracy required it. Archaic spelling has been retained in the extracts from Milton and Montaigne, and modernized in those from Spenser and Bacon; while Shakespeare's watchdogs bark 'Bowgh, wowgh', and his strutting chanticleer cries 'Cock-a-diddle-do'. These niceties—though not every one may be of one mind about them—are neither arbitrary nor pedantic. The one aim, whether in text or notes, is to attain precision and to make obscurity clear, to lead the reader on the right track of ideas. An occasional waft of irony is no hindrance. Read, mark, learn, digest is Mr. Bridges's counsel; let no doubt or difficulty escape. His argument on the versification and on the meaning and *morale* of Chaucer's *Truth*, on the style of Hobbes compared with that of Thucydides, on Emily Brontë's 'Tell me, tell me, smiling child', and on the passage from Aristotle on the 'Final Cause', show how practice may enforce precept. To cite one instance. Few lovers of poetry are unfamiliar with Keats's *Sleep and Poetry*:

Stop and consider! Life is but a day;
A fragile dewdrop on its perilous way
From a tree's summit; a poor Indian's sleep
While his boat hastens to the monstrous steep
Of Montmorenci. Why so sad a moan?
Life is the rose's hope while yet unblown;
The reading of an ever-changing tale;
The light uplifting of a maiden's veil;
A pigeon tumbling in clear summer air;
A laughing school-boy, without grief or care,
Riding the springing branches of an elm. . . .

But how many readers have paused over more than its beauty and music, and discovered the diversity of thought that underlies them?

'A good example of Keats's objective style [runs the note]. These images are of life considered first as a mere atomic movement in a general flux, then as a dream on the brink of destruction, then as a budding hope, then as an intellectual distraction, then as an ecstatic glimpse of beauty, and lastly as an instinctive pleasure.'

As regards the all-important question of inclusion and the far less important, but still significant even if baffling, one of rejection, we must keep in mind Mr. Bridges's warning—he has not sought to avoid in his own work the 'peculiarities and blemishes that mark any personality and any time'. 'He did not wish to put his honest likings'—it would be merely a gratuitous assumption to add his dislikings—'aside.' His range has been an unusually wide one. There are translations from the Hebrew, Greek, Latin, Persian, Russian, German, and Chinese—every one of which has been submitted to his own perhaps too fastidious revision. Only the selections from French authors appear in French—another little intentional discipline for the languid reader, but that also not without influence on the general impression of the book, especially since the greater part of these are from Amiel. Of our own poets Shakespeare, Milton, Shelley, Blake, Keats, and Coleridge are the chief contributors. Concerning more modern writers, the book is singularly rich in the work of Dolben, R. W. Dixon, and Gerard Hopkins—and friendship needs no better tribute and loyalty—and these, with the extraordinary and intensely effective passage from Lagerlof that follows, are among (in its exact sense) the most egregious craftsmen of Mr. Bridges's flock.

'We thought of that inquisitive spirit of self-criticism, who had made his entry even into our inner chamber. We thought of him, with his eyes of ice and long, bent fingers, he, who sits within in the darkest corner of the soul and tears our being to pieces, as old women shred up bits of silk and wool. . . .'

There is, also, an exquisite little poem of Andrew Lang's.

Rupert Brooke is in his place with the immortals. There are some beautiful and unfamiliar lyrics from Mr. Yeats, and, with one other example, a haunting visionary fragment from Mr. Lascelles Abercrombie's *An Escape*. One or two names appear that borrow, we think, more radiance from the suns around them than they themselves bestow. It is the index that reveals this rather than the text, and the reader's 'vainly curious mind' may be at fault. But, in an anthology so rich and various in beauty, wisdom, and tenderness as this, what explanation is conceivable regarding the complete exclusion of Vaughan, Campion, Patmore, and Christina Rossetti ? He may accept for consolation and happy surprise Dostoevsky, Jellaludin, Tagore, Nicias, the anonymous author of *XAPITEΣΣI*, and beautiful, unfamiliar extracts from the Salisbury Antiphoner, and yet speculate on the absence also of Browning and Mr. Hardy, and be reminded a little forlornly by one stanza from *A Hymn to God the Father* of Donne! Moreover, only one of the Poet Laureate's own poems has found a place, but that one essential to a true understanding of his book; though there are many fragments of original translation in classic metres, including 'one of the finest passages in Homer' (from the *Iliad* XXIV, 468–551), now printed for the first time:

> *O God-like Achiles, thy father call to remembrance;*
> *How he is halting as I, i' the dark'ning doorway of old age,*
> *And desolately liveth, while all they that dwell about him*
> *Vex him, nor hath he one from their violence to defend him;*
> *But yet an heareth he aught of thee, thy well-being in life,*
> *Then he rejoiceth an' all his days are glad with a good hope*
> *Soon to behold thee again, his son safe fro' the warfare.*
> *But most hapless am I, for I had sons numerous and brave*
> *In wide Troy;—where be they now? scarce is one o' them left . . .*

O God-like Achiles . . .
Thy sire also remember, having yet more pity on me,
Who now stoop me beneath what dread deed mortal ever dared,
Raising the hand that slew his son, pitiably to kiss it. . . .

Two other minor and positive characteristics distinguish this anthology from most of its kindred. First, it contains many fragments which are only a few lines long, from poems brief enough even in their supreme completeness. Of Herbert's *Easter*, for instance, there is only one stanza; and only one from Marvell's *To his Coy Mistress*. And, second, it is compounded of prose as well as verse. Both these departures, even if they need justification in a book so personal, are in much a gain. The economy keeps the all-connecting thread unburdened with digression and superfluity, the prose serves as a sort of bit and bridle to the flights of the poetic imagination. Its philosophy not only gives balance and stability, but, like evening sunshine, it calls out of the poetry it shines on its own colours and enhances what else might lie concealed. It may even at times cheat the poem into a meaning and allusion only vaguely its own.

One of the clearest lessons, indeed, inherent in these pages is that which teaches the inward reasonableness of all spirituality and proves that everything that we see and admire and love in the world is dark and unresponsive unless and until it is transfigured by the light of truth within us. 'La Beauté', says Amiel, 'est donc un phénomène de spiritualization de la matière.' Else, certainly, says Bacon, 'the earth with men upon it (the divineness of souls except) will not seem much other than an anthill'; and never was there a more pregnant parenthesis. Again, in the words of Rivarol, 'Tout Etat, si j'ose le dire, est un vaisseau mystérieux qui a ses ancres dans le Ciel.' And yet again, in a passage taken from Father Zossima's discourse to that strange company in *The Brothers Karamazof*:

'Much on earth is hidden from us, but there is given us in recompense the secret conviction of our living bond with another world, a celestial and loftier world; and the very roots of our thoughts and sensations are not here but there, in other worlds. And that is why philosophers say that on earth it is impossible to know the essence of things.'

It is, then, not the mere sequence of self-contained poems and fragments of prose that gives this anthology its intrinsic meaning, however valuable and truthful and beautiful they may be in themselves. It is their inter-relation and inter-communion one with another. Like a host of candles in the quiet air they congregate their light, but the ghostly shrine which they illumine is the mind that set them in their places. There is no absolute isolation. Every page echoes, colours, or refines its neighbour, and all these pages are needed to make up one book in its completeness. They impel and win the reader on from theme to theme, from sensuous delight to intellectual exaltation, by almost imperceptible gradations. Wherever we turn, we find this compulsory but happy collusion. With the Social Virtues and Freedom for subject, the Funeral Oration of Pericles from Thucydides gives place to a fragment from Montesquieu, 'L'Angleterre est à présent le pays le plus libre qui soit au monde, je n'en excepte aucune république . . .' and that to this from Lincoln, 'It has long been a grave question whether any government, not too strong for the liberties of its people, can be strong enough to maintain its existence in great emergencies . . .' and thence to his speech at Gettysburg in 1863, and thence to Burke on the Colonies, to Milton in his *Areopagitica*, and then the prose suddenly breaks like a sturdy northern tree into full flower, with Blake's *Jerusalem*.

Even the war-tired may take heart of grace. 'Oh how comely it is and how reviving To the spirits of just men long opprest! . . .' Keats, again, adds from his letters a postscript to his poetical vision 'on the true meaning of Poetry'—'A man's life of any worth is a continual Allegory, and very few eyes can see the Mystery of his life.' And from Amiel comes the penetrating corollary, 'Qui veut voir parfaitement clair avant de se déterminer ne se détermine jamais. Qui n'accepte pas le regret n'accepte pas la vie.' And the solemn, the marmoreal, 'Methought I saw my late espoused Saint' is followed by the forlorn passionate courage of:

If grief for grief can touch thee,
If answering woe for woe,
If any ruth can melt thee,
Come to me now!

I cannot be more lonely,
More drear I cannot be:

192

My worn heart throbs so wildly
    'Twill break for thee.

And when the world despises,
    When heaven repels my prayer,
Will not my angel comfort?
    Mine idol hear?

Yes, by the tears I've poured,
    By all my hours of pain,
O I shall surely win thee,
    Beloved, again.

But only a close study of the book can show the indefatigable pains of the artist to express an idea and an ideal with the world's masterpieces for his material. 'The teaching is only of whither and how to go, the vision itself is the work of him who hath willed to see.' What is made visible by this will is a serene solitude of the spirit, of a spirit not aloof from the hideous storm and terror of these days, but above it. Not unmoved by it, but its master. That idiosyncratic touch of strangeness which is essential, or is rather always a mark of poetry—just as the beauty of a face is stranger than the dust it must become—is a mark also of this anthology. But it is a strangeness with little eccentricity or quixoticism, and therefore perhaps it carries with it a certain frigidity towards the humours and homeliness, the common impulses and aberrations of human mortality. Scintillating with romance and dark with melancholy though many of these pages are, the romance at last, like the transmutations of a dream, is lost in the light of the spiritual imagination, and the dark shades conceal no shape or phantasm of the sinister, the grotesque, or the devilish. Mystery is here, not for the mind to dwell in, but transcend; peeping curiosity has no place, and wonder is not welcomed merely for its naïveté. A full but not refulgent or dazzling sunshine dwells over the scene, of a temperate heat; and so these waters flow on, beneath a shifting play of radiance and colour, ever varying in direction, now deepening, now shallowing, but always pure and clear, the hill-waters of a stream bordering earth and Paradise, and called by this interpreter of the spirit of man, Reality.

Times Literary Supplement, Feb. 3, 1916
193

EDGAR ALLAN POE

While artists and critics will dispute to the end of time whether the state of a man's soul has all or nothing to do with his work, the general public has quite made up its mind on the question. Poe it speedily comprehended. For, finding no definite defection in his history so far as appertains to Mrs. Grundy's own peculiar province of ethics, it summed up its indictment against him in the one word 'morbid'. It is a vague, borderland word, that may be used freely, and with effect, by all. Unfortunately, indefinite and partial charges such as these, besides being extremely difficult to meet, are impossible to rebut, since they are invariably founded on fact. It is certainly true that to America's most distinctive and most widely-acknowledged author mankind owes a debt resembling that which the rather sinister proprietor of the opium den solicits from his half-willing but regular devotee. If life on earth be but a brief series of reminiscences, then Poe has whispered in our ear many that might more prudently have been left undisturbed.

Take up his stories, and with fuming torch in hand he will lead you down into a labyrinth of gloom and foreboding as deep as that which Fortunato thridded in cap and bells to sip of the Amontillado. It is a region of the imagination—this principality of Poe's—to which fever, drugs, insanity give ingress. It lies deep in subconsciousness, all but undreamed-of by many, peeped into, and as hastily as possible withdrawn from, by less fortunate adventurers. Poe breathed at ease in its suffocating atmosphere. It was to him as fire is to the salamander. Whole and hale, who thinks of pain?—against whose unimaginable activites insensitiveness is only a door on the latch. So, too, for many wholesome minds fear and horror scarcely exist at all. But it is in early youth, before experience has taught one to appreciate the charms of sobriety in literature as well as in life, that

Poe waylays his victim. His monstrous tales, with their height-ened vocabulary, their crafty refrains, and all their bizarre and antique lumber, even their names, Ligeia, Morella, Berenice, capture the fancy. To come across them for the first time may be shattering; to read them late in life is still a remarkable, but it is not quite so overwhelming, an experience.

Had Poe in these stories 'of the arabesque and the grotesque', as they were first entitled, confined himself to horrors of the fancy and imagination; could he but, with his originality and enterprise, have foreseen the psychical enigmas that now engage us—his tales would certainly have gained in subtlety and power. But he habitually indulged an acute sense of the physically repul-sive. His tales are grey with mould and mildew. Poison, plague, consumption, death—he is an expert amateur in their cumula-tive, fleeting, or confounding effects. He never wearies of prying and probing, even of sniffing. He makes no apparent effort to surmount the humiliating facts of our mortality. He cannot charge with beauty even the torturers' tools, as does Webster in *The Duchess of Malfi*.

Swift has repelled many a reader, but his nastiness rarely failed to convey a hint of satire or irony. Poe was infatuated with the simple fact that when the golden bowl is broken tarnish sets in. Green graves fatten no mutton for him. He counts the maggots in Yorick's skull and ignores his jests. Never, perhaps, lived man before him so generously endowed with waking and articu-late nightmare; never, surely, one so fascinated by the parapher-nalia of the charnel-house. It is a venial weakness of intelligence if it revolt against the transmutations of disease and death. But Poe's mind, in this as in other respects, like the minds of so many men of genius other than the greatest, was out of focus with the normal experience of humanity. He surveyed the world now through a microscope, now beneath a minifying-glass. He never knew the quietude and peace that a judiciously restricted out-look may bring even to those who might as deliberately have chosen otherwise. It was the misfortune of his temperament, the defect of his wonderful qualities.

It is not only the power of his imagination that none the less makes him one of the few masters of the short story. Busy in its service were a logical lucidity, a keenness of intellect, a passion for proportion, for climax and crisis. The masterly combination of these diverse qualities is the secret of his art and its effects. However weird, however distorted, his theme may be—and it was rarely anything else—Poe's presence of mind never fails him. His plot advances, without haste, with the clearest attention to every detail, to its overwhelming conclusion. Beneath all the vapourings and incoherence of the subject, we see M. Dupin of the Rue Morgue, rational and alert, dotting his 'i's' and crossing every 't'. Each blur of the mind in mono-mania is set in place, each nuance of a horrifying situation exactly adjusted. We may be in a lunatic asylum, but Poe at least is physician in charge. In his earlier and more beautiful work, in *The Adventure of One Hans Pfaall*, in the *MS. found in a Bottle*, he has not yet discovered the secret of his method. He writes simply of what possesses him. The genius is clear and engaging, the exultation in the work simple and sincere. His later stories suggest the art of the conjurer who knows precisely what he is proposing to do and is a little tired of so often doing it, a little contemptuous of the spectator's credulity. And yet, after discovering virgin and golden soil for these imaginative and analytical faculties to work on in harmony one with another, and with perfect ease and success—the unravelling of crime—he founded only three short stories on such a theme, *The Murders in the Rue Morgue*, *The Mystery of Marie Roget*, and *The Purloined Letter*. With such excellent opportunities of theme as a talent for cryptogram and the hunt after buried treasure afforded him, he wrote only *The Gold Bug*. Others have garnered the grain he scattered. He was a pioneer. He staked out a claim; dug up a Koh-i-noor, and wearied, yet restless, struck camp and ventured further.

Ordinary human affairs, the jog-trot of life interested Poe, so far at least as his stories are concerned, scarcely at all. Even his murderer of the Rue Morgue is an orang-outang. He gloried in darkness, in gigantic and spectral light. His moon is bewitched. His seas are supreme in volume and mystery; and they stretch from Pole to Pole. His sense of the mere drip of time from the tiny phial of life into the unechoing silence of eternity is unique. The churchyard is his chosen haunt, but no Elizabethan glow-worm creeps upon its clods. He can fill a closet, a gallery, the firmament itself, with horror and darkness; he can mount into space with Hans Pfaall, and descend into indescribably horrible dungeons. His banquets would tempt a Beckford. His domestic economy resembles that of a Richmond Roy. He wanders craven and penniless in the solitude of a swarming and indifferent city in *The Man of the Crowd*. He squanders millions in *The Domain of Arnheim*. One week's diet in *The Narrative of A. Gordon Pym* includes olives, sea-rotted ham, pickled tortoise, barnacles, with a garnishing beloved of the Anthropophagi.

All is vast, abnormal, far-fetched. He scarcely alludes to quiet, delicate and lovely things; the familiarity and homeliness of life he left completely unrecorded. As for his humour, it is all but as revolting as the mesmerized death in life of M. Waldemar. When humour is wedded to horror, we get that atrocity, *A Predicament*. His nebulous characters are moved by hatred, suspicion, remorse, exotic passion. The conscience of 'Arthur Wilson' is retributory and hostile, not the still, if somewhat inaudible, voice that haunts the inward ear of most of his fellow-creatures. Had Poe written these stories only we should have gathered from them but a vague and incomplete knowledge of his personality. Hawthorne we know as intimately from his *Scarlet Letter* as we know Shelley from his *Epipsychidion*. But what precise ghoul, or phantom, is the author of *The Black Cat*, of *The Tell-tale Heart*, of *The Fall of the House of Usher*?

It is in his poems that we learn most of the man himself. Yet even here is evident the curious duality of his mind. He imagines and creates; he analyses and goes very near to destroying. However vigorously we may reject his own critical dicta (so often and so clearly expressed) *in their entirety* or in their extremes, his own practice follows obediently on his own principles. So completely in accord are they that we are tempted to believe that he discovered these principles by an arduous analysis of his own verse. He maintained that poetry has intrinsically nothing to do with truth or morals; that its only office and purpose is to give pleasure; that its only subject-matter is 'beauty'; that its aim is indefinite, and music its chief instrument and delight. He denied that a long poem was even possible. There is little to quarrel with here, so far, at any rate, as lyrical poetry is concerned. But subjected to the too stringent application of this test, the greater part of his contemporaries' verse melted away. Tennyson, Moore, Hood, he considered, remained in much unaffected by it. Longfellow, Emerson, and hosts of

lesser men he laughed out of court. But apply it to *Ulalume,*
The Haunted Palace, Israfel, Lenore, Poe triumphantly survives
the ordeal. Indeed, in one of his many hoaxes of a gullible
public he professed to have evolved his most popular poem, *The*
Raven, from its first emotional conception to its last technical
device of rhyme and metre, on the simple formula of supply
intelligently responding to demand. 'The average man has a
craving for this kind of thing: here it is.' Hoax though it was, it
betrays the analytical bent of his mind tampering with the
creative. In *The Fall of the House of Usher,* however, occurs the
following passage:

'But the fervid *facility* of his *impromptus* could not be so
accounted for. They must have been, and were, in the notes, as
well as in the words of his wild fantasies, the result of that
intense mental collectedness and concentration to which I have
previously alluded as observable only in particular moments of
the highest artificial excitement.'

That (except for the 'artificial') is a good deal nearer a true
account of the actual conditions that have attended the making of
every lyrical poem ever written, including Poe's own. Elaboration is a less instinctive, a more conscious affair. Even here Poe
supplies his own example. *The Bells,* as it was originally published, consisted of nineteen lines; that was its nucleus. Poe, the
craftsman, elaborated it into above a hundred. But he seems
never to have been content with his miracles; they must be
miraculous miracles. Not only must he possess genius, but, like
Aladdin, he must be absolute and conscious master of that
genius. And so he often wasted his rich mind on laborious
trivialities. He wasted time and reputation, too, reiterating
charges of plagiarism against his contemporaries, small and
great.

He had little need to fear. His poems are essentially original
in subject as in style; he alone made, he alone marred them.
The verse has little grace and flexibility of rhythm, and much
too much mere trickery. Even over so restricted a range of subject recurs a flatness of phrase, a deadness of thought in his
poems that casts a doubt on the sincerity of the emotion
that evoked them. Yet, despite salient and vital defects, Poe's
poems are saturated with some mysterious emanation. They
haunt the memory beyond the exorcizing of criticism and scoff-

ing common sense. In every one lurks something of his dark and enigmatic personality, that phantom which never ceased during his life on earth to absorb and to possess him.

It has been recorded by more than one of his biographers that a single glass of wine would suffice to intoxicate him. It is not difficult, by the aid of this one hint regarding his sensationality, to realize how solitary and how beset with the pains of over-sensitiveness such a man must have been. He lived in a world happily inconceivable to the great majority of his fellow-creatures. He not only lived in such a world; with unfaltering vigilance he watched himself, his every thought and action, during his sojourn there. He dissected every emotion, probed every wound, caged every fantasy. He analysed his love of beauty, his ideals; and the analysis endangered all. It is now conventional to talk of environment. Poe's imagination was his chief and his lifelong environment. All else by comparison was faint and immaterial.

America justly, but not always too warmly, claims his genius. He was, however, a man of no time and of no place. He was an Ariel who had hob-a-nobbed—a little too intimately for his own peace—with Caliban. He is himself, in many thin disguises, the acutely living and dominant character in all his stories and poems —himself and that clouded, unearthly, beautiful abstraction called in turn by every seductive name he knew. His heart was in his intellect; and both were keenly engrossed in every remote problem and fantastic theory he invented or encountered. And such a man—arrogant, impulsive, intensely egotistic, passionate, and capricious—Fortune, like the gentle Walton with his frog, used consistently as if she loved him. His father and mother died in his childhood in crippling poverty. In his youth he was pampered and spoiled by a capricious and wealthy foster-father, to be banished in early manhood into the maelstrom of American journalism. What that life of incessant struggle against such odds must have meant for him the author of *The Premature Burial* never deigned to confess.

Yet Poe has survived and triumphed. In his own chosen and definite province of literature few approach him in power or achievement. He squandered ideas which countless men of talent and more than one man of genius have worthily inherited. The skill, the scrupulous patience, and the imaginative reach of the best of his stories are a joy to his fellow-craftsmen. Mr. Guthrie, in a portfolio of beautiful drawings just published so opportunely in view of his centenary, is one more of the many artists who have found in him their impulse and inspiration. Work of vivid imagination is apt to oppress that of its reader. Poe's is vivifying and suggestive. Even if in these illustrations there is little of the extravagance and fantasticalness so conspicuous in his work, and a more serene beauty, they are not the less witness to the power of the poems they enrich. Whether Poe misused or wasted his talents are questions as graceless as they are vain. A passion for moral perfection—we cannot too often remind one another—is nothing but admirable if kept strictly for private use. But the world too gladly plays the cynical valet to its men of genius. The heart knoweth its own bitterness. And although few writers have striven as waywardly as Poe for their own undoing, it is now a matter of little moment that his friend and first biographer vainly endeavoured to bury his fame at the crossroads.

Times Literary Supplement, Jan. 14, 1909

FIONA MACLEOD*

In these seven volumes is contained all that William Sharp considered worth preserving of the work that he wrote and published under the pseudonym of Fiona Macleod. Mrs. Sharp has brought to the task of editing them full understanding and insight, sympathy and pains. By the aid of these and of her Memoir it is now possible to learn all that it was practicable to tell—though not, possibly, all that curiosity might desire to know—concerning an interesting, vigorous, and attractive man and his elusive and extraordinarily diligent 'ghost'. To write a faithful history of one near and dear, with candour and judgment, was not the chief of Mrs. Sharp's many difficulties. Confronted with the task of explaining, even of clearly setting down, the puzzling enigma of what has been called Sharp's 'dual personality', a gift resembling that of the second sight was surely all but indispensable. Pseudonyms are common enough, and are donned and doffed for many purposes. Writers, too, who are blessed with widely diverse gifts are by no means rare. In a world where the sweets of life hardly 'go round', versatility, indeed, is regarded a little askance. But the name, 'Fiona Macleod', was something more than a mask of identity. And the compact she made with her fellow-craftsman was a far less simple arrangement than a mere division of capital. A little dry scepticism is wholesome and excusable in such matters. But even now, over the reader familiar with the close-kept secret of these collaborators still steals the conviction of a wraith-like presence quite other than that of the handsome distinguished-looking man whose face looks out at him from the portraits in this fascinating Memoir. Surely it is a woman's voice we hear in

* *The Works of 'Fiona Macleod'*. Uniform edition. Arranged by Mrs. William Sharp. 7 vols. (Heinemann). *William Sharp* (Fiona Macleod). A Memoir compiled by his wife, Elizabeth A. Sharp (Heinemann).

The Sin Eater, The Washer of the Ford, in *Under the Dark Star,*
a woman with whom we sail these Hebridean seas, through
whose eyes their beauty and glamour become so rarefied and
charged. So keenly aware do we become of this insistent personality that we are willing to take refuge in the formidable
conclusion that William Sharp was truly not one but two, and
that, in a sense, the intangible and invisible companion was the
more definite.

Not only is this the case, but, as Mrs. Sharp points out in her
'Conclusion', a study of Gaelic tales reveals a gradual growth
and development in the mind and genius of Fiona Macleod. The
crudities, extravagance, and formlessness of *Pharais* and *The
Mountain Lovers* give place to serenity and mastery in *The
Divine Adventure.* Moreover, this springtime and harvest are
things different and apart from the gain of skill and form and
interest, in the writings of William Sharp. The efforts of each
collaborator seem in fact to have been chiefly directed to casting
out the traits of thought and expression specifically the other's.
At length it became imperative for the two partners to come to
terms, as it were, with this perplexing ménage, and the reins of
government, Mrs. Sharp tells us, were handed over to (or
rather taken up by) a third and dominant personality that lay
behind those of William and Fiona, and on him the name of
'Wilfion' was bestowed. 'More and more absolutely, in one
sense,' writes this 'Wilfion' in 1897, 'are W.S. and F.M.
becoming two persons—often married in mind and one nature,
but often absolutely distinct. I am filled with a passion of dream
and work.' . . . 'I am going through a new birth,' he adds in a
later letter. Such is the riddle which a close study of Mrs.
Sharp's extremely interesting Memoir elucidates, but does not,
possibly could not, succeed in fully answering.

Three parts Scottish and one Swedish, William Sharp was
born at Paisley in 1855, while the bells were ringing the fall of
Sevastopol. He was the eldest of a family of eight. His childhood was more than usually the best part of what seems to have
been a happy life. He had an old Scottish nurse, Barbara, who
told him haunting stories. Every summer the seas and shores of
the Western Highlands were his playground. Mrs. Sharp tells
us not only how venturesome he was as a child, but how he built
a little altar of stones to the beautiful Presence that is behind the

wind and sunshine. He dreamed by day in the company of tree-spirits, and of all Fiona's countless birds—'linties and shilfas and yellow-yites'—of her canna and bracken and heather, and slept by night in the company of ghosts, without fear. He learned, too, to shut away a visionary self, like some lovely Princess in a cupboard, spared by that Bluebeard called Adult only on condition that she never took her walks abroad. God-desses, too, he became conscious of—a stealthy raising of the eyes, and the vision of a tall woman standing in a mist of hyacinths, a Lady of the Woods, and a twilight 'Star Eyes', familiar to him long after as 'the woman who is in the heart of women'—Baumorair-na-mara. Here, quite clearly, are all the qualities of that rarer self, afterwards to be called Fiona, happy and at ease in the breast of a child, not unlike dozens of children of rare and poetical gifts before him. In boyhood—also by no means an unusual fact in the lives of dreamers—come symptoms of a dual nature not quite so surely at an equilibrium.

With school begins the blunting and the 'sharpening' of the world. Four times 'Willie' ran away, the last time with two school-fellows, one of whom became a venerable dean, the other (less fortunate) a cannibal feast. Later in life this roving and rest-less spirit persuaded him to 'take to the heather', and a whole summer was spent in the company of a wandering tribe of tinkers and gipsies. At nineteen he is studying and reading omnivor-ously twenty hours a day. Then followed rapidly a stool in a lawyer's office, his secret betrothal to his cousin—the writer of this Memoir, his first poem, *A Pantheistic Dream*, celebrating a stolen lovers' meeting in an out-of-the-way churchyard, an anxious illness, a voyage, and another stool, this time in a London bank. A warm friendship with Rossetti brought many friends, among them Watts and Morris, Holman Hunt, Brown-ing and Mathilde Blind, brought too, finally, aided by incom-patibility of temperament, emancipation from his bank and embarkation (with a book of poems and a study of Rossetti for cargo) on the treacherous seas of literature. For a time it was a frigid experience, but at last one desperate morning, when his pockets were empty, and his spirits at their lowest ebb, came a scarcely credible windfall of £240. It enabled him to travel, to complete his art training as a critic, to turn round. In 1884 he published a second volume of poems, and, better yet, married.

Thenceforward, though the pen is not the best of weapons
with which to set off for El Dorado, Sharp led an extremely busy
life, constantly moving from house to house, for ever roving,
making good and constant friends, writing, criticizing, editing
(not only an admirable collection of Sonnets, but *The Young
Folks' Paper*, to which he contributed a series of thrilling stories
of adventure). He wrote anything and everything which chance
and 'the idea' put into his way—Lives of Shelley and of Heine,
a Study of Browning, various novels, all of them mainly con-
sisting of just that 'blood and bones' of literature he was afterwards to scoff at so warmly, when as he wrote to one of his
dearest friends, E. C. Stedman, having taken down the board,
'William Sharp, Literary Manufacturer (All kinds of jobs under-
taken)', he substituted for it 'William Sharp, Given up Business:
Moved to Bohemia. Publishers and Editors need not apply.'
So pent up with energy and lust for 'life' was this 'Viking
in build, Scandinavian in cast of mind, Celt in heart and spirit',
that he had not only planned and published a magazine for the
elect entitled *The Pagan Review*, but under seven different
pseudonyms wrote every page which the first and only number
of it contained.

All these busy, vivid, courageous, and enthusiastic years of
life Mrs. Sharp tells of lucidly and delightfully, and joys in the
telling; mainly by means of diaries, and letters to and from
William Sharp himself. Excellent criticism we get incidentally,
from Meredith, Pater, Rossetti, Henley, Mathilde Blind;
though occasionally this flowing friendly interchange of
reviews with the edge off becomes a little wearisome. Meredith's blade, though, even in the cause of friendship, invariably
cuts clean. 'Always beware of the devilish in art,' he writes.
'It has the obverse of an intellectual meaning.'

Meredith's also is the genial fling at Matthew Arnold's 'very
lofty lift of a super-terrestrial nose over the Godwin nest'.
Pater, in somewhat stilted letters, confesses that 'to my mind
Rossetti is the most significant man among us', and confides to
his friend that 'it is always a sign to me that I have to some
extent succeeded in my literary aim when I gain the approval of
accomplished women'. Henley jubilantly brandishes the scalp of
an indolent *Saturday Reviewer*; Oscar Wilde languidly wishes
he 'could grave his sonnets on an ivory tablet'; Mr. Watts-

Dunton 'doubts if *Aylwin* ever *could* have been written save to dictation', and adds a postscript from Seaford, 'I and Swinburne are getting some excellent bathing.'

Not until 1893, when Sharp was thirty-seven, came the first assured tidings of that other self destined to make his fame. He had paid a long visit to Rome, filled with new hopes and desires, and there met the friend to whom *Pharais* is dedicated, the friend of whom he afterwards said to his wife that 'without her there would have been no Fiona Macleod'. He added, however, 'that development began, in a sense, long before I knew her, and indeed while I was still a child.' This reference to his childhood is full of significance. The influence of a friend, intimately appealing to the imaginative side of his mind, might evoke, it could hardly create, a new personality. The child we have seen, haunted in his solitude by dreams and visions, had, after all, merely been shut up in a cupboard all this time out of sight of the world. Mrs. Sharp relates, moreover, how that from early days her husband would speak of a momentary curious 'dazzle in the brain', preluding some fleeting vision 'of beauty or symbolic import', and how she had sat beside him in a trance and had 'felt all the room throb with heightened vibration'. To friends who knew nothing of Fiona Macleod he was a psychic and mystic. Not without peril had he fished in shadowy waters with Mr. Yeats, and had one night shared with him and Mr. Symons, though all three were at a distance from one another, the same vision in the darkness of Cnoc-na-Hurich of a woman, 'a shadowy archer shooting arrow after arrow against the stars'. Glimpses of 'F.M.' break through even his early Life of Shelley: 'Perhaps this almost fantastic yearning for the unattainable . . . is the heritage of many of us. It is a longing which shall be insatiate even in death.' And another passage tells of a wheeling curlew wildly wailing above Shelley's burning ashes, 'heedless of those who would have driven it away'.

It would seem, therefore, that although that other personality which at last took possession of this busy mind, opening up ever more freely its secret chambers, was dormant during these active and practical years, it sometimes stirred in its sleep. And when at last Sharp arrayed himself in his pseudonym, the mere name became the nucleus round which it swiftly gathered, took shape and form, broke free; it seems at times to have possessed him almost to the exclusion of that far less rare artist, that much more matter-of-fact, terrestrial but vivid and virile being who shared its earthly habitation under the name of William Sharp. They even sent their books to one another—this unprecedented pair; exchanged long letters of drastic criticism, and wrote home of themselves as 'we'. And when Fiona Macleod acknowledges the tributes of her numerous unknown admirers (one of whom proposed marriage) she sometimes mentions, and with an unmistakably feminine touch, her 'cousin' William Sharp, who, on his side, returns the compliment by sending, with letters of unaffected commendation, her successive publications to his friends.

Fantastic and affected though much of this may seem, Sharp paid heavily for the privilege of leading a double life. The advantages are obvious—a renewed zest, privacy, the winning of a wider, certainly of a more fastidious and appreciative, public. Carried away in his natural exuberance at the onset, he could not have foreseen to what extremes Fiona was going to lead him. The severe physical stress of this labour and expense of spirit was revealed at last by more than one serious breakdown in health, and by the real mental risks he became well aware he was running in the service of a divided mind. Yet so much the sacred and scrupulous keeping of his secret came to mean for him that rather than make public acknowledgment of it he surrendered the certainty of a pension on the Civil List, and endangered many a warm friendship.

It is easy to realize how much secret delight and isolation this wraith-like and feminine companionship must have meant, alike in the solitude and in the bustle and business of a literary man's life. It was a sort of tranquil retreat of the mind into which Sharp could retire at will, refresh his fancy, regain a long-lost freedom, and say out, without hesitation, the many unusual and unconventional things he found it in him to say. Any man might well pine for such green pastures. Possibly, indeed, if the gate were left ajar, most imaginative minds would some day discover a Fiona beneath the wild apple-blossom—though a strain of Celticism is probably the only sure introduction to such rare company. Celtic to the finger-tips Fiona Macleod undoubtedly was. Yet she herself once startled the Irish dovecotes, where so many eagles have their eyries, with such a repudiation as 'I, for one, care less to be identified with any movement avowedly partisan. . . . I am somewhat tired of an epithet that, in a certain association, is become jejune, through use and misuse.' This is refreshing and welcome commonsense (a word which, with a touch of irony, she remarked has no Celtic equivalent).

The danger for the critic in this unique case is that of rating a literary achievement too high for reasons other than its essential value and significance. The romance of the situation casts a glamour over its outcome. Sharp, at any rate, was not slow to take advantage of the kind of irresponsibility it conferred. He could write as if he were somebody else. And in the somewhat oppressive prefaces to one or two of 'F.M.'s' books there is an occasional want of balance, a hint of arrogance and overweening. Fiona loved to be a little esoteric, to fill up her sentences with obscure allusions, fine words and names, and snatches of Gaelic. And though the progress of such prose is like that of an army with banners, its final effect upon the reader sometimes resembles the impression left on the mind of the spectator when the army has gone by. In spite of all this, it is with English literature as a whole, 'F.M.' herself maintained, that her poems and tales, simply because her means of expression was English, would have to take their stand and be compared. Only by her original contribution to that will she finally be judged.

In the volume entitled *Poems and Dramas* the poems, we think, are few that positively survive this test. The far-reaching, unstrained, and quiet beauty that is for poetry its vindication and truth is rare. Rare, too, that single effort of the imagination, that punctilious elaboration of the reason, which fuse a poem into a consummate whole. Fiona Macleod's views regarding the 'prose-poem' were sound enough. 'Prose is prose and poetry is poetry. The two arts are distinct, though they may lie so close in method and achievement as to seem to differ only in degree.' In actual practice she often went astray. To a quick and facile fancy the prose-poem is the easiest means of expression. It allows of profusion and vagueness. It makes more demands upon the writer's feelings than upon his thought. It does not insist, as both poetry and prose must insist, on the rigorous necessity of leaving out. And so we find that just as 'F.M.'s' poems are for the most part not quite poetical enough, the earlier stories are a little too much so. They are exaggerated and lavish. Their violence is not strength, but weakness. Words abundantly used for their mystical effect become in reiteration merely conventional counters, not less conventional than the 'gales' and 'rage' and 'swains' of the Augustans. The fantasy, too, of this earlier work is at times as hard and unplastic as realism. It does not seem to have passed through any slow process in the mind, but to be the efflorescence of an impulse, aided apparently by a voluminous note-book.

The later stories are freed from these defects and are admirably restrained. Each definitely fulfils its purpose, each is told with economy, is well-wrought, and closely finished. Their chief fascination is their still and clear atmosphere, as of a dream. Widely and subtly different though the characters may be—Gloom Achanna and the Sin Eater, Silis and Ahèz, Cathal, St. Colum, and the lovely vision of Iosa the Life, and many others—seldom, if at all, does any one of them escape out of the kind of mirage in which they move, into the fresh free air of life. In all the violence and wildness, as in the quiet and solitude, the voices are faint. Saint and peasant and Celtic hero walk, and bodies hang where they have been crucified, in an emerald twilight. The most perfect of these stories is a kind of lyrical reverie. Few there are that are not based on some excess, that do not traverse the borderland of consciousness shared alike by poet and primitive, the one its master, the other its slave. And so we read of the occult, the frenzied, the ominous, the forlorn; we are caught up in 'ecstasy'; return in sorcery back to lives remote; share the long night with the fey and the possessed. To keep the immediate effect of the colour, strangeness, and music of these tales we must not read too long. The nerves soon weary when at stretch, and when, as sometimes happens, the common light of day intrudes the illusion vanishes.

All this bewitched and alluring country lay for more than a score of years forgotten or undiscovered in the mind of its wizard. Inspired by the solitudes of his island seas and steeps, by their old legends and folklore, by their haunted, isolated, fate-ridden inhabitants, he suddenly renewed his life. He threw off the amassed tedium that middle-age sometimes means, and went a-fairing with this wonderful 'comrade'. It became possible for him to pour out his moods and exaltations, to enwrap in a tessellated prose the beauty he desired, the spiritual significance that lies in, and yet beyond, the appearance of things.

'To see things in their beauty is to see them in their truth,' said Matthew Arnold. So, too, Fiona Macleod: 'It is loveliness I seek, not lovely things.' All that she claimed for herself she claimed for all the Celtic peoples:

'This has been given to us, a more ardent longing, a more rapt passion in the things of outward beauty, and in the things of spiritual beauty. Nor, it seems to me, is there any sadness, or only the serene sadness of a great day's end that, to others, we reveal in our best the genius of a race whose farewell is in a tragic lighting of torches around its grave.'

That fascinating 'Celtic' melancholy is 'Fiona Macleod's'. But the other and equally characteristic side of the same temperament—its vivacity and easy charm, exuberance, courage, defiance of circumstance—is not less conspicuous in her self-sacrificing host and collaborator, William Sharp.

Times Literary Supplement, Nov. 17, 1910

P

RUSKIN'S LETTERS*

With one other volume yet to follow, which will include a detailed bibliography and an index of 'something like 100,000 references', these two collections of letters complete the library edition of the works of Ruskin. And even a single glance at the backs of their thirty-five Brobdingnagian comrades calls instantly to mind the rather repellent word monumental. 'We come to bury Caesar, not to praise him,' they seem to insinuate. And it may well prove that some young mind which is now bent on tadpoles or daisy-chains may faint a little, twenty years hence, at its first confrontation with the complete works of the wizard who took all nature for his hobby. But we may be sure that out of the womb of this thirty-eight-volumed behemoth will spring an innumerable progeny suitable to every age and circumstance. No monument of stone or paper, criticism, or scholarship will ever crush to the dust the heart of one who exulted in all things beautiful—from the earliest days of childhood, when in his mother's garden at Herne Hill he stood entranced before the clustered lamps, ruby and amber, of the currant bushes, to those of extreme age, when, no less a child in spirit, he could write with untroubled joy to his 'dearest Susie' of the Alpine cyclamen and the craft of a woodcock's bill.

Through all these seventy years of ceaseless effort, until he surrendered his arms for a peace he ever longed for—but disdained, until destiny commanded it, to accept—Ruskin never for an instant let his standard trail in the dust. Few minds of much account in the last half century but acknowledge an immense debt to this unflinching knight errant. *Don Quixote* he rebelled against as a romance—for the reason that it may have brought into contempt, in the minds of the many Sancho Panzas of the

* *The Works of John Ruskin*. Library edition. Vols. xxxvi. and xxxvii. Edited by E. T. Cook and Alexander Wedderburn (George Allen).

world, all great and forlorn causes because the sorrowful knight's were those of phantasy. It is the Don Quixote, none the less, in Ruskin that will catch men's hearts and enthusiasm. Dully and witlessly we have all scrawled that old inexorable maxim in tear-blotted copy-books, 'It is human to err'. A little knowledge of life gilds its triteness. And in spite of Ruskin's half-jesting, half-serious repudiation of the affection that was poured out on him instead of the intelligent *attention* at which he aimed, it is in part because of his wilful humanity that we do attend so eagerly to his work. To the absorbed, assiduous intellect, to the patient and almost impeccable automatism of mind that selflessly sifts and classifies, peers and experiments, humanity owes the tremendous advance of a Science that makes certain of the smallest fraction of an inch in one generation, in sure and certain hope of the ell of an aeon. But to Ruskin, however real and various was the actual accomplishment of 'the most analytic mind in Europe', the majority of his readers owe what is at least as valuable, the clearer eye, the keener delight, the braver heart, that are the best comrades of a man in any and every chance of life.

Throughout the whole of the preceding volumes of this splendid edition there is, of course, scarcely a chapter, even a paragraph, that does not reflect Ruskin's pervasive personality. It was almost impossible for him to state the simplest fact without clothing it with all the provocations, the capriciousness, and the intense individuality of his style. To this in part is due the fanaticism of friend and foe alike. It is easy to accept, to combat, or to ignore a frigid statement of opinion or conviction when the pen that composed it is dipped in the ichor of pure reason; but Ruskin's ink was his life blood. He could only with the utmost difficulty be dispassionate; and even then the effort burns through his prose. He detested the lukewarm. His superb powers of mind and of language were merely the faithful servants of his aspirations and ideals. Every fragment of hard-won learning and bitterly-gained experience went to enrich and enforce the message which he believed, in spite of contempt and hostility—even his own—it was the sole aim and intention of his life to deliver to a darkened and deafened world. And throughout the twelve hundred pages of these letters there can be scarcely one that entirely fails to bring this home to us.

To write a letter that will outlive both sender and recipient is a fairy godmother's gift rather than an art. It comes of genius more often than of talent. It must be familiar yet not too lax. The least conscious hint in the writer's mind of a wider target imperils its charm and much of its appeal. Sincerity it must have, even if it be only sincere in its want of candour. And it must, unless the priceless odd little scribble be a Marjorie Fleming's, come out of a sustained though not, maybe, a wide experience. All else it may have—every quality and tone and turn, opulence and eccentricity of literature, the most far-fetched or the most ordinary of subject-matter, the meanest, oddest or rarest of characters to make manifest—so long as it still remains personal, arresting and human.

If these are some of its chief and necessary ingredients and conditions, then Ruskin easily enters the rather scanty ranks of the great English letter-writers. And it is our lasting good fortune that he scattered and squandered through a long life letters in almost every conceivable mood, on every conceivable topic, with an inimitable mastery of language, out of the undisguisable sincerity of his heart—and these addressed everywhere and to almost everybody. From 'My dear Prince,—I venture to write thus to you', and 'My dear Mr. Rogers,—I only returned to town on Monday, and to wait on you tomorrow will be the first, as it is always the happiest, of my duties,' to 'Darling Charles, —What a venomous old infidel you are!' and 'My precious little May,—If you *were* but here instead of March', the letters range through every degree of friendship, through every degree of formality. Bubbling over with the humour he proudly professed himself to be 'eminently deficient in'; withering with the scorn the most listless of his readers must know so well; arrogant, dictatorial, exquisitely lucid, madly fantastic, packed with wisdom, counsel, and understanding; quietly tender and simple, and broken with sorrow, there is nothing quite like them. 'You had no intention of being to me like a dose of arsenic or of strychnine,' he reassures an author modestly presenting his literary offspring. 'Oh my Susie, what is to become of me in the next world?' he cries, when he is 61, to his dear old friend and neighbour, Miss Beever, of 74, to whom five years before he had sent 'a crystal, and a little bit of native gold, and a little bit of native silver', because, in the old joke between them, 'today you enter upon your "teens".' When the truth bids he joyfully contradicts himself; 'Every man does his best things easiest,' he repeats again and again, and yet spends hours in imploring Kate Greenaway to study perspective and to paint feet, legs, arms, and hands bare. 'Finished the rats, have you! But you ought to do dozens of rats with undulating tails'; 'Oh dear, think how happy you are, with all that power of drawing, and ages to come to work in, to paint Floras and Norahs and Fairies and Marys and Goddesses and—bodices. Oh me, when *will* you do one without any?' He is simple and loving, and never condescending to children, tender to the aged, merciless to a fool, perfectly candid to the pretentious and the false.

He hits straight from the shoulder, when he must, friend or enemy; sometimes for two Olympian pages he storms, with only the merest crumb of comfort in a friendly postscript—'Sheer blurting out is best.' His frankness spares no man. 'I don't say you do wrong,' he tells Rossetti, 'because you don't seem to know what *is* wrong, but just to do whatever you like as far as possible—as puppies and tomtits do.' 'The two terrific mistakes which you and Mama made', he confides to his father, and 'I am an incomparably nobler and worthier person, now, when you disapprove of nearly all I say and do than when I was everything you and my mother desired me.' 'My dear M——,' he writes to Miss Gladstone, 'I find it will be quite impossible for me to come to Hawarden this autumn. . . . The chief of all reasons being . . . that, in my present state of illness, nearly every word anybody says, if I care for them, either grieves or astonishes me to a degree which puts me off my sleep and off my work and off my meat.' Himself he spares less than any man: 'I've had my heart broken ages ago, when I was a boy, then mended, cracked, beaten in, kicked about old corridors, and finally, I think, flattened fairly out. . . . I suppose everything I have chosen to have been about as wrong as wrong can be.'

Even when he is gravest, most desperate and sorrowful, there peeps out that wistful humorousness which springs from the depths of gravity and sorrow: 'If grief would only let one's stomach alone I could manage the heart well enough.' 'I begin to think nobody can be a great painter who isn't rather wicked—in a noble sort of way.' 'If I could make a toad of myself and get into a hole in a stone and be quiet I think it would do me good.' And he tells Norton in 1860 that the only relief he has, his sole alternative to choking from his 'disgust and fury at the way the mob is going on (meaning by mob chiefly dukes, Crown Princes, and such like persons)' is to go to the British Museum and look at penguins till he gets cool. 'One can't be angry when one looks at a penguin.'

His judgments and criticism leap delightfully from Pole to Pole. 'Your sister should exercise herself in the severest commonplace of metre until she can write as the public like. Then if she puts in her observation and passion all will become precious. But she must have the Form first.' So he writes regarding Christina Rossetti's unexcelled sense of verbal rhythm! But, 'Atalanta, the grandest thing ever done by a youth', goes far to redeeming such a slip. 'I think Aurora Leigh', he assures Robert Browning—and not Robert Browning only—'the greatest *poem* in the English language . . . *not* surpassed by Shakespeare's *Sonnets*.' 'Read poetry as prose to find its merit' seems rather a dangerous deliverance, but he forthwith puts the method into practice by taking some of his own early verses and scornfully rending them to tatters for the rather doubtful entertainment of a doting parent!

Not too much stress, as Mr. Cook warns us, in this, the last of his invaluable series of introductions, must be laid on what is written in haste to a friend, and can never be amended or recalled. But however whimsical Ruskin may be, however gaily the needle veers, due north was his daydream. And one may be forgiven for quoting what may seem light and trivial things in the belief that these, too, can reveal character and personality as delicately as the stormy eloquence, the matchless beauty, the enthusiasm, irony, and indignation that are almost as conspicuous in these pages as in the most characteristic of Ruskin's work. Perhaps of all these letters none shows us the author of *Modern Painters* so clearly as those addressed to his father. There is a sobriety, a nearness, a tenderness, a bitterness in them which no extract could reveal. To read quietly straight through the two formidable volumes, page by page, is at the conclusion to become aware of, and in part to understand and appreciate a man whom, maybe, one begins by indiscriminately admiring, by rebelling against, or even, in the supremacy of one's egotism, by ridiculing; and whom one ends by loving as very few men can be loved—with a mind as gifted, a temperament as fitful, and a life as noble as his.

Step by step we watch that life advancing, from the brooding, self-conscious little boy of eight to the shy, vain, zealous, and tempestuous despot of middle age. Steadily, almost without being aware of it, he follows where he thought to lead, discarding one by one every belief or judgment that is no longer true for him; confessing his pride proudly; childishly acting the man; carrying along his own insistent solitude with him wherever he goes. Simpler and simpler the letters get, in thought and style. The 'thunder answering to thunder' of his eloquence gradually dies down; and a pale gold sunshine leans across the rain-sweetened air upon the towering and stormy bastions sinking in the East. Defeat, disappointment, utter desolation of mind and weakness of body—those hunting dogs that follow on every lonely track—waylay and pester him. Sorrow brings its peace; love its renunciation. There are few things in books so likely to trouble the reader's heart as Ruskin's record of his severe illnesses in 1878 and 1881:

'But both these illnesses have been part of one and the same system of constant thought, far out of sight to the people about me, and, of course, getting more and more separated from them as *they* go on in the ways of the modern world, and *I* go *back* to live with my Father and my Mother and my Nurse, and one more—all waiting for me in the Land of the Leal.'

Few things are likelier to rouse him than the eager docility, the courtesy and patience, and the fine surrender in the correspondence between this aged and tired-out Galahad and the young squire of science, then Professor Oliver Lodge.

As with the greatest so with the least of men—each goes his own narrow way, however vociferous of applause or of contempt the phantom spectators of this world may be; however urgent the viewless witnesses of another. A man takes up his candle, and in its clear but baffling light must push his way through the darkness of life's corridor past every hindrance, stopping his ears as best he can against fear and the conflicting voices, towards the glimmer of the window at the far end, only to stand at last confronting in the dark glass, against the deeper darkness of the night without, his own weary and haunted face;

bravely aware that even the candle that has been his guide and comrade must be extinguished before he can see beyond—such, out of their courage and energy, out of their final peace, is one of the after-thoughts these letters seem to suggest.

Times Literary Supplement, March 18, 1909

PORTRAITS AND SKETCHES*

Since the value of any literary portrait depends upon the artist, an insistency on certain features is essential—those which appeal most strongly to his mind, affection, and imagination. Whether instinctively or consciously, he selects. He may idealize or he may caricature, but in any case he emphasizes. A mere glance at Mr. Gosse's index will reveal his most enviable good fortune in the choice and variety of his subjects. There are thirteen portraits and sketches; among them, those of Swinburne, Aubrey de Vere, Whittier, Mandell Creighton, Shorthouse, Lang, André Gide, and Eugène Melchior de Vogüé, the very syllables of whose name should suffice for the inspiration of a bouquet of sonnets. Many of these familiar names recall to Mr. Gosse a long and intimate friendship, numberless salient and happy memories; the rest of them bring back to mind 'flashing glimpses' and an occasional talk. With one and all, the contact was direct and personal. Twentieth-century biography, as Mr. Gosse remarks in his preface, is too often the record of a distinguished man under the observation of 'his most cautious relatives'. It is all to the good, then, if in one case a published estimate 'too pre-eminently ecclesiastical' is here refreshed by a livelier and more secular touch. As regards the author of *John Inglesant*, on the other hand, what Mr. Gosse considers 'an actually false impression of a very singular person' has been corrected—but without the slightest diminution of singularity.

As in this private view, then, there is no portrait without intrinsic and peculiar interest, so too it is all clearly and delightfully 'one man's show'. A keen and sedulous eye, a sensitive consciousness, a supple hand have been put to its service. And although Mr. Gosse is never so gay and pungent as when he is recording in his sitter some queer little twist or bizarrerie, some ingratiating foible—and playing upon him a humour, acid or

---

* *Portraits and Sketches*. By Edmund Gosse (Heinemann).

217

tender but never malignant or sentimental—a sound judgment and the warmest admiration keep the result from belittlement or the grotesque. 'La cinématographie d'une abeille dans le mystère de la mellification', that is what Mr. Gosse likes best in literary biography, and that is what his reader who is not less interested in bee than honey will watch engrossed in these pages.

Not entirely so, for cinematography is the handiwork of an agent far too callously truthful even in its wildest effrontery of deception to be human. And a portrait is not a photograph. Upon many of Mr. Gosse's memories time has spent its faint and magic gilding. They have been left to ripen and clarify, to lose the raw flavour of the notebook. The best of them, or at least the warmest and most vivid, go back to the seventies and eighties. Youth is the hotbed of enthusiasm, though its causes, like its fashions, vary with the years. In those blissful days poets and painters might hope 'for honours which were private indeed, and strictly limited, but almost divine'. Fresh to the azure, Mr. Gosse was then bestriding a coltish Pegasus. With impassioned eyes he saw the high gods through a flattering mist of shyness, rapture, and curiosity, and the lesser gods with not less ecstatic curiosity, though more at his ease.

In the summer of 1871, for instance, in the long First Sculpture Gallery at the British Museum, he first bowed the knee to Tennyson. All day long he had himself been 'palely baking, like a crumpet, in a singularly horrible underground cage, made of steel bars, called "the Den", a den scented with rotten morocco and an indescribable odour familiar in foreign barracks, when down came dashing long-bearded, six-feet-six W. R. S. Ralston —reporting lions. "Come upstairs at once and be presented to Mr. Tennyson!"' With pounding heart and brain in a whirl Mr. Gosse vehemently obeyed—and there, singularly majestic in repose, stood that magnificent presence, bare-headed among the Roman Emperors, the 'God of the Golden Bow'. Only one slow, deep-voiced remark Mr. Gosse has retained of a conversation in which the poet (while Ralston kept off Spedding) was 'vaguely gracious' about his devotee's own 'stammering verses'. They had paused before the black bust of Antinous: 'Ah! this is the inscrutable Bithynian!' There was a pause, and then he added, gazing into the eyes of the bust: 'If we knew what he knew, we should understand the ancient world!' Soon after, the gates of heaven were closed, and Mr. Gosse returned down three flights of stairs to his hell of rotten morocco.

But Tennyson was then in his sixties. Swinburne was only a little over thirty when—four years after *Poems and Ballads* had crashed about (a literary) Mrs. Grundy's ears—Mr. Gosse first made his acquaintance. 'Algernon', wrote his hostess on the occasion, 'took to you at once, as is seldom the case with him', for he was 'constitutionally unfitted to shine in mixed society'. By 1873 acquaintance had ripened into intimacy. And the result for us is a portrait of endless detail and vivacity—a Swinburne that was 'not merely a poet, but a flag; and not merely a flag, but the Red Flag incarnate'. The orange ruddy hair (never better displayed than when he sat, wrapped up in his nakedness in a spare sail, after being hauled half-drowned out of the sea at Etretat, and declaimed to his horny-handed rescuers the doctrines of the Republic and the poems of Victor Hugo)—that fan of hair, those marvellous eyes, the shoulders so narrow they hardly outledged his prodigious head, the thistledown body, almost as immaterial as that of a fairy, the spasmodic action of arms and legs, the untirable agility, the moods of wildest excitement and rhapsody, of trance-like dejection; his gentleness, noble-mindedness, and dauntless courage—Mr. Gosse celebrates them all and once for all, with the gayest of stories and an unbounded appreciation for a setting. For example:

'He required very little sleep, and occasionally when I have parted from him in the evening after saying "Good-night," he has simply sat back in the deep sofa in his sitting-room, his little feet close together, his arms against his side, folded in his frock-coat, like a grasshopper in its wing-covers, and fallen asleep, apparently for the night, before I could blow out the candles and steal forth from the door.'

But of Swinburne and Tennyson posterity will have ample evidence. Lang, Mandell Creighton, Aubrey de Vere, were friends of Mr. Gosse's maturity; and of them, as of Shorthouse, Carl Snoilsky, and the rest, Mr. Gosse writes with as sound a judgment and as genuine a regard, but rather more critically and with less scintillating zest. For this reason in part, and because also two other of his portraits depict men 'of one book', and that book in ever-deepening danger of oblivion, many of his readers will best enjoy his festive and exhilarating pages on

Philip James Bailey and 'Orion' Horne. Horne, like the author of *Festus*, somehow missed his chance of dying young. His honey has now lost its virgin sweetness, but he still makes a most exciting bee. When Mr. Gosse first set eyes on him he was a little curly, white-poodleish, fat, tiny old gentleman, and he was seated on the floor at a Pre-Raphaelite wedding feast, trolling out, in a 'funny little cracked voice, Spanish songs to his own accompaniment on the guitar'. From this humiliating pose and from the ribaldry of his audience Robert Browning rescued him. His whole life was like 'a book for boys'—as romantic in his telling of it as it was independent of brute fact. He had bathed in Niagara at the expense of two broken ribs, had tramped in moccasins from the St. Lawrence to Halifax, and earned the captain's tearful and eternal gratitude by quelling a mutiny that broke out on board a timber ship in mid-Atlantic. But that is all nothing compared with the fact that as he 'came bounding out of school' one winter afternoon he espied a young man sunken deep in reverie, beside the chaise of a Mr. Hammond, the local surgeon. The temptation was too savoury. He threw a snowball at him and hit him on the back of his head. And that young man was Keats. Such, and much else, was Horne's tribute to life. His gift to literature was *Orion*. This epic was first published priced a farthing; and Elizabeth Barrett ordered (but was refused) a shillingsworth. Carlyle, Mr. Gosse tells us—and Carlyle after his own brief activities in rhyme was kind to few poets under six feet tall 'and broad to match'—Carlyle declared that 'the fire of the stars was in him'. But by the time Horne's crafty publishers had steadily raised the price of *Orion* to seven shillings, that constellation was dipping towards the west, the goal of how many never-returning poetical stars! Lost reputations need extort no more tears than spilt milk. After all, Horne's flower blossomed before it withered, and full many a flower is born to blush unseen. Mr. Gosse has rescued those 'milky ringlets' a while from the clutch of destiny. His *Portraits and Sketches* indeed will inspire one particular joy and only one regretful reflection in his reader—the joy that Mr. Gosse has met so many poets to such an account, the regret that there were not, in the sterile nature of things, more poets for Mr. Gosse to meet.

Times Literary Supplement, Oct. 31, 1912

SHELLEY'S TRELAWNY*

Two books of an unusual kind stand in the name of Trelawny, *The Adventures of a Younger Son* and *Records of Shelley, Byron, and the Author*. They are in their own fashion books that are deeds. Trelawny was first and last a man of venture, impulse, and action, but unlike most such men, he had an extraordinarily vivid (though erratic) gift of writing. He lived and did as he pleased, wrote and spelt as he pleased, and out of his books and out of these letters steps a man like a masterly character in a masterly play. He seems to have cared as little for what the world thought of him as for what the world knew of him. And though there are many such things in this volume as few men usually care to share with all comers, it is very doubtful if Trelawny's shade in the Elysian Fields will much lament their publication. It is true that he did once caution his chief correspondent, Claire Clairmont, Shelley's and Mary's honeymoon companion and the mother of Allegra, to see to it that a certain exchange of views should not see the light. But 'she did not see to it,' says Mr. Buxton Forman. And it is now a good many years ago since with enterprise and alacrity he paid down Miss Paolo Clairmont's price for Trelawny's letters, and 'brought them home with joy' to add to his collection of biographical miscellanea regarding that Pisan circle 'which is not one to be soon forgotten'. The anthropophagous reading public does not inquire too closely about its contents so long as the literary pie is sapid and eats 'short'. And for all, at any rate, who have an insatiable appetite for anything and everything that concerns Shelley, or Shelley's 'set', this volume will prove as entertaining as it is indispensable.

---

* *Letters of Edward John Trelawny*. Edited, with a brief introduction and notes, by H. Buxton Forman, C.B. (Henry Frowde).

Mr. Buxton Forman is an admirable editor. He knows to the last iota everything there is to be known about Shelley and Keats. He is crisp, exact, and punctilious in all such things as dates, notes, and appendices. He deftly steers his way through the shoals of such a question as that of Trelawny's imaginative veracity, and would not graciously permit any 'outsider', we hope, to indulge in his own witticism about 'roast poet'. This being a book not for the general but for the particular reader, voluminous biographical notes and explanations were scarcely necessary; though concerning one thing in its preparation many readers, we think, will share our regret. We cannot help being sorry that Mr. Forman has considered it incumbent on him to touch up Trelawny's spelling and construction, and, if we understand him aright, now and again to correct his facts. Seeing that he has left undisturbed such fascinating wild-fowl as 'missel' (? missal, missile, or missive), 'scrool', 'arrivising', 'rendazous', is it possible not to hanker after more of a like feather?

The headlong candour and directness of these letters are their rarest qualities. Few men of note, very few literary men, even in their most intimate correspondence, long forget that they are in part public property. Trelawny, although he was a man out of the common ruck, and knew it, when he sat down to write a letter wrote it from beginning to end without blotting a line. He never even read his letters over. 'If I did, I could do no better—and should only be dissatisfied.' Without care or caution, the slave of the vivid moment, he poured out his mood. Partly because of this, partly because Trelawny was Trelawny, there is extremely little 'niceness' or fine writing in these pages, no cant (unless it be the cant of outspokenness), very little sentiment or reflection. He hardly ever improves the occasion, and if he preaches at all, his sermon, like the traditional sermon of Herrick's, takes the form of a missile flung at the head of a congregation of one. He was a man of immense bodily vigour and vitality—one of that very various class, the typical Englishman. Like all the best letter-writers, he loved to compare notes on life, to get at the real things, and so he loved to talk about himself. When nearly eighty he gives more than one correspondent, and the same correspondent more than once, an account of his day's round. He tells of his morning ice-cold bath, of his dinner at one, of his favourite drink—light home-brewed and small claret, of the fruit and trash he lives on as of old, of his four pipes per diem of rarest latakia 'bacce'. 'Old and grizzled', prowling at last in ever-narrowing circles nearer his den, he still exults in life, sound in wind and limb, with senses clear, joints flexible, memory intact, and energy undiminished, to the end possessed with Shelley's mania for water, to the end a scorner of great-coats and underwool, weighing still the stones he weighed when he was thirty-nine, a lover, if not exactly of humanity, at least of horses and dogs. And yet, 'I have lived quite long enough,' he goes off at a tangent; 'and am quite ready to be extinguished'; 'nothing's worth much after thirty.' Age is indolent and procrastinating—hope extinguished—so are our wants: for what is life?—an intermittent fever, hot and cold fits in a world of fools and mad people; a Donkey Sweepstakes—and we are all in the race; living and dying like other animals, to be replaced again and again—'When will the cant and humbug of these costermonger times be reformed?' It was just this medley, this passion for life, and carelessness of it, this lifelong revolt against its shackles which embarked him in his youth on a privateer, despatched him in an old tub to Greece with Lord Byron, and when he was little beyond that critical 'thirty' inspired him not only to purchase a grave beside Shelley's, but to ask Claire and Leigh Hunt for an appropriate epitaph, and to offer Mary Shelley the privilege of sleeping on the other side.

It is difficult, and Mr. Buxton Forman does not help us, to discover to what exact extent Trelawny was married. Tell-tale names and children are dotted about. He offered his hand and heart to Mary Shelley, and never ceased to resent her refusal. 'Purse and person' seem to have been absolutely at the disposal of any lady in distress who needed them. He execrated that vampire, Poverty, yet generosity kept him ever bewailing his want of funds. But so far as these letters tell us, it was Claire Clairmont who most severely and for more than fifty years enslaved his affections, stirred his rapture, and tried his patience.

'You! You! Torture me Clare—your cold, cruel, heartless letter has driven me mad—it is ungenerous under the mask of love to enact the part of a demon.' 'And can you, Clare, resign me and my hopes—can you leave me for the gelid north?'

'Dear Claire,—Why will you not dedicate one spare hour

to me? . . . I consider you very fish-like—bloodless—and in-sensible—you are the counterpart of Werter—a sort of bread, butter, and worsted stockings—like Charlotte fit for "suckling fools and chronicling small beer". Adieu, old Aunt.'

And again nine years after:

'Clare, hollo!—do you hear? Are you alive, or, indeed, trans-formed into a tree girdled round by the axe—leafless, lifeless—my dropping gall into your milk was not in wantonness—but to make you into something better than a dish of skimmed stuff—have you not lived long enough in your present way of life to prove that it was never intended for a being gifted with soul or sense—when all around is dismal—damp and devilish—and the ground sounds hollow under our feet—is it not time to move? Well, then, will you come live at Putney?'

A candour that he allowed to play over himself so freely was scarcely likely to spare his friends. Mary becomes at last 'the blab of blabs, who lives on hog's wash, writing mawkish cant, namby-pamby stuff—as different from her real character as Hell is from Helicon'. Byron, who shared with Hunt and Trelawny that amazingly told experience on the desolate beach near Via Reggio—Byron he grew to detest more and more as life went on. 'It is well for his name and better for Greece that he is dead,' he could write—not many weeks after Tennyson had spent a dramatic half-hour confiding his grief to a beech-tree. Could he, indeed, easily forgive 'the world's greatest man', who, when it came to a question of helping Mary with money, remarked concerning his connexion with Shelley that he had 'let himself down to the level of the democrats'?

Shelley, for whom Trelawny 'designed the treacherous bark which proved his coffin', Shelley, and no other, is the idol, the lode-star of these letters. Trelawny never weaied of lamenting and praising, of quoting, vindicating, and fighting for that 'lorn and outraged poet', for those few months of 1822 his 'noble friend'.

Saturday Westminster Gazette, Dec. 31, 1910

JOHN D. ROCKEFELLER'S REMINISCENCES*

To a reader with the faintest memory of his childhood's delight in a fairy-tale still lingering unquenched in his elderly fancy the title of this book suggests treasure trove indeed. Here is the record of an unparalleled prince among men, if ever wealth can confer distinction. Here are the reminiscences of a plutocrat who could bestow 'second-best beds' of purple and ivory on a hundred times as ample a household as the wisest of mankind enjoyed at his zenith; who could commission a Caesar, outbuild a Kubla Khan, carry off for residential gate-posts North and South Poles, buy up all the world's lollipops, 'have an egg with his tea' every day of his life, and still have sufficient greenbacks in his old stocking to purchase a comfortable annuity for a respected and enviable old age; a Nabob who could quell the North Sea with oil-bunkered Dreadnoughts; could even make temporarily happy every one of the 'loyal' 60,000 *employés* of the most gigantic Trust the world (we hope) will ever see; and his poor little volume no more resembles Sindbad or Aladdin than these old dreams a tract. Things there are, one is driven to confess, past the purchase even by a billionaire.

It is a real disappointment; for although, perhaps, with that shadowy knowledge which we already possess of its author it would have been ungracious to look to his volume for the more precious or the lighter graces of literature, yet it was merely reasonable to expect a convincing apology for the art and science of indiscriminate money-making, a rousing 'Veni, vidi, vici!'— something racy and cute and pre-eminently Transatlantic. All that is actually given us is a groping and rather dull account of a few commonplace business transactions, a few as commonplace

* *Random Reminiscences of Men and Events.* By John D. Rockefeller (Heinemann).

225

Q

associates. As for character and personality, if, as one is never tired of quoting, style is the very man, then so far as this author is concerned, we must pity while we shun. What Imp of the Perverse, the reader asks in vain, could have enticed Mr. Rockefeller to don this sackcloth and to chatter amid these ashes? One thing, and one thing only, shines in these chapters—an inimitable naïveté. Simple Simon is a German philosopher by comparison. Here is a man revered, or at any rate envied, by the children of Mammon all the world over; he has ventured to appear as he would like to appear before the narrow and retired world of literature, the world that has for its boon companions Montaigne and Lamb, Rousseau and Gibbon and Cellini; Pascal and Traherne; Penn, Emerson, and Hawthorne; and he is to be distinctly observed actively using the same primitive methods, the same astute and trivial persuasions that sell oil and 'push business'.

'For myself', Mr. Rockefeller confesses in his preface, 'I had decided to say nothing, hoping that after my death truth would gradually come to the surface, and posterity would do strict justice.' Mr. Rockefeller is not the only frail human being who prefers an autopsy to vivisection, and the inaudible judgment of posterity to that of the American Press. And of course mercy is rather a crude term. But when we turn these pages to enjoy his self-effacement and a gallant vindication of his partners and subordinates, it is at least discreet so far as the latter are concerned. 'That some of these *employés* were over-zealous in going after sales, it would not be surprising to learn, but they were acting in violation of the expressed and known wishes of the Company.' It is not surprising. Of the few associates whom Mr. Rockefeller finds space to mention by name, perhaps the most representative, certainly the most taking, is 'that bright and active young fellow, full of vim and push, Mr. H. M. Flagler', who 'drew practically all our contracts'. He had such simple faith in his fellow-creatures that he accepted the phrase, 'the line runs South to a mullen stalk,' in a contract drawn up by the unsophisticated proprietor of the land on which 'one of our refineries was built. . . . "It's all right, John, I'll accept that contract; and when the deed comes in, you will see that the mullen stalk will be replaced by a proper stake."' It is the most inspiriting episode in the volume. This, too, is the Mr. Flagler who 'got on his conscience' a certain little German 'baker man', desirous of selling a small plant, which Mr. Flagler 'felt sure would not succeed'. I like the walrus best, said Alice, because, you see, he was a little sorry for the poor oysters.

But, indeed, in spite of the author's intention to say nothing for himself, his reminiscences are little else than rambling and colourless gossip around his own extraordinary personality. An uneasy fame seems to haunt him. He tries manfully to be the great historical figure, the Oil King. But all we actually succeed in seeing is a kind of drab little mole-like creature, scuttling helter-skelter out of the searching rays of day, with a more than Boer-like skill for taking cover. He gives us a glimpse of his father, who loaned him a legacy of $1,000 at the age of 17 at ten per cent interest, and as a spiritual tonic demanded it again when the boy most needed it. 'My son, I want that money back,' was his almost Biblical request. His mother just appears, who midway in the thrashing of the budding millionaire with a birch-switch for some unfortunate doings of which he proved in his roarings that he was innocent, remarked good-humouredly, 'Never mind, we have started in on this whipping, and it will do for next time.' If only one could be even partially certain that this procedure applies to one's whole earthly existence! Both of Mr. Rockefeller's parents were martinets, it seems. 'How many different kinds of friends there are!' is one of the author's *bon-mots*.

Far from any self-glorification, he himself casts the whole burden of the Trust's triumph on other shoulders. He repeatedly disclaims any but the littlest of fingers in the pie. All the long spoons came uninvited. He merely lives, he avers, like an old 'farmer', with a hobby for 'views that invite the soul', and for transporting full-sized forest trees from one of his estates to another, on a scrupulous profit-and-loss basis. He jogs on and on, washing his hands of horrid scandals by the way—poor Mrs. Backus's refineries; the rail-road rebate system. 'I well remember a bright man from Boston,' he tells us. He delivered himself of the conviction, 'I am opposed on principle to the whole system of rebates and drawbacks—unless I am in it.'

He is most generous of counsel, and that of the most excellent sentiments. 'I know of nothing more despicable and pathetic than a man who devotes all the working hours of the day to making money for money's sake.' 'From my earliest youth, as my successes began to come, I have seldom put my head on the pillow at night without speaking a few words to myself in this wise, "Now a little success, soon you will fall down, soon you will be overthrown. Because you have got a start you think you are quite a merchant; look out, or you will lose your head—go steady."' Once upon a time, of course, this being quite a merchant by no means precluded the possibility of losing one's head, even though that merchant were a student of the Emperor Marcus Aurelius. Of his heart the author makes no mention.

As for the Standard Oil Company, Mr. Rockefeller is satisfied that it is a national benefactor. Does it not pour every week of the year into the coffers of its shareholders from foreign parts alone 'a million dollars gold', leaving behind it just such hire as the labourer is worthy of, 'no less, but no more'? Its standards of business are not only beyond reproach, but 'getting better all the time'. 'It has never crushed out a competitor who adequately cultivated his field of operations.' But the adequately remains undefined. 'It is a most happy association of busy people.' 'It pays its workmen well, it cares for them when sick, and pensions them when old.'

Blow, blow, thou winter wind;
Thou are not so unkind
As man's ingratitude!

we seem to hear this Trust-Maker murmuring, looking doubtfully in the direction of his 58,000 or more *employés*.

Even at the confessed risk of immodesty Mr. Rockefeller devotes two whole chapters of his very meagre seven to the subject of his charities, and heads it characteristically 'The Benevolent Trust—The Value of the Co-operative Principle in Giving'.

This Trust, we gather, expends annually the sum of about £500,000 in benefactions, and is aided by doctors, clergymen, lawyers, as well as many 'high-grade men of affairs'. Without danger of looking a gift-horse too closely in the mouth, it may be remarked that Mr. Rockefeller's wealth is now popularly reputed to amount to anything between 60 and 100 millions sterling. These royal charities, therefore, reduce his income to a total of anything between three and ten million pounds. We have not space to recapitulate his arguments proving that the State would be no better custodian of his wealth than himself. Hard things have been said in all ages against the devotee of riches; but for Mr. Rockefeller himself Fate has oddly enough reserved the privilege of saying the hardest and the worst, in this tawdry and charmless little book. To the enemies of Trusts it should prove Excalibur itself.

Times Literary Supplement, June 3, 1909

'WITHOUT MISGIVING'*

'**M**rs. Meynell's Papers are little sermons, ideal sermons,' said Meredith, writing of one of the small volumes which have gone to the making of this collection of *Essays*. He could fancy Matthew Arnold being refreshed by their profound limpidity, Carlyle listening with no weariful gesture to his wife's reading of them: 'This woman thinks.' What names, what touchstones would Meredith's fancy have lighted on today to enforce a renewed and intensified appreciation? It is difficult, indeed, to realize that these Essays, which only the other day, it would seem, one avidly awaited every Wednesday in the columns of the *Pall Mall Gazette*, take us back so far. None of their distinction and individuality has faded under the furtive influence of time. Their wisdom is independent of fashion and ways of thought. Their delicacy—scrupulousness, balance, fineness, skill—is as rare in life and in art as ever it was. A flood of turbid water has flowed under the bridge since Meredith's fancy extorted that characteristic exclamation from Carlyle, and yet how easy it would be to echo it now. And, as Mrs. Meynell herself comments on a Sultanic passage in the *Mahabharata*, 'Nothing but extreme feminine lowliness can well reply . . . to this Hindu profession of masculine reverence.'

Feminine lowliness, however—pensive, seductive duplicity—is no more the mark of Mrs. Meynell's *Essays* than is that dryish and furious activity *in vacuo* which man is accustomed to call thought. However intellectual her work may be, its intellectuality is as near to feeling without peril of 'sensibility' as it is near to life without being noisy and boisterous. It comes from a quiet, vigilant mind, at ease with a hospitable but discriminating heart. Intuition has lost nothing of its spring and inexplic-

* *Essays*. By Alice Meynell (Burns and Oates).

ability by acquiring the stability of a considered judgment. And if Mrs. Meynell's shafts have any target, that (comparatively spacious) target is certainly Man. She may add a chillish word of comfort to her suggestion that he should make a strenuous effort even at this late day to attain to 'a certain human dignity in the clothing of his natural body'—'the best leg is the man's.' And while he is yet a small boy—'A Child of Tumult', 'That Pretty Person'—her love and understanding refuse no forgiveness. But whether she is considering him as 'a sensitive Municipality in tears' over the grass that defies forbiddance to spring up in its tramway; or as the poet who says nothing in terms of the eternal and wastes his craft on a common hoard of erotic remembrances; or as a critic who for dapper sentimentality's sake would dismiss Swift's beloved Dingley from all share in his idolized 'M.D.'; or who lavishes cheap satire at the expense of the all-consoling wife of Johnson—well, when these come into view Mrs. Meynell shows no mercy. Poor Gulliver writhes under whispering volleys of wit, irony, raillery which he is powerless not only to repel but to locate.

It is against facile judgments, facile admirations, in literature no less than in life, that Mrs. Meynell gravely directs her fastidious attack—the silly modern habit of laughter to evade the stress of silence, the indolent unintelligence of the 'Life' that mainly consists of a death, a lover's language 'imitated from the children they doubtless never studied, and perhaps never loved', the importunate sentimentality of an age that finds in pathos a refuge from the simplicity of truth, that accuses itself of nothing under cover of a universal excuse of everything. 'Perfect personal distinctness of experience would be in literature a delicate innocence'; and nothing is clearer in these essays than the assurance that every word of them comes straight out of such an experience—the experience of a quiet, piercing, meditative scrutiny, of a mind stable in poise yet instant in response, of a sensitiveness quick to suffer but heedful of surrender. The charm of many writers consists as much in their own as in our surprise at the bright and beautiful ideas they have chanced on. These essays, rather, convince us of a definite and sustained habit of life and thought. 'Happiness is not a matter of events, it depends upon the tides of the mind.' 'Remorse itself does not remain—it returns.' 'It is in the hours of sleep that the mind, by some divine paradox, has the intensest sense of light.' Truths, like these, are a distillation of naked experience, not mere treasure trove. They come of a discipline that has been learned, suffered, as well as divined. So, too, with the expression of it. 'The stroke of the raindrop which is the drop and its path at once'; 'lines of poetry that cast sunrise shadows'; the felicity of such writing is the rare truth it tells. It is the revelation of an habitual poetic consciousness. And, as with the phrase, so with each individual essay—its brevity is the soul of thought. And when that thought takes flight on the wings of the imagination, beauty dwells in the words, and so lives on in Memory.

Times Literary Supplement, July 2, 1914

RUSTIC SPEECH*

The *English Dialect Dictionary* enshrines for the use of one per cent of its students thirteen hundred synonyms of the word fool, and there are more than a thousand with which to upbraid a slattern. The former may be anything from a goffeny goavey to a nornigig, the latter is unquestionably a slommocks and a wally-draigle. Every tiniest pig in a litter, even, has a hundred and twenty names to his christening. The squeaking squab is a true-born treseltrype. Literature dressed up in the latest mode in silk and satin is accustomed to look askance at these boldacious and fancical country cousins. Yet to a lover of true English, Mrs. Wright's learned and enchanting volume on Rustic Speech is rich with music. ''Ow the birds bin singin' this mornin'!' the reader may well exclaim; 'the coppy's all on a charm!' Her book appears at a moment, too, when the 'Society for Pure English' is in process of formation, one of whose worthy objects it will be to welcome homespun terms into high literary society, to expose this ignorant contempt, even to encourage the gifted amateur in feats of word-craft and neologization. A living language is in sad straits when it becomes the passive prey of the grammarian and ceases to be the despair of the lexicographer. Every tome of Sir James Murray's gigantic undertaking bears witness to the incessancy of word-coinage. But back to the land we must go for words and phrases racy of the soil and encrusted with homely associations, words that are not mere bodiless spectres, but as expressive of the things they represent as a biggin is of a baby, its song of a blackbird.

For a while such terms will strike queerly on the ear; they will sound 'low'. So once did *budge, coax, sham,* and *quandary* to

* *Rustic Speech and Folk-lore.* By Elizabeth Mary Wright (Oxford University Press).

Dr. Johnson. Nor can more than a tithe of them be redeemed. Like the men who make and use them, words die a natural death. Not even the English Bible has saved *charger* (dish), *clout, cocker, leasing, magnifical, wist*; nor Shakespeare, *bolter, codger, inch-meal, melch, squinny, minikin, moble*. And all are worth a scatter of flowers upon their graves. But how gladly would one welcome every course of the ceremonious and otiose dinner in respect to which one had been 'bidden', discard one's decent black to don one's 'bravery'! Who would look twice at a blue Persian if he possessed an English 'chintz', would refuse the consolations of a hot-water bottle if proffered in the guise of a 'piggy', and who, unless mimpsey-pimpsey to the last degree, would hesitate to confess to a distaste for onions on the plea that 'they upraids me' and induce internal 'chunnerings'?

Neither the East nor the West End can properly define a gentleman. To the Midlands we must go: there he is a fellow-creature that need not work. And the term is not confined to the less busy sex. Should such a supercilious idler listen to a chance acquaintance recounting a dream of how, after the crowner had obleedged his poor waughy body with a verdict, and the sexton had laid it darkling with a showl, his soul took its journey under a serene fleece of siller clouds, along an alablaster causey, sweet with laylock and nodding with apricocks unforboden to the pilgrim unafeared, his sneer would be the mark not, perhaps, of a cappernikious snool, but certainly of a too fastidious purist. For all these forms are of a wholesome stock. As for pronunciation, let the Cockney pause. There are, says Mrs. Wright, who has searched the land through, seven main groups of English dialects following clear phonological laws, and he who refuses to recognize *earth* as his *home* may pronounce each of these terms in four-and-forty different ways and be no less a patriot at the end of it.

But Mrs. Wright's book is not confined to Rustic Speech. It is reinforced and illustrated with a wealth of folk-lore—proverbs and graces, devils and ghosts (from Tankerabogus to Knocky-boh), fairies ('a kind of fabled beings', as Dr. Johnson defines them), and Derricks (from Nanny Button-cap of Yorkshire to Phynnodderee of the Isle of Man), physics and cure-alls, omens, portents, forebodings, fairs and feasts, charms and talismans. One thing alone is wanting—an index. Well indeed has she proved the truth of her quotation from *The Great Frost of January*; and although the quotation that follows might well be manna and marrow out of one of the Wessex novels it is actually out of the mouth of a countryman of 1600:

'We old men are old chronicles, and when our tongues go they are not clocks to tell only the time present, but large books unclasped; and our speeches, like leaves turned over and over, discover wonders that are long since past.'

Edinburgh Review, Jan. 1914

PURE ENGLISH

Of the innumerable associations and leagues and missions in this crowded tumultuous world the S.P.E. may at least claim to be one of the most unassuming and quiet. Its only assumption is that those who use English in speech or in writing should use it heedfully, and its quiet is one neither of lethargy nor stagnation. Nor of age; for this year marks the completion of but its first decade, and in 1914 it suspended 'proceedings until the national distraction should have abated' —a characteristic fragment of its corporate style. It has therefore enjoyed only four years of activity—an activity not easily detectable, perhaps, as positive progress. For though its principles are open to the day, their practice is more or less a secret gratification.

Its members are still few in numbers, but they are one and all—as the mere fact of their membership attests—scholars, in either meaning of the term, and they have had for counsellors masters of their cult. Their aims, moreover, are 'finite', and chiefly anti-pedantic—destructive, that is, only of the destructive—and they are expressed in publications which are dryly entitled tracts. The term tract, however—though now distantly —is related to 'treat', and since these particular treats are of the workmanship of the Oxford University Press (and are sent in return for an annual subscription of only ten shillings) they are an economical pleasure to possess and handle. While the S.P.E. presents these substantial foundations on which to base them, its appeal is nevertheless to 'the preferences of individuals'; it relies, that is, on 'suggestion'.

Only to mere modesty must it be due, then, that among the societies and institutions 'scientific, artistic, religious, philanthropic' listed in Whitaker, the Society for Pure English has failed to find mention, and in its earliest infancy at once took

cover behind but three initial letters in all, and these symbolic only of a fraction of a hope. Backwaters, eyots, oases have
their charms just now, and to be 'side-tracked' is to be given
the opportunity of collecting heaven's dews and earth's mosses
as well as rust. A society at any rate that incites its members to
practise precepts almost privately intimated rather than pub-
licly enforced more closely resembles a haven of refuge than a
crusade. None the less, the Society for Pure English merits at
least three of the four classifying epithets used in Whitaker.
Tracts on the Language of Anatomy, on English Influence on
the French Vocabulary, and on that queer and questionable
quartet, 'Shall and Will, Should and Would', are nothing if not
scientific. The use of language is of little literary merit if, however modest in intention it may have been, it is devoid of any art
but the 'artistic'. Reverence for one's mother tongue, delight in
its long history, and the desire after a lifetime's usage to have
refrained from contaminating its purity, and even perhaps to
have infinitesimally enriched its treasury, are incentives that
may claim to be philanthropic. 'And if ony man gessith himselff
to be religious, and refreyneth not his tunge . . . the religion of
him is veyn.'

If all human societies boasted only of bees in their bonnets as
harmless as these, their honey perhaps might be the sweeter and
more wholesome. To incite men to take action may be well or
ill; to persuade them actively to take thought cannot be ill.
Indeed, the longer we patiently practise ourselves in speaking or
writing, the clearer becomes the evidence not only that it is
immeasurably difficult to express ourselves in truth, but that it
is ultimately impossible to express anything else. Our words
delimit as well as free mind and heart. A work like the *Oxford
English Dictionary* is therefore not merely a verbal reservoir,
but a narrative in symbols of the pilgrimage of the English race.
The *Dictionary of National Biography* recounts the exploits,
achievements, heroisms of rarely endowed and signally for-
tuned individuals. That of our words recounts the creative and
imaginative exploits not only of the erudite, the man of science,
and of the channering bookworm, but of the people, the folk.
There could be no more beguiling proof of this than Mr. Pearsall Smith's recently published Tract (No. XII) on English
Idioms—a hedgerow dense and fragrant with the wild flowers

of speech. The hospitality of a dictionary, moreover, embraces
not only the dead but the living, and it awaits the as yet un-
born. Here in obscure medley are the complete manifestations
of a certain racial order of human consciousness, revealing the
actual and potential scope of its freedom of thought, the degrees
of its sensibilities, its powers of discrimination, its lost and forlorn, its vivified and vivifying causes. To find its equal, even
for mere concision, in the revelation of human adventure not
only physical but spiritual, one must open an atlas. And many of
us are all but blind to the riches of either.

Even a cursory scrutiny of the objects which have collected
themselves about us instantly proves that they are almost inextricably bound up with their names. There are interesting,
beautiful, significant objects cursed with bad names. There are
unworthy objects blessed with good ones. However that may
be, the sensuous or intellectual appropriation of an object is but
partially attainable without the appropriation of its name. Any
attempt, for example, to recall the wild flowers seen in a hedgerow in a spring-time morning's walk is likely to retrieve with
positive definiteness only those we can name. It is not only the
savage who finds it difficult to discriminate between them. If we
but breathe the names—thyme, hawthorn, wallflower, are not
the flowers themselves instantly ours again in sense and spirit?
Rather than debase a secret coinage, are we not betrayed at
times into calling a Mr. Jones Mr. Robinson? What true
familiarity with the birds has any benighted soul who *cannot* tell
a hawk from a handsaw; with the stars who cannot give name to
Orion, Cassiopeia, Leo, the Great Bear—with its 'Jack-by-the-
middle-horse'?

But a day or two ago a London child aged nine gently shook
her head when as gently asked the name for the palm of her
hand and the sole of her foot. In Glasgow, it has been whispered,
the children have to be taught the meaning of the word 'sky'.
Sterility of terms entails sterility of mind. The mere learning of them by rote is like the ploughing of a field. It will
afford an irresistible welcome to whatever seeds the winds
and birds and Providence may bring. Weeds have their dangers,
maybe, and an otiose vocabulary—any vocabulary at all, for
that matter—entails the risk of becoming word-ridden. For to
have constantly at the very tip of one's tongue the name of an

object or of a sentiment may eventuate in the partial loss of response to it, or in the failure to perceive that any such object or sentiment is most valuable because it is unique. Keep a close and vigilant eye and attention on both name and thing, and all is well.

A man, of course, may express himself in other things than words: in facial contortion and gesture; in manners and dress; with needle, saucepan, spade, and axe; with sword and gun; in paint, in metal, in wood and stone. The merest nincompoop realizes at sight of works of this order—a farm, its barns, its furrows, the vermin dangling on its shed, its plough and wains, its furniture, the pictures on its walls, its ploughman's smock, its goodwife's cradle, cider, and embroidery—that they are one and all the outcome of taking thought, that skill in their accomplishment cannot be attained without practice, that they represent the result of an arduous and prolonged process. Chiefly perhaps because we suck in our vocabulary with our mother's milk, we may utterly fail to realize that words are the most delicate and most easily blunted tools of any we possess, and that endless toil and effort and circumspection are needed for their efficient use.

In a degree, it is true, words are *common* property. Bricks, Stevenson called them—and one looks, for that very reason, a little more closely at his style. For words surely are as fluent and chameleonic in practice and effect as the hues of a humming-bird. The enormous mass of them has none the less been inherited. It is the mass that intimidates. For Shakespeare's purposes, after all, we need only fifteen thousand of them or so— 'the best'. And yet, apart from men of letters, writers, how few of us attempt to acquire that comparatively modest total, or to use well even what we have mastered, to make a definite choice among them, or to achieve anything in the nature of innovation. Practice in them is not only audible. We think in them, can dream in them. We make magic with them, may comfort and solace with them beyond belief, or injure and wound irrevocably. We pray in them, and we die with a poor last few of them on our lips. Should we not then be a little bolder, more human, humorous, bold and original in our efforts to acquire and use them, to become fully articulate?

There are families who enjoy private countersigns. We all of us value the names of our personal friends. Beyond this few of us venture. Invite an imaginative child (if the phrase be not tautological) not to repeat M or N, or even To-be-or-not-to-be, but out of the livingness and innate abundance of its eye and mind to invent its own apt name for toy, doll, flower, or insect, room, place, sensation, or acquaintance:—and be astounded at the result. It is, alas, the grown-ups who are *not* children in these matters. None the less, might we not in the silence of our hearts compile a small choice private vocabulary, 'a little language' of our own, if merely for purely personal delectation, and maybe for the sharing of it with the deserving?

To state that every word in our language was once used for the first time by a single human being is no less animating a truism than the reminder that somewhere throughout the day the sun is setting (and rising) may be a disconcerting one. But the mimicry, the sensitiveness, the apprehension, the creativeness it implies! To inquire how a word—lighter than thistledown, secret as the odour of violets—spreads from tongue to tongue, from mind to mind, is almost as idle as to inquire what song the Sirens sang. But to debate which of them one would most gladly (and most easily) have fathered is amusing— digladiation, terminological, quodlibetically, heterogeneity, soul, flea, pantechnicon, omnibus, slops, cuspidor, pink, heartsease, comfrey, rhinoceros, skunk, ant, weevil, hyssop, Aldebaran, Betelgeuse, meu, rue, or bald-money? On the one side the needs and adventurings of the scholar, the philologist, the Groves of Academe; on the other those of the herd, the sailor, the craftsman, the housewife, the people, youth with eyes in its head and a tip to its tongue.

Each variety comes and goes. The delicate, shade-loving, night-folding *Oxalis acetosella*, whose snowy flowers are at times 'dashed over with a small show of bluish', and whose sour relishing juice 'maketh a most dainty clear syrup', is, as Mr. Bridges cites in Tract V, for exquisite exactitude's sake the *Oxalis acetosella*, and—botanically—it is nothing more. But how happy is the country polyonymosity that hails it also as sheep-sorrel, cuckoo-spice, hallelujah, ladies' cakes, and God Almighty's bread-and-cheese! Need it be added that it is also Saint Patrick's one true shamrock?

The desire, however, to refresh our English vocabulary with

words that are not lost but have fallen a little behind in the march of making ourselves understood, and the hope of encouraging its members to try their hands, 'prentice or otherwise, at word-making (not without the reminder that to the 'uneducated classes' we owe the best of our homespun terms, and that for a word to call a machine by we should go not to the inventor of it but to his workmen)—these are not the sole aims of the S.P.E. Its 'pure', it will be noticed, is not *good*. It counsels its members not on how to write, but on what words to write with. It deplores 'foolish interference with living developments', while welcoming 'the scientific alliance of the best linguistic authorities'. Pure English, in its esteem, then, is English truly characteristic of the language, howsoever derived, whether only of yesterday's standing or hoar with the centuries—an English unpedantic, exact, vivifying, and so, of its nature, racy, musical, idiomatic; a decoy to the imagination, a standfast to the reason.

The Society, therefore, no more contemns the precise sesquipedalianity of chemical terms—which, fortunately, have little connection with literature—than it despises 'the picturesque vocabularies of local vernaculars'. Only 'where there is choice, the English form is to be preferred.' For this reason it casts a jealous and grudging eye on the alien if, as a novelty, it has been borrowed without due need. On the other hand, it exhorts us one and all to keep what is ours ours.

There is a tendency nowadays, owing perhaps to the ubiquity of education, to become morbidly anxious regarding a word that wears any self-evident trace of its foreign origin (even in face of Mr. Bridges's pungent exorcism). Just as certain phonologists would reduce our commonest vowel sounds to an indiscriminate *er* ('We went frerm Margit ter Brightern ernd then ern ter Bernmerth'), and certain versifiers would sacrifice metre and rhyme to their passion for the 'free', so there are genteel writers—and Mr. Pearsall Smith vouches for it—who prefer to write *impasse* or *cul-de-sac* when they mean blind alley; *résumé* when they mean summary, synopsis or abstract; *mêlée* for mellay, *naïveté* for naivety, *flair* for flair, *technique* for technic, *clinique* for clinic, and will not only presently italicize vogue, bouquet, cab and wig and war, but with a concert for theme will tell us that 'the *ideae* of *music* implied in the *chori* suggested the inmates of rival *asyla*'. A little knowledge is indeed a maleficent

241

R

thing when it indulges in nasturtia, pæonia, miasmata, lexica, and apices. Yet it is as bad manners thus to advertise a domesticated alien term as it would be to introduce an old friend of Huguenot descent with 'Thees ees Meestare ———.' As vast a proportion of our language consists of borrowed words as of hidden metaphors. Ask only, Is this term now English? i.e., Has it, happy creature, ceased to be an exotic? The Society's tracts are rendyvouses for memorandums (in mass rather than in single file) on all similar malpractices. Let us at least take the wrong path—if we so insist—not blindly.

Then, again, those who take pleasure in delving in old books and so win (for *use*) an occasional charming makeweight in the shape of some half-forgotten rich and crusted word or phrase, will be fortified by the thought that there are other enthusiasts as blithely eager as themselves in the quest for such pelf— enthusiasts who will not shun as futile or heinous any proof of an attempt to preserve from 'the limbo of silence' what for generations has been on the tongues of the people, but is now merely the sorry spoil of the lexicographer. In this sentence alone are half a dozen obsolescent words for which Mr. Pearsall Smith entreats a further lease of active life. Not that there is any occasion to fash oneself in search of such foison. There are writers fastidiously nesh in these matters. Do they realize that, in spite of the 'standard' style into which our language is in danger of falling, 'the hog and sow still have their pigs and are all of them swine'?

There are little niceties of syntax and grammar, again, in which not even the adept need be ashamed to realize that he is still something of a novice. Even past masters in the cutting down of suspended relatives, in the nice use of compound passives, of 'whether' and 'unique' and 'somewhat', *and* who are ready, if need be, to neatly split an infinitive rather than to for mere propriety's sake or with a pedantic craving for grammatical precision leave it uncloven, may have their moments of torturing hesitation. Only the dead languages after a postmortem dissection can be reduced, it is true, to an absolute grammar. The living defy the process. Still, it is prudent to be aware that verbal problems exist—problems and puzzles seemingly trivial but exceedingly vexatious. The propriety of 'as to', the judicious manipulation of the hyphen. E.g.—As to whether lay writers, Academy committee men, ex headmasters, and such like, who have a *bona fide*, up to date, and not *ex parte* prejudiced interest in the use of English, are likely, none the less, to be over severe on their fellow men is hardly a matter of doubt, since literature, at any rate, is ill served when those interested in the Pure English campaign have the ill grace and will to scold business men for not vaunting themselves as men of letters or for at least paying something better than mere lip service to an easy going common sense in matters of composition. Fortunate indeed is the writer who (even after study of Mr. Fowler's Tract VI) can unhesitatingly hyphenate such a sentence as this. And there is virtue in modesty.

'It is an error' (wrote Charles Lamb to Southey) 'more particularly incident to persons of the correctest principles and habits, to seclude themselves from the rest of mankind, as from another species, and form into knots and clubs. The best people, herding thus exclusively, are in danger of contracting a narrowness. . . . If all the good people were to ship themselves off to Terra Incognita, what, in humanity's name, is to become of the refuse?'

Such is the risk remotely incident to membership of the S.P.E. A trivial one, so long as it be clearly realized that the Society's primary purpose is not to lay down laws, but to influence practice; not to stereotype, but to some extent to systematize. Its members then are not at all likely 'to look awful upon their poor friends'. Their ideal is to learn not to dictate. Apart, however, from other little disadvantages, the elderly (and few writers are in life's heyday) may find instruction, even self-instruction, dull and tiresome. And composition —as Newman agreed with Johnson—is one of the severest of occupations. To endeavour to write a pure English is the best means of achieving a good English. The scope of this ideal is extensive. For language is a growth—in part natural, in the sense that human beings talk as the spirit moves them; in part artificial, since scholars are apt to write according to rule. It cannot but have its imperfections, then. As yet we have no one word for his-or-her, for he-or-she. Again and again a writer of any experience discovers that his pen is in the middle of a sentence without a grammatical exit. He finds himself in a blind alley, and to get out must turn back. He now and then discovers, too, that

243

language, like the human eye, is a defective instrument—a refreshing experience, if anything, after the more frequent one of discovering that he himself is an incredibly poor performer on it.

Every language is rich in some respects, less rich in others. All languages go borrowing, but at haphazard, for as yet, it seems, we, for our part, are in ignorance of what refreshment, what syntactical elasticity, what innovations English actually needs. To welcome the neologism, to hark back to the bygone, is mere common sense. Posterity will filter. Children, once more, country people, players of games, users of tools and machinery, and pioneers are, by nature or necessity, makers of words, whereas the sciences are hot-beds of technical terms. And literary men themselves—novelists, critics, even poets—tend to write technically. 'De Quincey once said that authors are a dangerous class for any language. And Ascham: "He that will wryte well in any tongue must folowe this council of Aristotle, to speak as the common people do, to think as wise men do."' (Tract V.) The wise men, having thought, should know what words they need and where to seek them. But as yet there is no compendium of the wanted. It would be enlightening and useful.

Since, moreover, English bids fair to be the chief language of civilization, it must be adaptive, catholic, hospitable. There is America—a comparatively large and vocal country; and there are the Colonies. They are all of them rapidly moulding an inherited English into their own forms, and are swamping it with novelties—crude, racy, striking, dubious. But theirs, too, is the expressed ideal 'to maintain the tradition and foster the development of our common tongue'. A further use for the S.P.E. and for similar bodies would be a friendly family consultation on this and on similar activities. Its truest success, once more, will be revealed in the practice of individuals.

For progress in this direction must be by little and little. Personal impulse is as necessary as conscious practice and elaboration. To love a thing is to treat it well and to wish it to be itself as much as possible. It is to be zealous for its powers and privileges, its being and life. That is why the reading of grammars or treatises on style may be far from a stuffy occupation. Nevertheless it is prudent to be frugal in the use even of a grammar. There are certain writers who for obscure reasons have a sterilizing effect on the minds of their readers. Their books have fine qualities; they engross attention. But, unlike the books that free the fancy, set the wits spinning, excite the imagination, and simply cry on us, Go and do likewise! these whisper, Thus far and no farther. We rise from them sated, devitalized, a little depressed. Theirs is the peculiar secret of turning off the fountain, so to speak. Treatises on composition are at times of their company. They may incite us to excellent intentions; we have to wait until their influence has subsided for an opportunity to carry them out. And the constructors of that invaluable pillory *The King's English* would magnanimously agree that protracted study of it is a rather morbid amusement. The S.P.E. wisely prescribes its tonics in small doses, and membership therefore entails no excessive risk of becoming grammar-conscious and word-bound.

For though some exact knowledge of the laws of syntax is desirable, example remains better than precept. It is therefore unfortunate that grammarians can hardly avoid exemplifying their rules with infectious infringements of them. It is unfortunate also that grammarians are compelled to submit to reason what is largely a matter of intuition and taste. Merely to know that there are commandments makes the keeping of them more difficult. We become aware of the delicate nuances of signification in words all but synonymous almost as naturally as we become aware of the differences between the leaves of trees, or tints, or human faces, or the meaning of speech-tones. Style can no more be taught than euphony. Attention to rules—to be simple, lucid, concise, unaffected—will help a man to write decently; it will not teach him to write. And even if it could, *what* to say, he will discover, is a more exhausting and exacting problem than how to say it. He is faced with that curious difficulty—the coincidence of content and form. And at long last the acquisition of a technical mastery in any art—too rare a feat perhaps to cause anxiety—is by no means nothing but gain.

This may in part be why heedful writers are a peevish and ungrateful folk. They are apt to fear ink at length as much as a cat dreads water. Flaubert is their high priest, and the commination service their daily fare, and it was hardly the craftsman in Stevenson that pooh-poohed them as *filles-de-joie.*

Having imprudently contracted a habit—scratched cacoethically where they itch—they rebel against its dictates. And yet, however undeserving of it they may be, they occasionally enjoy a queer and unpremeditated reward. How rarely refreshing an experience is that told of by Gibbon in his Autobiography—after a prolonged and feverish spell of reading or writing to turn back from these peculiar silent haunts, to shake free of verbiage and to discover the world of the real patiently awaiting a long-deferred tryst. Above, the dark open ample sky, powdered with its stars! A sweet air that is of the immortal springtime of the spirit moves in space. And to see again the face of the constant moon is to see again the face of one loved, and the more lovely for having been for a while unremembered.

Times Literary Supplement, May 3, 1923

PETER RABBIT, BEATRIX POTTER
AND FRIENDS

'It was many and many a year ago' . . . there lived a child called, not very prettily, Beatrix Potter. And a child, in all that matters most, she remained all her life. She did not live, as did Annabel Lee, in a kingdom by the sea, but resided in London with her parents at No. 2 Bolton Gardens, Earl's Court —which is not so very far from Mayfair. It was a large and very quiet house, but gloomy, and it was known to the irreverent as 'the Mausoleum'.

Both parents had inherited Lancashire cotton fortunes, but they had been by now a whole generation out of trade, which makes all the difference. They were carriage-folk, and thoroughly genteel; but although Mrs. Potter bore a remarkable resemblance to Queen Victoria, they were not 'in Society'. Nor did they entertain.

Miss Margaret Lane, in her enchanting *Tale of Beatrix Potter*, which is a marvel of insight, judgment, wit and humour, and as rich with plums of the quotable as was Mrs. Tiggy-Winkle with quills, says little about Mrs. Potter. Nor is she eloquent concerning Mr. Rupert Potter. Professionally, he was a barrister. But the only brief said to have come his way proved to be a hoax. He was a friend of John Bright's (and so was Beatrix) and he spent much of the day at his club, the Athenaeum. Why in his photographs he always looks so angry and indignant, and why his much-bewhiskered countenance should invariably remind me of the explorer du Chaillu, is now only a small matter—as Captain Kidd remarked when only the cabin-boy was left to walk the plank.

Both parents, it seems, had unusual ideas about the 'bringing up' of children. Their only son, Bertram, a staunch comrade of his sister in childhood—but no Mausoleumite—later made a secret and happy marriage with a farmer's daughter. For Beatrix, there was a clean starched piqué frock every morning, accompanied by 'cotton stockings striped round and round like a zebra's legs'. A cutlet and rice pudding came up the back stairs every day for her lunch.

She sometimes visited a wonderful old grandmama. There, munching ginger-snaps and seated with her black doll, Topsy, or her grimy once-white flannelette Pig, on the cross-bar beneath the large oval table, she would listen intently to the old lady's untrammelled conversation. *She* was a Crompton, one of many attractive sisters, a toast and a beauty, and in her day she had refused three proposals of marriage in a week. One of her beaux, alas, was found drowned in the lily-pond.

Later, when Beatrix was too tall to fit this cubby-hole, she privately, Boswell-fashion, scribbled down some of her grandmama's romantic conversation in a home-made cipher and a tiny script resembling Charlotte Brontë's, under that grandmama's very nose. She was never sent to any school; and so, bless her heart, was largely self-taught. In due course she was supplied with a visiting governess for French and another for German, who, after leaving Mrs. Potter's to get married, remained a lasting friend.

Never, surely, had any child of Beatrix's age and station such prolonged savannahs of solitude—or spent them to such unique effect. For books she had the Waverley novels—from which she learned to read, and Miss Edgeworth's complete Works. But not, it seems, Edward Lear or Lewis Carroll, not Shakespeare or Christina Rossetti, *The Girl's Own Paper* or *The Bow Bells Novelettes*. Extremely vivacious company besides her own, however (and *can* Mr. Potter wholly have been aware of it?), she had in plenty. As many small birds and little animals of every variety, indeed, as she cared to keep. Also, *in excelsis*, she had the images and creations of her own mind's making which no one could deprive her of, that 'kingdom'—for so many children who are never less alone than when alone—called the Imagination.

Not that Beatrix Potter was a 'dreamer'. Nor, it seems, was she ever accused of being one. From her earliest years and to her last, the seventy-eighth, she was a rarely practical, common-sensical and sagacious child and woman. And never idle. Even in 1943, and within hearing of the bombs and guns, she was helping in the fields on one of her three little farms at Sawrey, a village between Coniston and Windermere.

However, this present occasion is specifically Peter Rabbit's Jubilee, since in September 1902 his *Tale*, the first of some twenty-four of its kind (roundabout only 50,000 words in all!) was published by Frederick Warne and Co. As were all the others, it was illustrated by its 'onlie begetter' with twenty-seven little coloured plates; 'slowly and laboriously' executed. Its price was one shilling; and it carried a royalty of threepence a copy. Miss Potter considered the royalty very liberal, but ventured to inquire about the copyright, adding the comment, 'Mr. Potter is a little formal, having been a barrister.' It was to the youngest partner in this firm, Norman Warne, she afterwards became engaged—a step, although she was in her late thirties, vehemently opposed by her parents. Was he not merely a publisher, whereas the Potter forbears had been in cotton! Alas, a few days before the Christmas of 1905—and their wedding—he died.

A few days ago I inquired of an unrivalled authority how well Peter was now doing. The prompt reply was 'As well as ever'.

So much for Peter's *public* birthday. And although in her later years, long after she had become Mrs. Heelis, she became positively sick of poor Peter and was quite unable to understand why he was so popular; she would surely be overjoyed to hear that it was being celebrated two thousand miles away, and in America.

Possibly her weariness of Peter was in part owing to the fact that *The Tailor of Gloucester* puts him completely in the shade. And this contains perhaps the most exquisite little drawing—a Miss Mouse in sumptuous silks and a huge mob-cap—she ever achieved.

When Peter was actually conceived, who can say? He *appeared* first in a letter to a small boy beginning 'My dear Noël' who was ill in bed. Noël was the first-born of her German governess, now Mrs. Moore. And—as a shining example of the value of after-thoughts—in the printed tale, but not in Noël's letter, is perhaps one of the tastiest morsels of understatement, downrightness and secret humour characteristic of *all* these tiny books:

' "Now, my dears," said old Mrs. Rabbit one morning, "you may go into the fields or down the lane, but don't go into Mr. McGregor's garden: *your father had an accident there; he was put in a pie by Mrs. McGregor.*" '

She was affronted rather than flattered when one of her devoted admirers and afterwards greatly valued friend, who was the editor of *The Horn Book*, declared her little pictures comparable with Constable's. Contrariwise, she was intensely pleased when another critic remarked on the mastery of her prose. Absolute essence indeed it is, clean as a whistle, delicious to utter, and precise as a formula of Professor Einstein's.

Since, however, in the faded little bundle of clear and beautifully spaced letters from Dunkeld, of which this to Noël dated 'Sep. 4th., *93*' was one, several others of her characters—Hunca Munca, Jeremy, Nutkin, among them—are mentioned, can this really have been the beginning? My own fancy is that, named or nameless, they were in her imagination years before her twenties. Moreover, from the age of sixteen there is a gap of ten years in her life of which even Margaret Lane can give very little information. Nor did Peter *stay* in a letter before the English-speaking nurseries engulfed him. He was privately printed at a cost of eleven pounds, sold to amiable friends and kind aunts in fours and fives, and brought in about one pound profit.

Finally—and how much I wish it hadn't to be—there are three things which seem to me paramount in any account of Beatrix Potter, all of them rare. First, she not only had a true-blue and formidable character, she was also *a* Character. Such Beings are beyond all price in this rather stereotyped and grossly over-populated world. Work, she was convinced, was man's earthly salvation. Next, whereas nearly all grown-ups are able to retrieve only the minutest recollections of their early childhood, she herself could recall clearly *being* five. And how blessedly and triumphantly she proved it! And last, she possessed, as she herself declared, 'the seeing eye'. Habitually intense and intent was the use she made of it. It is of course not only a heaven-sent possession but also the grace, inspiration, and joy of every poet that has ever walked this earth, and shared the stars.

New York Times, Sept. 7, 1952

'MY MIND TO ME . . .'

When the unmethodical traveller packs his knapsack (or Saratoga trunk) he may forget a few little necessities that he will need on his journey—and most of them may nowadays be easily reacquired *en route*. Yet, however little or ample his need or aspiration may be, it remains beyond his power to pack his mind. His own nature and what life has given, or surrendered, have done that for him already. Whether he is off and away to the Sahara or to the South Seas; whether his quarry is a broiled frog, in a once 'gay Paree', or the angels of William Blake's childhood on Peckham Rye, he must put up with what he has. No shopman will sell him plenty—or even peace—of *mind*.

Indeed, his secret incentive for setting out may have been rather to lose, to jettison, than to gain. He may be a fugitive from the rat-trap of his own thoughts; he may be seeking—Utopian dream—a home away from home; his one corroding impulse may be to escape from ennui, and therefore from himself. But that, as every refugee with a pinch of Montaigne for philosophy knows, is likely to prove a vanity. The self within will remain as faithful to him as his own shadow; and it is (blessedly) easier to forgive than, by mere trying, to forget—almost anything. In any event, new scenes and nothing to do will make exacting demands on his resources. Which, then, of these resources are of most value, use and comfort? If he retains in lively activity his seven senses and his five wits, then *all* his mind will be the least of it he will need; and especially a rich and ready memory and, for starry zenith, an imagination which bestows on him a universe compared with which the round world itself, safely circumnavigated, will prove to have been but a bubble—however lovely, iridescent and inexhaustible.

Any mere 'Sweet Stay-at-Home' will, however, be astonished

251

at the little which even the wide and practised traveller may appear to have brought back with him. Or is it that the wallet of his mind is packed to bursting, yet words wherewith to share it are wanting? On the other hand, a twilight expedition even to the nearest pillarbox may present another order of traveller with an evening star that seems in its serene and solitary beauty to have been awaiting the assignation until that very moment; with a common bird, the meaning of whose cadences his ear had never really caught before; or with a wild flower until that moment never *seen*; and, perhaps, even with an Idea! It is not distance that counts, or hope, or even longing; but the mind's looking-glass, which not only reflects but transmutes to its own purposes all that it receives. Whatever, then, the journey may be, the wayfarer must bring to it at least as much as it offers.

For although there is a trace of the bagman, something a trifle smug and mainchancy in travelling chiefly to acquire memories —and the best will come and stay unsought—Memory itself is of capital importance. Its aid alone can bring full recognition of all that is encountered, and of the slight novelty which that encountering may secure. And this is no less true—physical activity for the moment entirely in abeyance—of travelling into the Past; a venture which, like the astronomer's cipher-infested sallies into the black and icy voids of space, is almost wholly of the mind. For memory, even when childhood is left behind, may retain the grace to keep for its owner's use and pleasure the best and brightest, however wantonly meagre that best may be; and, with a sovereign irony or humour or absence of self-conceit, may even gild what once was lead. That hapless little picnic when the rain dripped minute-drops from the rusty railway bridge over the river into the salad; the tryst she failed to keep; the comfortless inn; the wrong and vacant train; tedious company; the flies; the mob—all such little distresses may at length give a pleasing edge to recollection; and what was once the mind's fast may, in retrospect, resemble a feast. And although recalled travel, a remembered journey, can in duration surrender little more than moments, and these chiefly perhaps when one was at rest, how gay a patchwork mere Memory's loose stitchery may make of them. There are curious unguents and life-revivers in that nebulous and magic box—up that conjurer's sleeve.

Moreover, the travelling mind moves, like that which gave it being, in a mysterious way. Its caprices are unpredictable, its rapidity is Ariel's, its geography chaotic. It cannot be said to mock at time, since of time, for the time being, it is unconscious; and therefore space almost ceases to be. We can hardly be said to be engaged in travel, since, apparently, a moment or two *before* even we asked for our ticket, we have found ourselves already there! No place thus retrieved, whether one's mother's arms at the age of three, or where a last good-bye was said, or where the eye seized one of life's few glimpses of what it took to be Eden, or where mortal existence for the moment seemed to fall into ashes—nothing shows any sign of wear or tear, of date or destruction. Any such memory may be little more than a momentary fraction of the original source from which it came; it is in itself no more than a phantom image, but one, it may be, all but unendurably dark and tragic; or how dear!

Travellers' 'tales' are proverbial. It is indeed a little dull, as well as difficult, to pass on even an anecdote without fringing it with an aura which we alone can bestow on it. It restores the bloom of novelty. Must we be equally strict when one's only credulous and delighted listener is oneself? What would Conscience have to say to the sheer invention of *imagined* memories—inventions, that is, rather more substantial than excursions into a forlorn or remorseful might-have-been? Would there be any fatal mischief in the attempt provided it were kept (as indeed it could hardly help being kept) clearly distinguishable from what has actually happened, but which is now, except in memory, no more? Dreams, in sleep, do their best and worst for us in this respect. But might not the rational day-time, less capricious in the recognition of what we want and would be most enriched by, lend its aid? The severe moralist will have no doubt of *his* answer.

And yet, in Memory's all but patternless mosaic, the insertion of a few lustrous cubes, which we realize were of pure fancy's setting, would at least enhance the general effect. That being so, must they concern solely ourselves? If we seldom endeavour as we well might, to think *out* a true friend, a process that will never eventuate in thinking him away—endeavour, that is, to traverse his heart and mind and all that they mean to us— does it really entail any treachery to truth, or to him, or to ourselves, if we *imagine* memories of him in our chosen time and place that never, except in imagination, were, but where we could secure him solely and wholly for ourselves? After all, there are even more childish occupations than these. Even fugitively to fall in love is to fall into 'fancy'; and every ardent ideal is to the eager mind, possessed by it, a sort of paradise, although others may dismiss it with contempt as the limbo reserved for fools.

Indeed, all travel into the past may be only the better for a little method and for a little quiet preparation. What, then, of the Present and the Future? All flesh is grass; even a mind of the strangest energy wearies, and has to await its own moments. Nevertheless, it is astonishing how seldom it may so much as heed the invitations squandered on it, let alone accept them. Yet let the meditative eye rest but for a moment on the most familiar of objects in the most familiar of rooms, the image thus welcomed may transport the self within into regions not of the bygone or the might-have-been, but of the *is* or the never-to-be; and that perhaps a radiant one. How many times, on the wings of the ether, have we flown off to envied places no more to us than names in fact, though not in fancy?—solitudes, cities, valleys, waters which we have not only never seen, but never shall see—not with the naked eye. But this is usually chance-work; there is little system. We may begrudge even opportunity. What if we took a little more trouble; if we examined the conditions; if we really tried? The last question, until we do try, is unanswerable concerning this order of travel as it is concerning Nature and her exquisite handiwork. Have these regions any actuality? We build up our small-orbited universe of Earth and sea and sky and their inhabitants by means of our physical senses. And of what else besides? Is the imagination compact solely of what has been so devised? Do we not impose on Nature herself—apart from anything that assures us of the divine—fully as much as she confers upon us? Whence comes this except out of the mind and out of the heart that life has given us, wherewith the spirit feels its joys and pangs. This, then, is the veritable goal of every true explorer, whether he pines to scale the topmost peak of Everest, to tread the sands of the uttermost solitude, to give Death the countersign or—merely to dream on.

However that may be, and whatever our views on the waste-fulness of reverie, the vast savannahs of the future await the mind's survey. And even now, since something of that daydream future *may* eventuate, we are only on the outskirts of fantasy. It is here that the imagination itself must take us into its keeping, an imagination timorous or daring, groping or swift. Love may then give that mind the wings of the condor, and pining and passion—even a child's—may exhaust it. A heart of furious fancies—which, through the stupidity and malice of his fellow creatures, brought 'poor Tom' to Bedlam—is, mercifully perhaps, only the occasional boon, or bane, of the few. But let that heart begin to beat—say, ninety-nine to the minute —then the Horse of Air, silently champing his golden grain in his grass-green stable, will instantly whinny his reply; leagues are no journey; and the world's end is precisely where we like to place it. And all this without the aid of a single grain of any drug —from opium to hashish. Instanter, we may find ourselves in the dubious presence of the Old Man of the Mountains; for the travelling mind not only materializes, like some Tibetan lama, what the inward eye sees, but is its own kingdom; and countless other realms are open to its quest. We can think as we please— pretty nearly; we can imagine what we can—wholly. And every writer, who has, as far as may be, surveyed the outskirts of his own mind, lies in wait for us with what is all but an infinitude of territory, his pen for Sesame. Every story we read, indeed, if it is an escape, or a homecoming, into the imagined, and is not a wallowing in the pigsty of what is falsely called 'realism', is such an adventure—at second-hand. Coleridge, after a brief meal of Purchas's *Pilgrims*, sallied out from his chair, in his three hours' armchair sleep, to Xanadu—and returned to the man who had come knocking at his door from Porlock, and a fragment entitled *Kubla Khan*. A more miscellaneous menu presented him with that other exorbitant journey—supreme in light, colour, music and the remote—the Ancient Mariner's. How far he could have gone solely on his own crutches, who can say?

Milton also chose his route; as did Dante; as, in their several degrees and fashions, did Robert Burton, Sir Thomas Browne, Shelley, Peacock, Lewis Carroll; while Wordsworth, even with 'poor Susan' for company and immaterial daffodils for bliss, stayed chiefly, but by no means always, at home. And what reader worthy of print is not, at mere mention of such names, or after a few lines or sentences of their incantations, immediately among their mountains of the moon; or those (with their spectral moonshine) to which Webster gave his name; or Beddoes his; or Vaughan—ethereally transmuted mountains of his own beloved Wales; or Poe—where lies the dark tarn of Auber in the misty mid-region of Weir.

> *He gave the bridle-reins a shake,*
> *Said ' Adieu for evermore*
> *My love!*
> *And Adieu for evermore.'*

Every travelling mind, of course, is, to put it crudely, skull-confined. Nevertheless, when we share that of a man of genius, both the rarest and the most beloved, then his travels are, to our own degree, ours for the mere wishing—his birds, flowers, streams, valleys, wildernesses, gulfs, peaks, seas, vision of paradise and celestial ocean; and, beyond all this, the company of such humans as he knew well, divined deeply, adored and delighted in. In such travels of the mind as these—and better and stranger even yet our secret own!—all holidays are 'staggered'. There in truth we are never less alone than when alone; we may even taste, it may be, of an order of existence that may be awaiting us after the last journey of all, a journey, perhaps, often obscurely contemplated, but whose goal evades us. Poor worn August, there, is fresh as May; the snows of winter wear a silence that only we ourselves can break; there is danger—but that goes into every true traveller's knapsack; and however freely the Lotos may blossom, there is an enchantment even in its longest afternoon. Knowledge-ridden, obsessed with mere circumstance, bandaged by convention, and *tied* to mother Nature's apron-strings, the mind is in a prison house. But, 'It came to pass at the end of forty days, that Noah opened the window of the ark which he had made: and he sent forth . . . a dove from him, to see if the waters were abated . . . and the dove came in to him in the evening; and, lo, in her mouth was an olive leaf pluckt off. . . . And he stayed yet other seven days; and sent forth the dove; which returned not again unto him any more.' And, like this old patriarch of the Flood, the mind itself can dispatch also a 'raven' out of its window over its inscrutably mysterious and unfathomable waters—and Noah's also never came back at all.

Times Literary Supplement, July 9, 1938